Pardon My French

Pardon My French

How a Grumpy American Fell in Love with France

Allen Johnson

YUCCA

Yucca Publishing books may be purchased in bulk at special discounts for sales promotion, corporate gifts, fund-raising, or educational purposes. Special editions can also be created to specifications. For details, contact the Special Sales Department, Yucca Publishing, 307 West 36th Street, 11th Floor, New York, NY 10018 or yucca@skyhorsepublishing.com.

Yucca Publishing® is an imprint of Skyhorse Publishing, Inc.®, a Delaware corporation.

Visit our website at www.yuccapub.com.

10 9 8 7 6 5 4 3 2 1

Library of Congress Cataloging-in-Publication Data is available on file.

Cover design by Zoran Opalic for Yucca Publishing
Cover photo by PHB.cz

Print ISBN: 978-1-63158-064-2
Ebook ISBN: 978-1-63158-078-9

Printed in the United States of America

For the people of Pérols, France

TABLE OF CONTENTS

CHAPTER 1

First Encounter of the French Kind

I DIDN'T KNOW WHAT TO SAY TO THE NAKED FRENCH GIRL lounging at the edge of the pool when her eyes met mine and she said, *"Bonjour"* as casually as asking for the time of day. I wanted to be hip and say something witty and smart like "Nice tan line" or, cutesier, "Would you like to be my pen pal for, I don't know, forever?" But I was new to the French language, and the only thing I could think of was "Where is the railroad station?" which really didn't seem to fit the situation.

It was not the first time I had been befuddled in France. That started on Day One of a yearlong language course in Grenoble. It was 1971 and the Vietnam War was raging. I was a conscientious objector and was granted an alternative service with the Mennonites. My wife, Nita, and I enlisted for a three-year term: one year in Grenoble to learn French followed by two years in Algeria where we taught English in a Berber mountain village.

When the summer of our first year in France had arrived, I decided it would be a good experience for me to attend a two-week acting camp sponsored by the University of Grenoble drama department. The camp was to be held at a retreat center near Dijon, which was about two hundred miles from Grenoble. I would have to be away from Nita, but I was excited about the possibilities. Acting had always been a passion for me—in college I had played Shylock in *The Merchant of Venice* and Henry Higgins in *Pygmalion*—so a French acting camp felt like a good fit. Besides, it would surely improve my French.

My wife and I had been married for less than three years. As a married couple, we had never been separated for more than a day or two. As much as I was looking forward to the new experience, it was hard to say goodbye to my beautiful bride.

"Now, don't you be seduced by some French floozy," Nita said, when she kissed me goodbye.

"Honey, you're the only floozy who interests me," I said, quickly tightening my embrace to avoid a punch to the chest.

When I finally began to pull away, she put her lips to my ear and whispered, "Don't you ever forget that I love you."

"Don't you ever forget that I love *you*."

Four hours later, I was tripping over my suitcase and guitar while mumbling something incomprehensible to the naked floozy at the retreat center pool.

"I'm sorry, do you know where I can register for the summer acting camp?"

"Why are you sorry?" the floozy asked.

She had me there. "No reason I guess. You just seemed so much at ease, I didn't want to disturb you."

"Why should I be disturbed?"

She had me again. "Well, I suppose. I mean I just . . ."

"Yes?"

The floozy was clearly in control. Like me, she must have been in her early twenties, but when it came to self-composure, she was decades ahead of me. She had reason to be composed. She had a sleek body that glistened in the play of sun and olive oil. Her wet, boyishly short bristles of blond hair crowned an impish, sculpted face. I had seen women like her before, but only from afar: women who had been reminded of their beauty so often that they had come to accept the praise as routine and inarguable.

"My name is . . . uh, Allen."

"You sound like you're not sure."

"Oh, I'm sure. It's Allen. It's definitely Allen."

She paused long enough for a slow smile to cross her lips. She was enjoying this. "*Bonjour* Allen. My name is Caroline."

"Nice to meet you, Caroline." My French was quickly dwindling. There was still no lead-in for a question about the railroad station. "About that registration?"

"You're American, aren't you?"

I rolled my eyes. "What gave me away?" The obvious answer was "my accent," but she surprised me.

"Your nervousness."

"Huh? Who me? I'm not nervous. What . . . what makes you think I'm nervous?"

"Oh, I don't know. Maybe it's the way you're biting your lower lip. I'm afraid you're going to put a hole in it."

I released the grip on my lip and massaged it with my tongue. I took a breath, set my guitar down, flipped my suitcase on end, and sat down on it. "You're right. I *am* nervous. Excluding my wife, this is the longest conversation I've had with a naked woman."

"Oh, this makes you nervous?" she asked, slowly lifting and turning from her outstretched lolling position. Now she sat with her back straight and her feet to the side. She brushed her hand over her hair, which released a spritz of mist. "I'm sorry. I would not have imagined. I thought you Americans were a liberal-minded people. You know, *Bob & Carol & Ted & Alice* and all."

I was silent for a moment. She peered into my face with that look of supreme confidence. "Let me make you feel more comfortable." She then stood, walked three paces to a lawn chair, lifted a black summer dress from the back of the chair, and slipped it over her head. "Would you help me with this?" she asked fumbling for the zipper pull at the curve of her back.

I smiled to myself. I knew I was being played, but I loved the music. I zipped her into her black spaghetti-strap dress in one slow stroke.

She turned and faced me. "Thank you, Allen. You are a gentleman."

"Anytime, Caroline," I said, already feeling more comfortable. "Oh, by the way, do you remember the ending to *Bob & Carol*?"

Caroline nodded.

"Then you know they couldn't make the switch. That is also American."

I asked her again where I would find the registration desk. She pointed the way. A few minutes later, I was registered and in my room where I met my roommate, Jean-Pierre, a graduate student from Lyon.

The summer acting camp was a stretch for me. My upbringing had been pretty sheltered. I was not living in San Francisco during the Summer of Love. I was at Northwest Nazarene College in Nampa, Idaho, wrapping up my bachelor's degree in language/literature with a minor in secondary education. The most infamous event in my college days was lived, not by me, but by my rebellious girlfriend who sneaked out of the girls' dormitory at midnight and went skinny-dipping in the public pool with her roommate. When she confessed to the adventure, I felt both titillated and scandalized. That was as close as I got to anything remotely salacious, if you don't count skipping out on morning chapel.

At the end of the first week of camp, Jean-Pierre and I decided to go to Dijon for lunch. Caroline and a couple of other girls asked if they could join us, to which we happily complied.

It was a beautiful summer day, so we chose to sit outside under an umbrella on the cobblestoned square of Place François Rude. The conversation was playful with an undercurrent of sexuality.

"Did you see Annette in the improvisation she did with André yesterday?" Jean-Pierre asked.

I knew what he was talking about. Annette and André had set two folding chairs side by side and pretended to be sitting in the front seat of a powerful sports car. André was at the wheel. As he jammed through the gears and accelerated around the corners, Annette responded with one simulated orgasm after the other. Just when we thought she was totally spent, André would shift down, which sent her screaming into even higher realms of ecstasy. She was astounding. No, that's not strong enough. She was a mythical alien from the planet of Erotica—that's what she was. When they had finally finished, even I felt like having a cigarette.

Jean-Pierre continued. "Did you notice when Annette spread her legs?"

"Et alors?" What about it? Caroline asked.

"She wasn't wearing any panties," Jean-Pierre said with staccato precision and puerile delight.

"And what is your point?" Caroline asked.

"No point," Jean-Pierre said. "I just enjoyed the view."

"And why shouldn't you?" Caroline said. "You're a sexual being."

"We are all sexual beings," Jean-Pierre countered. "Except maybe Allen."

"Hey, wait a minute. How did I get into this conversation? I'm just as sexual as the next guy."

"Really?" Jean-Pierre said.

"Yes, really."

"I'm not so sure."

I could see that Jean-Pierre was cooking up something in his elfin brain.

"I'll tell you what," he said. "Let's have a little contest between you and Caroline."

"What sort of contest?" I asked skeptically.

"Oh, something very simple. You can think of it as a little exercise in acting. Both you and Caroline will speak the same line, one to the other. The contest is to see who delivers the most sensual performance."

"What's the line?" Caroline asked.

"Let's see," Jean-Pierre said, stroking his chin for a moment. "Here's the line. 'I love you. I have always loved you. I want you now, this very moment, or I will die.'"

"Je peux faire ça," Caroline said.

"I know *you* can do it," I said to Caroline. I have always been a pretty good actor, but suddenly I felt like I was a miniature poodle in a dogfight going up against a gray wolf with a sticker in his paw.

"All right, Allen, you go first."

"Why do I go first?"

"Because you're the one who said you were as sexual as anyone else."

"Okay, okay."

I sat tall in my chair and put on my best sultry look, which must have been unconvincing because it made everyone at the table laugh.

"Hey, I'm working here! Give me a break."

The table of scoffers stifled their giggles. I looked at Caroline, who was seated at my side. She tipped her head down and looked at me from under her eyebrows, which was fantastic motivation for me. I returned her gaze, feeling certain that my expression was seething with passion. "I love you. I have always loved you. I want you now, this very moment, or I will die."

There was a polite smattering of applause.

I looked at Jean-Pierre, who sardonically covered a yawn. "Not bad, not bad my American friend. Now, it's Caroline's turn. Are you ready Caroline?"

"I'm always ready."

Caroline reached over my body, gripped the arm of my chair, and gave it a hard tug. I was now facing her straight on. She put her hands on my thighs.

"Whoa Nelly," I said in English. "No one said anything about touching."

"No one said anything about *not* touching," Caroline said.

She was already in character. Her voice had taken on a low, husky timbre somewhere between Lauren Bacall and Barry White.

"Oh my God, I am screwed," I heard myself say out loud.

Caroline purred *sotto voce* like the idling hum of a jungle cat. "Only if you want to be, sweetheart."

I swallowed hard.

Caroline was the iconic picture of seduction. She was wearing the same low-cut black summer dress that I had zipped her into on the first day of camp. Knowing exactly what she was doing, she leaned over deeply at the waist. She was not wearing a bra. Oh so slowly she slid her hands up my thighs until she was a whisper away from Mr. Whimple.

"I love you. I have always loved you."

Then the huntress moved in with feline concentration onto my lap and held my face in her hands. "I want you now, this very moment, or . . ."

I . . . will . . . die." And then she pressed herself into me, commanding the stage with a long, hard French kiss with a lot of English. The café customers who surrounded us were whooping and whistling. And still Caroline was kissing me, her warm body writhing against my chest, my gut, and lower still until I felt my toes clench.

I have been tempted in my life. In my early years the fear of hell kept me physically chaste, if not mentally pure. But at that moment I was not thinking about hell. I was thinking about grabbing Caroline by the hair, throwing her on the café table, and taking her right there in the Place François Rude. No sacrifice was too great. I was ready to be handcuffed, tried, and imprisoned for public indecency. But then, at the most inconvenient moment, the sound of Nita's voice was whispering in my ear. "Don't you ever forget that I love you." Suddenly I was back. I understood the grave consequences of accepting Caroline's invitation on that weekend in Dijon. The cost would have been more than giving her my body. It would have required surrendering my soul (not to mention a stay in the clink).

When Caroline finally pulled her lips from mine, she capped the performance with a wicked smile, puckered and touched her lips with two fingers, and then pressed her fingers to my lips. Only then did she return to her chair, cross her legs, and tip her head to her adoring fans, who were now clapping in rhythm.

"I'd say Caroline won that competition," Jean-Pierre said through his laughter. "You still have some work to do, Allen."

"Uh huh," I said, slumping into a pool of sweat.

That was not the last of the unforgettable moments at the acting camp. There was the evening after our last class of the day when I pulled out a harmonica and started playing the blues. To my amazement everyone started to dance. I got the idea of leading the dancers outside and then to the pool where everyone stripped to the waist and jumped in. I felt like the X-rated version of the Pied Piper of Hamelin.

Then there was the evening I was playing my guitar and singing love songs to the entire camp, about thirty university students in all. We were sprawled out on beds in the girls' dormitory. After a few minutes I realized that couples were fondling each other to the sound of my voice. My God, I was the film score for a French lovefest! (The movie title would be *Coeds Gone Wild, French Style*.)

As I surveyed the room, I noted that my roommate, Jean-Pierre, was nowhere in sight. Then I remembered. The night before he had slept with one of the campers. Now he was sleeping with his wife, who had driven up from Lyon for a surprise visit—nearly too surprising. But Jean-Pierre was undaunted. The following day his wife returned home, and he trippingly rejoined his lover.

I was afraid. I left at midnight before the last day of camp. I did not say goodbye to Jean-Pierre. Nor did I say a word to Caroline; I did not have the courage. Her spirit had beguiled me, nearly bewitched me, and so I ran. Over the years I have wondered if her alluring presence had been tempered. Could she be tamed? Would she one day become a conventional businesswoman or a loyal wife and mother? Or would she always conspire to shock and tantalize? Would she inevitably follow her own feral, nonconforming heart? I do not know. I never saw or heard from her again. But wherever she is, whoever she is with, I truly hope that she is happy.

It was three-thirty in the morning when I rolled into the driveway of our Grenoble apartment complex. I looked up at the bedroom window of our fourth-story apartment. The lights were on! It was the middle of the night. What was going on? Suddenly my mind warped from unconditional love to a manic suspicion of Shakespearean proportions. My imagination was on fire.

It was all self-evident now. I had come home a day early. In the last two weeks my wife had been stalked, charmed, and seduced. Now, at this very moment, she was entertaining a filthy French libertine—the supercharged male equivalent of Caroline. Sure, the country must be swarming with them. But this would not stand. I would throw the swarthy French weasel off the balcony and watch him splatter on the bicycle rack like a bladder of Camembert cheese.

I could feel my heart pulsating in my throat. This was not happening—not to me, not after all the temptations that I had endured and cast aside. I had been loyal, blameless—even saintly. Well, loyal anyway.

In the elevator my head was throbbing. *Premier étage.* I would slam my fist into the weasel's gut and finish him off with an uppercut to his stubbly jaw. BAM, BAM. I could see him fall to the ground like a sack of spuds. *Deuxième étage.* I would take his ten-speed bicycle and cram it up his . . . *Troisième étage.* This was it. This was my floor. Prepare to die, you greasy frog.

I was breathing heavily now as I strode down the hallway that suddenly seemed to lengthen with every step, like looking backward into a telescope. Now the periphery of my vision had blurred. I had to snap out of it. I had to be clearheaded for what would surely be the fight of my life—maybe the fight of anyone's life.

I guided the key into the lock and slowly turned the knob. I opened the door just wide enough to slip through. I was in the living room. I shut the door behind me and dead bolted the latch. The room was dark and empty. I stopped and listened for heavy breathing. There was nothing.

The bedroom door was closed—like that could stop me. A band of yellow light poured out beneath the door. I crossed the room, stood before the door, and turned the knob—bit by bit, tick by tock—and then pushed forward. The door did not give way. A chair had been braced against the knob from the inside. I pressed harder, rattling the doorknob.

I heard my wife's voice. "Honey, is that you?"

Who else would it be? "Yes. Are you all right?"

"Oh, honey. I'm coming, I'm coming."

I could hear Nita slip the chair away from the door. I reached for the knob again, but before my fingers touched the handle, the door flew open. Nita's face was before me. Her eyes, still heavy with sleep, were gleaming with tears. But there was something else, something strange in her gaze, something I could not quite make out.

She leapt into my arms, kissing me again and again. "You're home, you're home."

My heart melted. "Yes, I'm home now."

"I missed you so much."

"I missed you too."

"Just a tiny bit or a great big humongous bunch?"

"You will never know how much."

"Good."

As I held her in my arms, I could not imagine any reunion so perfectly sweet. I squeezed her so tightly that she said, "Ouf," and then again, "Ouf."

"Honey, you have me curious. Why were the bedroom lights turned on?"

"I was so scared. I couldn't stand sleeping in the dark."

"And you braced the door."

"Uh huh."

"Every night?"

"Every night. Oh, sweetheart, you were gone so long, so very long."

I looked at her again and suddenly realized what pathos had escaped me in her eyes. What I had seen were the remnants of terror. She had been terrified to be left alone in a dingy apartment with peculiar scents, islanded in a city where people seldom smiled, within a country that was so very far from home.

I knew then that if we were going to make it in France, not to mention Algeria, it would have to be as a couple who would trust wholeheartedly, encourage indefatigably, and lift each other up when our hearts were dispirited. We would have to be intrepid soul mates. Whatever might come—the misunderstandings, the bewildering culture, the conundrum of language—we would need to be there for the other like a wash of bedroom light that deflects the shadows and offers a beacon of hope for the homeward bound. We would have to be each other's savior.

On that early morning when we went to bed, Nita laid her head on my chest. I had one last thing to say before I drifted off. "Honey, don't you ever forget that I love you."

CHAPTER 2

Thirty-One Years Later

IN 2002 NITA AND I RETURNED TO FRANCE. And once again, we would spend a full year in the country we had come to love.

The first week of our year in France was a blaze of impressions that overwhelmed my senses. I felt like a kid in a Willy Wonka candy store. Everywhere I looked, there were inscrutable delights to ponder. Every few minutes, I would turn to Nita and say, "Did you see that?" "How do they do that?" "Can we go into that bakery?" "Oh my goodness, look at that cathedral. Isn't that incredible?" The synapses in my brain were snapping like voracious piranha.

Strolling in Montpellier, I again witnessed the French penchant for style. The fashions had changed, but the sensuality remained constant. We saw it in their choice of clothing, their walk, even their attitude.

As our heels clicked on the narrow cobblestoned streets, I was reminded of Caroline's confidence and her enticing black summer dress. That had not altered. Everywhere we walked, our eyes were dazzled by the simple, yet sensual presence of proud young Mediterranean beauties. And they all seemed to own a black dress. In one afternoon, we saw all variations: sleeveless, spaghetti straps, single strap, and, yes, strapless. This provocative black basic came in all lengths—both miniskirts and full-length—some slit to the hip, others shaped like petals at the hem. It occurred to me that I could create a luscious coffee-table book of images on the French black dress alone.

By day's end, I felt certain that these women—in spiked heels and dresses two sizes too small to accent their slender figures—were supremely sure of themselves. I saw none of the awkward self-consciousness that is so prevalent among American young women. Frenchwomen have a grace about themselves that is noticed in every step they take—with pointed toes, one step in front of the other, like an elegant dancer gliding across the stage. Compare that with the all-too-typical American high school student with baggy pants draped below butt cleavage, waddling down the hall like Charlie Chaplin: feet akimbo, shoulders rolled forward, eyes focused on the cracks in the linoleum tile.

Frenchwomen have a *je ne sais quoi* about their bodies that is astounding to Americans and dismissed as completely normal by the French. A French woman's choice in clothing is seldom layered and rarely pretentious. But it is sexy (the French have adopted the English word).

A few days after arriving in France, our longtime French friends, Jean-Marie and Monique Ducros, drove us to the prefecture in downtown Montpellier to begin the process of obtaining our *cartes de séjour* (official identification papers for those wishing to stay in France for longer than three months).

Through American eyes, the woman who served us looked to be more suited for the beach than the office. She was a beautiful, slender woman with hair the color of school brick, strategically disheveled, the tips frosted in golden sienna. She must have spent a good deal of time in the sun, for her skin was deeply tanned to a copper perfection. All that was impressive, but what really caught my eye was her dress, a solid bright-orange number held in place by one strap over her right shoulder, exposing a bare left shoulder à la Wilma Flintstone. What is the word for the effect? Oh yes, "sexy."

When I recounted this vision to a twenty-three-year-old Frenchwoman, I was told that what I saw was the current rage and that Frenchwomen will typically wear the most stylish outfits to the office. From this man's perspective, the Frenchwoman's approach to business wear makes casual Friday in the States—blue jeans and a football jersey—a national embarrassment.

What Frenchwomen wear in the office is just a warm-up for what they wear on the street. For example, at a local sporting goods store, I saw the sinuous details of a woman's thighs and buttocks sealed in a hallelujah chorus of black spandex pants—no underwear I can assure you. (I nearly tripped over the barbells in my journalistic zeal to confirm that cultural detail.)

In the same store I saw a pregnant woman merrily strolling down the aisles in stretch jeans and a chopped t-shirt that exposed her bare protruding tummy.

My point is that regardless of the situation, many Frenchwomen—particularly those in their twenties and thirties—have an uninhibited, self-assured sensuality. Their method is calculated. Their effect is, for at least the uninitiated, enough to make you trip over your shoelaces and bump into things. "Uh, that is . . . I beg your pardon. I was distracted by this really cool . . . er, soccer ball. I've never seen a soccer ball quite like this before. It's black and white and round and everything. Really spiffy, don't you think?"

Nor is French sensuality limited to the country's youth. My first week in France, I watched a fifty-something-year-old man with a fringed black leather jacket board a bus with his girlfriend in tow. She, a lovely blond woman in her early thirties, wore the ubiquitous spaghetti-strap black dress, thrown over a pair of jeans that was rolled up at the cuff like pedal pushers.

With no empty seats in sight, they stood, feet splayed, in the middle of the bus. The man took the face of the blond woman in his hands and kissed her hard on the mouth as if he were going off to war. Then, to punctuate the embrace, he caressed the woman's breast as though he were checking for ripeness. She didn't seem to mind—nor did the French passengers, most of whom were looking out the windows or smoothing the wrinkles out of their black cotton dresses. As for me, I was wildly scribbling notes. "What a show!" I thought. "This is better than *Le Cirque du Soleil*."

The indiscreet Frenchman, understandably overheated in his leather garb in the ninety-degree Mediterranean weather, stripped off his jacket, unbuttoned his long-sleeve white shirt, and began brushing a carpet of white chest hair. At that moment a seat opened up, and the two of them sat down and immediately launched into round two of deep-throat kissing. As I ogled the middle-aged biker's beautiful blond companion, I timidly tapped my chest and whispered an ignominious prayer for a wooly thatch of chest hair.

When I shared this experience with a French friend, he assured me that the couple's behavior was inappropriate, but that, despite the indiscretion, the French would never vocally object. I agree with my friend. I think the incident was a French anomaly and just as likely to be witnessed on a New York subway as on the bus to Montpellier. Still, it was entertaining.

* * *

AFTER THE FRENCH AFFINITY FOR STYLE AND SENSUALITY, we noticed a second quality that has been misinterpreted by American tourists. Americans often label the French as closed or even cold. They are not. However, they are private.

When I stood on a street corner with a shipwrecked expression and a crumpled map in my hands, the French would never approach me and ask, "May I help you?" That is not their way. (In contrast, I found Germans ready to help at the first sign of a pinched brow. "You seem to be having difficulty," they would say in perfect English. "May I be of assistance?")

However, when I asked a French citizen for help, he or she happily obliged. The first time I lost my way in Montpellier, I pulled off to the side of the road and asked a gentleman for directions. *"C'est très simple,"* he said. *"Vous verrez."* And to prove just how simple it was and how quickly I would see, he pulled out a map from his own glove compartment, spread the map across the hood of his car, and traced the correct route with his finger. When I thanked him, he smiled broadly and said, *"Bon voyage, monsieur,* and have a marvelous stay in France."

My point is that the French can be most gracious and quite friendly, but they must be wooed first. For example, during our first year in France, I developed the habit of going for a morning bicycle ride. On nearly every outing I would come across a young man jogging. In all the times I passed the runner, he never once acknowledged me with a nod or a *"bonjour."* That is not surprising. Unlike Americans, the French do not say "howdy" to everyone they meet on the street. They do not nod; they don't even smile. In fact, when I smiled and said *"bonjour"* to a stranger in town, I was always greeted with the same expression, "What mental ward did you escape from?"

So when I decided to break the ice with the young jogger, I'm sure it seemed a little bizarre. On that day, I saw him just ahead. I picked up speed to catch up and then eased in beside him, pedaling slowly now to match his pace.

"Bonjour," I said. "I've seen you many times along this path."

"Ah oui? I don't remember seeing you," he said.

How could he remember seeing me? We had never made eye contact. "You are a very fast runner," I said. "I imagine that you're training for a race."

"Yes," he said, "I'm training for the Marathon de Reims in October."

"Well, you are certainly in good form."

"Oh, pas mal," he said in a typically French self-defacing style (more about that later). Then quickly, to escape the spotlight, he added, "You're in good shape yourself."

"Not bad," I said, mimicking his modesty. "I try to do something physical every day."

"Il le faut." One must.

"This is a wonderful place to train, don't you think?" I asked.

"A little too flat," he said.

"Oh?"

"I haven't been here long," he volunteered.

"You live in Pérols?" I asked.

"Yes, but I've just come from a town near Les Gorges du Tarn. It is more hilly there—a better workout. You know it?"

"Only by reputation," I admitted. (Later in the year, the Ducros, Nita, and I would kayak down the placid Tarn River, which is framed by a 1,500- to 2,000-foot vertical limestone canyon. It is a magnificent float.)

"Where do you come from?" he asked.

"Washington State," I said. "Have you ever visited the United States?"

"No," he said, "but if I do well in Reims, I will qualify for the New York Marathon."

"I hope that works out for you," I said.

The conversation continued for several minutes until we arrived at my turnoff point. In that conversation, I learned a great deal: where the young man lived, where he used to live, and what he hoped to accomplish. That is not information that he would have volunteered, but with just a little encouragement on my part, he was happy to engage in a fruitful dialogue.

Related to their respect for privacy, the French also like their fences—particularly in southern France. Not chain-link fences, not chicken-wire fences, not even wooden fences, but rather concrete-block barriers finished in stucco—from four to eight feet high, some topped with broken glass.

I have even seen signs on French gates that read DANGER DE MORT. Danger of death! In the States you might see PRIVATE PROPERTY, DO NOT ENTER, or maybe BEWARE OF DOG, but I've never seen an American sign that warned, "Stay out or I'll kill you."

I grant you, I have not seen a lot of death threats on French portals. What I have seen are enclosures that come equipped with a locked gate and a bell. Visitors who seek entry must first ring the bell. Someone from within the house will come to the gate. If you are a friend, the gate lock will be manually or electronically released. If you are not a friend, you will be carefully scrutinized and not with a surplus of smiles.

Why are the French so enamored with high walls? "For two reasons," one Frenchman explained. "First, to protect one's privacy and, second, to deter thieves from breaking in."

"Are there many thieves?" I asked.

"*Ça arrive,*" he said. It happens.

On another occasion, I noticed that my French friend closed all the window and door shutters just prior to sitting down for dinner. That seemed peculiar to me. His home was one of only a dozen in a mountain hamlet. What could he have to fear?

He answered my question with another question. "Why would you want people looking in, seeing what you are doing? No, that is not good," he said emphatically.

"Oh?"

Seeing my uncertainty, he added, "There is a French proverb: '*Pour vivre heureux, vivons caché.*'" To live happily, live hidden.

I don't want to be too critical of the French. When you think about it, they have good reason to be a bit cautious about strangers. After all, the French have had their share of invaders: Celts, Romans, Moors, English, Germans. And they have also engaged in their own civil and colonial conflicts: religious wars, the French Revolution, the Napoleonic wars, and the Algerian War. With such a deep history of conquests and conquerors, the formation of an instinct for security and self-preservation is understandable, even natural. Is it any wonder then that strangers may be seen as a potential enemy? *Il faut se méfier*—one must be mistrustful.

How long does it take for an *outsider* to become an *insider*? I once visited with a French couple who owned a bed-and-breakfast chateau in a small village in Provence. Although they were originally from Paris, they had lived in the village for thirty years and yet, by their own account, they were still not accepted by the community.

"How long does it take?" I asked innocently, expecting them to say "a lifetime."

"Three generations," was the answer.

To an American, whose nation is less than three centuries old, three generations sounds like an eternity. But if you look at time from a French perspective, you may be a little more forgiving. After all, the first traces of human life in France date back 1.8 million years. The oldest city, Marseille, was founded by the Greeks in 600 BC. Consequently, traditions—including the process of building allegiances—have had a very long time to evolve. Moreover, those traditions are held with a deep and enduring respect. You do not discard a way of being that took hundreds, even thousands of years to mature. I believe that for the French "tradition" and "safety" are synonyms.

You see Gallic mistrust expressed in a variety of ways. I've already mentioned their reluctance to greet a stranger on the street. What is more interesting is the French aversion to introducing themselves—even in business. In my first week in France, I bought a bicycle, a used car, car insurance, and a ton of groceries. I made transactions in banks, bakeries, and real estate agencies. At no time did *anyone* offer his or her name!

For example, when Nita and I completed the paperwork for a used car at the Chrysler dealership, an attractive young Frenchwoman served us. We signed the forms and counted out one hundred euro notes (curiously, the dealership, which also sold Porsches, would not accept traveler's checks or even a Visa card). During the exchange, I noticed, like the sales clerk before her, that the young woman did not bother to offer a name. After our transaction, I asked why.

"Oh, that's not done. We are not like Americans where all the clerks wear nametags. I like to keep my anonymity," the woman said. "We are a very private people."

All of this information was interesting to me—particularly coming from a woman who was wearing a body-hugging gold dress with a plunging peek-a-boo neckline and a perfunctory drawstring loosely laced through a half dozen eyelets. I walked away with a new understanding about France. Your name may be anonymous but not necessarily your bustline.

While writing this chapter, I received a telephone call from a friend of the Ducros.

"Is Jean-Marie or Monique there?" the caller asked.

"No, they are on vacation," I reported.

"You must be one of their American friends," the mystery man said.

"C'est ça, et qui êtes-vous?" That's right, and who are you? I asked.

"A friend," the man said.

"And what is the friend's name?" I asked, knowing I was starting to get under the caller's skin.

"We are friends of Jean-Marie and Monique," he repeated.

Pause. I could feel him squirming.

"Alors?"

"Eh bien . . . je suis . . . Pierre, et voilà."

That must have hurt. When I told this story to Jean-Marie, he laughed and said, *"Eh oui, c'est comme ça."* That's the way it is.

When I asked why, Jean-Marie had difficulty explaining. *"C'est comme ça,"* he repeated. "In business, the custom is easier to explain. One does not like to be held responsible. You see, a client doesn't really telephone a person; he telephones a company. And you are given information from the *company*, not the person."

"But a company is a thing," I argued. "You can't get information from a thing."

"Eh oui," Jean-Marie said, shrugging his shoulders in typical Midi fashion. "But one does not want to be at fault. It is never my fault. It is the fault of the *patron* (the boss) or the company."

I had a follow-up question. "But why would the French want to defer responsibility?"

Jean-Marie was stymied. But I have a theory. I think it has to do with the way the French see a glass, not as half full, but as half empty.

Like my new friend, the self-deprecating marathon runner, the French are modest about praising themselves—or others for that matter. When I asked the Ducros' son, Yann, how one says "good for you," his response was telling.

"We don't really say that," Yann said. "That's one of the big differences between Americans and us. You are very free with praise. We are not."

Not willing to give up, I offered another alternative. "Perhaps you say *'félicitations.'*"

"Not really," Yann said, "at least not in the sense you mean."

"How about 'bravo?'"

"Rarely."

"Hum."

Later, I discovered that Yann's assessment of French behavior was accurate. As an entertainer and public speaker in the States, I became accustomed to receiving praise. It was a common and natural occurrence for members of the audience to slap me on the back after a performance—even performances that were less than stellar. That rarely happens in France. They are not opposed to applauding in public. That is not a problem—in fact, they can be quite raucous. But it is rare for them to seek you out, shake your hand, and say, "Great job." That is not their way—even among close friends. If, on that rare occasion, you are praised, you can be sure that your performance was something truly extraordinary.

One night Yann and I went to a jazz club. Between sets, I congratulated a saxophonist's performance by shaking his hand and saying, *"Cela a été très bien fait."* That was very well done.

Later, Yann told me, "That is not really said, Allen."

"Not ever?"

"If it is used, it is usually sarcastic."

"What? Are you kidding me?"

"No. Imagine that a child is cautioned not to run in the house. The child ignores the warning and falls down. That's when you might say, *'C'est bien fait pour toi.'*"

The light went on. *"C'est bien fait pour toi"* was equivalent to saying "serves you right" in English. "I never knew," I said.

"And now you do."

That conversation with Yann was my first introduction to the French malaise with praise—both given and received. Later, I learned about a major contributor to that cultural characteristic: their educational system.

As a former high school teacher, I wondered what I would find in a French *lycée*. After sharing my journalistic curiosity with a school principal, I was given permission to visit his school. After a few visits, I discovered that classrooms in France were dramatically different from those in the States. First, French professors are not your friends; they are your rulers. French educators have little contact with their students outside the classroom. And inside the classroom, the relationship is always formal and hierarchical—the students using the formal "you" when speaking to the instructor, the instructor using the informal "you" when addressing the student.

French students are not in class to have fun; they are there to learn—perhaps more accurately, to be drilled. As such, French students tend to possess a wealth of knowledge, but minimal creativity. (Perhaps the opposite can be said of American students.)

In French schools, papers are scored on a scale of zero to twenty. Very seldom, if ever, does a student score a perfect twenty. When I asked why, I was told that a grade of twenty is reserved for the professors. To be given a score of twenty would suggest that the student is as knowledgeable as the teacher, an untenable supposition by French standards.

When a student earns a grade of eighteen or, on rare occasions, nineteen, the paper is likely to be accompanied by a comment of *"pas mal"*—a negative fashion of offering congratulations.

Eventually, students learn that they can never be perfect and that even a superior performance is valued as "not bad." With such powerful conditioning, it is not surprising to me that store clerks and business associates are reluctant to offer their names or take responsibility. Why would one choose to take responsibility when it is so easy to become a target of criticism or, at best, lukewarm approval?

I noticed early and throughout our first year that the French language and *usage* of language encourages negative thinking. For example, even the French idioms for saying "you're welcome" are couched in negativism: *de rien* (of nothing), *il n'y a pas de quoi* (not at all, or it is of no matter). Indeed, the more formal *je vous en prie* (I beg of you) is a kind of self-deprecating means of saying "you're welcome."

One day, after thanking a jovial, stocky woman for teaching me the French word for zucchini (*courgette*), she chirped, *"De rien de rien."* Wow, a double-barrel shot of negativity. "Of nothing of nothing."

After a while Nita and I became very familiar with the French propensity for negative responses—especially responses to praise. One of our French friends, Elizabeth, a beautiful and talented artist and cook, is a master at deflecting praise.

"What a delicious soup," I said one evening at a typical Elizabethan gourmet feast.

"Oh it's nothing really," Elizabeth said, actually blushing. "Just something very simple and everyday."

"And the table setting is so elegant too," my wife added.

"Not really," Elizabeth said, "but I just don't have anything finer."

Eventually, Elizabeth's instinct for sidestepping compliments became a running joke between our two families. Elizabeth's daughter, Christy, was a young opera singer, who at the time was studying in London and dating an American student. One evening she brought the issue to a head.

"*Maman,* just take the compliment!" Christy blurted out. "That's what my American boyfriend taught me."

"Yeah," I said, squeezing Elizabeth's hand across the table, "Just take the compliment."

To which, unbelievably, Elizabeth protested, "But I don't deserve it."

We all giggled over that, which of course made Elizabeth blush an even deeper rose.

I don't think that Elizabeth is at fault (not that fault needs to be assigned). It is simply evidence of a culture that is light on receiving and giving praise.

* * *

WHEN AMERICANS CRITICIZE WHAT THEY CALL "FRENCH COOLNESS," they often follow with querulous accusations regarding customer service. On this score, I have to side with my American compatriots. Nita and I learned very quickly that the French have a different concept of customer service. For the French, the customers are *not* always right. More often than not, they are seen as gravely misguided if not flat-out wrong. But it's not personal. Visitors from the States must recognize that clerical curtness in France is as common as Roquefort cheese and spread democratically across all clients.

After buying a used car in France, I told the car dealer that I was surprised that he had not filled the tank (the tank was only one-quarter full).

"Oh, that is not done," he said flatly, "even with new cars."

There was nothing apologetic about his tone—simply a dispassionate explanation of French traditions. (By the way, he made no offer to make an exception and fill the tank.)

I once went to a small shop to have a key made. The task was completed in less than three minutes.

"How much will that be?" I asked.

"Five euros, fifty centimes," the clerk said, which at the time was approximately $6.60—a little steep I thought to have a key made, but still something I could live with.

I poured out a fistful of change from my coin purse. Finding the five euros was no problem. I had a five-euro note wadded up with the change, but I wanted to unload some of my small ten-centime pieces. As I was counting them out in my hand, the clerk reached over the counter and poked his finger at a fifty-centime piece.

"*Et voilà*," he said.

"Yes," I said, "but I would like to get rid of some of my small change."

With that the man actually clucked his tongue. "*Dépêchez-vous. J'ai du travail à faire.*"

I couldn't believe my ears. "Hurry up, I have work to do."

My face flushed as I handed him the fifty-centime piece. "I'm sorry that I have been so bothersome," I said, more embarrassed than angry.

"Oh, you haven't been bothersome," he said. "I just have work to do."

Even the French would find that behavior annoying. When I told the story to a twenty-year-old French friend, he said he would have taken the key, pocketed the fifty centimes, turned on his heels, and left.

On another occasion when I had become a little more aware of the game rules, I stepped into Castorama, a large hardware store akin to our Lowe's or Home Depot. I was looking for a plastic bracket that held up a closet shoe rack. I walked up to one of the yellow-shirted employees.

"*Bonjour, je . . .*" That was all I got out.

"That is not my department. You have to go to the right department," the man said as he swished past me.

Now, I was a little more street smart by this time, so I actually grabbed the yellow hornet by the arm, which stopped him cold. "Wait a minute," I said. "How do you know what I want isn't in your department?"

"*J'ai du pif,*" he said, tapping his nose.

A "*pif*" is slang for "nose." So, when he said, "*J'ai du pif,*" he was saying, "I have a nose or flair (for that kind of thing)."

"You have a nose?" I repeated. Oh, brother, isn't that cute?

"I'm gifted that way," he said.

"Fine. I get it, you're gifted. But look, maybe you can at least point me in the right direction. This is what I want," I said, digging out the broken bracket from my pocket and waving it in his face. "Can you tell me where I can find this?"

"That's not my depart . . ."

"Don't even go there!" What I actually said was *"Ne dites pas ça"* (don't say that), but the tone was "Don't even go there!"

The man froze for a moment and stared right into my eyes. I thought, "Here's a guy who would really like to deck me." I stared right back.

"You might try the department just past the kitchen cabinets to your right."

"Merci," I said. "Now, that wasn't so hard, was it?"

I blame that kind of cold customer service on poor management. The French are certainly capable of doing better. When I ordered my phone service from France Telecom, it was all taken care of within minutes over the phone. The representative was absolutely charming, polite, and exceedingly patient with my less than perfect French. That kind of service only comes from good training, and good training only comes from good management.

One last example to make my point. In researching this book, I wanted to find out a little more about the phenomenon of the French *supermarché*, the huge department stores that carry everything from nuts to entertainment centers. I was particularly interested in knowing the square footage ("square meters" in French). So one day I drove to Carrefour, the biggest supermarket in our area, and walked to the welcome desk.

"Bonjour," I said. "I am writing a book about my French experience, and I am fascinated by your store. Would you be able to tell me how many square meters of space you have?"

"Ah non, that is something that only the director would know."

"Okay. Could you call the director and ask him?"

The woman laughed out loud. You would have thought I had asked for the director's personal bank account number. *"Mais non, monsieur,* not for a question like that."

So much for the welcome desk. Later, ironically enough, I met a store department manager (we attended the same dance class). When I told him the story, he merely smiled. "Yes, that's right. Only the director would have that information."

The department manager was not critical of the receptionist's behavior (as I was certain he would be). In fact, he felt just the opposite—that her action was most appropriate. She had protected her manager and that was paramount.

From my American business mentality, both the receptionist and the department manager are victims of a suffocating French business practice. At all costs maintain the sacred line of command. The tradition is so strong that, as in this case, hierarchy has usurped the organization's mission, which, at least by American standards, is to serve the customer.

The French are not unaware of slipshod customer service. In fact, sometimes they make jokes about it. One sixty-year-old man told me, "When it comes to service, you must realize that we French adhere to the 'five d's.'"

"What are the five 'd's'?" I naturally asked.

"It works like this. You walk into a store for a specific item, and the clerk says, *'D'accord'* (agreed). That is the first 'd.'

"But, upon searching, the clerk discovers that he doesn't have what you want, so he says, *'Demain'* (tomorrow). That is the second 'd.'

"You return the following day as instructed, and the item is still not available. The clerk's only consolation is to say, *'Désolé'* (sorry), the third 'd.' 'Please come back tomorrow,' you are told.

"The next day, you faithfully return and, again, the item is not in. At this point you are a little steamed, and the clerk sees it in your eyes. *'Doucement,'* (take it easy) he says. That is the fourth 'd.' Still, the clerk assures you that the item will come on the following day—this time without fail.

"So, always the optimist, you arrive the next day just before closing, and before you say a word, the clerk says, *'Débrouillez-vous'* (cope with it yourself). And that is the fifth and final 'd.'"

I'm not trying to make the French into Americans. No one would want that, certainly not the French, I can assure you. What I *have* tried to do is express my wonderment toward another culture and, as in the case of marginal customer service, my admitted frustrations. When I think about it, annoyances (and, yes, happy surprises) are what drove me to live in France for a year in the first place—to be simultaneously bedazzled and puzzled. For surely, when it comes to France, there is, without a doubt, a sixth "D": delightful.

CHAPTER 3

The Language

ONE NIGHT I WATCHED A FRENCH TELEVISION QUIZ SHOW where the following question was asked:

How do you spell "great grandfathers"?

A. *arrière-grand-pères*
B. *arrière-grands-pères*
C. *arrière-grands-père*
D. *arrière-grand-père*

The contestant guessed "A": *arrière-grand-pères*. HONK. Wrong. (The correct answer is "B.") Although the host admitted that he, too, did not know the correct answer, the unhappy contestant lost his shot at a million-dollar jackpot.

My meaning is that the French language is a complicated web of genders, conjugations, and prepositions that even the native speakers can't keep straight. This gives me some solace because, frankly, I speak ballpark French. My apologies to l'Académie française, but I just can't remember if the verb *préférer* (to prefer) requires a preposition when followed by a second verb infinitive (it doesn't, I looked it up).

And why is it so complicated to say the word "ninety-nine"? How complicated? Well, the answer is *"quatre-vingt-dix-neuf,"* which is equivalent to saying "four times twenty, plus ten, plus nine." I don't have enough fingers and toes to calculate all that.

Or how about this? Did you know in French you *"visit* a church," but *"render* a visit to a person"? I didn't know that for the longest time. So when I said I was going to "visit a friend," it must have sounded like I was going to climb up his steeple.

Then there are *les faux amis* or false friends. A *faux ami* is a French word that looks like English but carries a different meaning. By my count, there are hundreds of these linguistic traps. For example, in French *rester* doesn't mean "to repose"; it means "to stay." A *librairie* is not where you go to check out books; that's a *bibliothèque*. *Ancien* does not mean "ancient"; it means "former."

You would think that *malicieux* means malicious. Nope. It means "mischievous." When I use *malicieux* in French, it always sounds too harsh to me, but I shouldn't worry. If a French friend is teasing me about, say, my American accent, I might counter with, "And why are you so *malicieux*?" And while I half expect him to say, "Malicious, I'm not malicious!" he doesn't bat an eye. He just gives me a wink to let me know that it's all in good fun.

And a *dent* is not "a depression" that you might find on the side of your car. It's "a tooth." I learned that the hard way. I once noticed a caved-in fender on a Peugeot belonging to a French friend of mine and said, "What an ugly *dent*." My friend, whose teeth were, coincidently, less than perfect, covered his mouth—partly for shame, but more out of glazed dismay for my insensitivity.

* * *

To truly enjoy the French experience, you must have a decent working vocabulary. The best way to do that is through full immersion. You have to mingle with the French. Those who lock themselves away in a hotel room will, of course, learn nothing—except perhaps a few novel ways of using the bidet.

You could probably get by in France with a 500-word vocabulary—hello, goodbye, come, go, sit, stand, eat, drink—and a lot of American tourists make do with considerably less. But to be quasi fluent, I place the number of indispensable vocabulary words at 3,500. That will not make you a native speaker because, like Americans, the French have an active vocabulary of 20,000 words and a passive vocabulary (words understood but not used) of 40,000 words. I know that 3,500 words is a sizeable number, but given a common Latin base, it is not insurmountable. Thousands of French words have been incorporated into the English language, which accounts for about thirty percent of our vocabulary. All an Anglophone needs to do is learn how to pronounce those words in French, which is not as difficult as it might seem. (See Appendix C for resources that will help you build and pronounce French vocabulary.)

One invaluable source of vocabulary for me was the local hiking club. I was continually pummeled with new words: flowers, trees, animals, weather conditions, all together mixed in with the constant chatter of everyday life. Sometimes, when I was lucky, I learned more than one sense of the word.

On one hike in the mountainous Cévennes region north of Montpellier, Nicole, a slender blond Frenchwoman with a passion for English, led me to an oak tree at the edge of a clearing. She cupped a seed in her hand and asked me what the word was in English. I rolled the oak fruit between my fingers for a moment.

"We call it an acorn," I said.

"Acorn," Nicole repeated.

"Yes, acorn. What is the name in French?" I asked.

"*Un gland*," Nicole said.

"Ah, *un gland*," I echoed. "I see."

After that brief botany lesson, I walked back to the group, all of whom were taking a breather in the shade. I stripped off my backpack and propped it against a granite outcrop. I was taking a draw from my water bottle when Guy and Michel, two of the group leaders, drifted over to where I stood.

"Should we tell him?" Guy asked Michel, grinning like a teenager in a locker room with a wet towel, sizing up the vulnerable array of behinds.

"No," Michel said, turning away with a chuckle.

"Tell me what?" I asked Guy.

"Never mind," he said with the same lewd grin smeared across his face.

And then, finally, Michel turned back to me. "Okay, I'll explain," he said, pulling me off to the side. "A moment ago, you were fingering an acorn."

"Right?"

"An acorn has a second meaning."

"Okay."

"It has to do with a man's . . . well . . . private parts. And playing with *un gland*—especially with a woman present—could be interpreted as an invitation . . ."

Okay, you don't have to paint a picture. I acknowledged the expansion of my French lexicon with a quick adjustment of my "acorns."

Guy howled. "He understands," he whooped, whacking me on the back as if I had just scored the winning touchdown.

In that moment, I was initiated into the official locker-room clubhouse of the French Republic.

Later, I wondered if my female botany teacher considered the double meaning when she introduced me to the hooded oak fruit. Could her lesson have been a veiled flirtation? A harbinger of a secret midnight rendezvous? I doubt it (although one can always hope). All things considered, I think it's safer to chalk up the experience as just one more vocabulary lesson and leave it at that.

There are so many French rules to follow, so many linguistic landmines that sometimes a new speaker will take extraordinary steps to simplify the language—including faking understanding.

The French have a wonderful one-word exclamation: *Bof!* It is used to express indifference, which is fantastic. It is so noncommittal that it becomes a perfect response for a multitude of questions.

"Do you like seafood?"

"*Bof.*"

"Would you like to go to the movies?"

"*Bof.*"

"So what do you think of the weather in this part of the world?"

"*Bof.*" Or to be a little more verbose (a chapter from the *advanced* course in French idioms), "*Oh bof.*"

On our first visit to France in 1971, when I could barely utter "*bonjour,*" I was so keen on the word that I was using it at every opportunity—even in response to questions I didn't quite understand. So, it wasn't long before my little ruse was uncovered.

One day, our neighborhood baker finally gathered up the courage to pose a personal question.

"*Comment vous vous appelez?*" What is your name? he asked.

And for some reason, I did not make out the question, so I said, "*Bof!*"

From that point on, I was known by one French baker as *Monsieur Bof.* I just didn't have the courage to correct him.

Here's a little French characteristic that tickles me to no end. The French—at least the French in the South of France—have a couple of variations in the way they say "yes" and "no."

Let's start with "*oui,*" the one-syllable word for "*yes.*" Although this is not practiced by all, there are many among the French who actually inhale when they say "*oui.*" It sounds like an audible but discreet gasping for air. It always struck me as funny. So whenever it was said (or, more precisely, "sucked in"), I would gleefully point out the linguistic aberration. The French never had anything to say about it. They would just smile, cock their shoulders, and look at me as if to ask, "Yeah, and this is important for what reason?" Of course, it wasn't at all important—not in the grand scheme of things—but it was curious, and when it comes to the French, I'm curious about most everything.

Now, on to "*non.*" I'm fudging a bit by calling it an oddity on the word "*non.*" It is more of an expression of indifference that can be used in the place of *bof.* It's not a word; it's more of a sound. Here's how you make it.

1. Tightly close your lips and roll them in as if you are imitating an old man with no teeth.
2. Create a small pocket of air at the front of your mouth, just behind your front teeth.
3. Now "spit" the air out. No spray please—just dry air.

If you did it correctly, you would have made a wonderful plosive sound—a tiny imitation of a wine bottle being uncorked. I call the sound "phutt."

The French don't know the roots of "phutt," but I have a theory. I imagine that in medieval France the serfs would literally spit when they were disgruntled or in disagreement. Eventually, spitting was frowned upon. (In the 1970s, I remember seeing a sign in a French village post office that read, "No spitting allowed.") So spitting evolved into "phutting." Of course, I have no empirical evidence to support my claim—I wasn't there at the time—but that's my story, and I'm sticking to it.

History aside, I like to tease the French by suggesting that when they are conflicted, not knowing if they want to say "yes" or "no," they sound like a *deux chevaux* Citroën struggling to start on a cold morning: gasp-phutt-gasp-phutt-gasp-phutt. The French don't find my Victor Borge routine nearly as funny as I do, but hey, I've borne my share of playful rebuffs about my French pronunciation. What goes around comes around.

I remember a playful conversation with my French friend, Guy, early in our first year. At one point, the bantering swung around to my American accent.

"I know, I know," I said, "my accent is terrible."

Frankly, I was expecting Guy to protest like a used car salesman pressing for a sale. Surely, he would give me a side-hug and tell me that my pronunciation was nearly impeccable.

"Oh, no, Allen," he said. "You are too hard on yourself. Your French is not terrible; it is only abominable." (By the way, the French use the same words for "terrible" and "abominable." In fact, we adopted the words from them, so I had no problem in understanding the gibe.)

Funny, Guy. Real funny.

Despite Guy's impish review, my pronunciation is getting better. It used to be that whenever I asked a French person a question, they would stare at me in complete puzzlement—their heads cocked like French poodles, their brows crinkled, their eyes turned to slits—an expression that said, "Oh, I'm so sorry, but I don't speak Swahili." How I hated that look.

I don't blame the French. A slight difference in pronunciation—particularly in vowel sounds—can make the difference between a compliment and an insult. For example, "to do the *queue* [kø]" means "to stand in line," but "to do the *cul* [ky]" can only be roughly translated as "humping." To American ears, the difference of those two vowel sounds—[ø] and [y], sounds not found in English—is miniscule, even nonexistent. But to a francophone, the difference is as distinctive as the flavors of red and white wines.

I will never forget the day I asked a Frenchwoman in the Pérols post office if she wanted "to make a *cul*." Her eyes flashed, and her nose flared. I thought she was going to roundhouse me. Three or four other Péroliens who had overheard my indiscreet proposal whipped around, staring in disbelief. There was a deathly silence, as a drop of sweat trickled down my spine. At that moment, I wondered how the food was in a French maximum-security lockup. And then, thank God, they laughed. Frankly, I think it was my blue jeans, tennis shoes, and baseball cap that saved me. "*Et voilà*. An American. What do you expect?"

In 1971, when Nita and I knew only a handful of French words, I was introduced to the infamous blank stare of incomprehension. We had just landed in Paris and had taken a bus to the train station. It was my task to buy train tickets to Grenoble. So I looked up the word for "tickets" in my English/French pocket dictionary. "*Billets*" my dictionary said. What I didn't know was how to pronounce the word. I pronounced it "bill-its"—like any red-blooded American. That pronunciation, however, makes no sense to the French, who pronounce the word "bee-yea."

So with my dictionary in hand, I marched up to the ticket master, flashed a smile, waved two fingers in front of his face, and said in a voice that was probably too loud, "Two bill-its, Grenoble!"

He said nothing, he did nothing. He just gave me that French poo-dle look, shrugging his shoulders for good measure, and then turned his attention to the customer standing behind me.

Despondent but not yet beaten, I walked back to Nita, who was doggedly guarding our four suitcases. "What's the matter with that guy?" I whispered. "I said 'bill-its.' Don't these people know their own language?"

We stared at each other for a moment, then at the dictionary—yep, the word was "bill-its" all right—and then at each other again.

"Try one more time," Nita said in her you-can-do-it-Bunkie voice.

So I charged the ticket master again. This time I was definitely shout-ing. "BILL-ITS, BILL-ITS, BILL-ITS, okay?"

Nothing. Just more French poodle.

"Okay, look," I said, slamming my finger into the word in my dic-tionary. "Here it is, right here in plain English . . . er, French. BILL-ITS. BILL-ITS. Grenoble. Get it?"

"Ah, BEE-YEA," the ticket master said, along with some gibber-ish that sounded like, "Why didn't you say so in the first place?" And ten seconds later, I was the proud owner of two crisp train tickets to Grenoble.

One thing is certain about the French language. In comparison to Ameri-can English, it is terribly diplomatic and ingratiatingly polite. They do not, for example, end their business letters with, say, "Sincerely yours." They are more likely, by tradition, to use one of a number of diplomatic (I would call them stuffy) formulas. *Veuillez agréer, Monsieur, l'expression de mes sentiments distingués* (Would you accept, sir, my expression of dis-tinguished sentiments). When I pointed out this deferential sentence to Jean-Marie, he just laughed and said, "When we get to that part of the letter, we stop reading."

In general, if Americans want something, they get right to the point. The French are not that way. There are very precise rules of *étiquette*. (Wouldn't you know that "etiquette" is a French word?)

I am far too direct when speaking to the French, and it continually gets me in trouble. In Montpellier I once went to the city hall and asked the receptionist, *"Où se trouvent les toilettes?"* Where does one find the bathroom? It seemed like a perfectly proper question to me.

But, to my amazement, the receptionist glared at me with a look reserved for drug dealers and child molesters. *"Quoi?"* she asked.

"Où se trouvent les toilettes?" I repeated, even slower than my usual ponderous pace.

Her head snapped back as she poked her finger in the air. "Over there," she snarled.

I followed the vague line of her finger. "Where?"

Now she was poking the air like an impatient executive jabbing at an elevator button. "Over there, over there!" she squawked.

That evening I related the incident to Monique. Even before finishing my story, Monique asked, "Did you say, *'S'il vous plaît*?"

She had me. "Ah, no," I admitted, "I just smiled."

"Quand même, that is not sufficient," Monique said. "One must always say 'please.'"

Monique is a good teacher. She also taught me (as had our Belgian friends in the States) to drop the habit of saying *"Je veux quelque chose* (I want something)," and say, instead, *"Je voudrais quelque chose* (I would like something)." That makes sense. "I want something" is even a little harsh in English. But in French, it turns porcelain faces into dried prunes.

Learning the formulas for greetings and departures can be tricky. For instance, I noted quickly that the French often end a transaction with *"Bonne journée,"* in the same way we might say, "Have a nice day." But I was never quite certain of the proper response. The English translation is "The same to you." But do the French say *"À vous le même"* or *"À vous de même"*?

To find out for sure, I went to my favorite bakery and bought a *royal* (a chocolate mousse pastry with a delicious wafer crust, one of my favorites). As the store clerk handed me my treat, I quickly said, *"Bonne journée,"* and squinted my eyes to better hear her response. Would it be *"À vous le même,"* or *"À vous de même"*? *Le* or *de*—what's it going to be?

One click of the clock later, the clerk smiled and said, *"Également"* (the sneaky devil).

I found out later that the correct response is *"À vous de même"* or, more often, *"Vous de même"* or, shorter yet, *"De même."* But don't be surprised to hear someone squeeze in an *"également"* (equally) or even a *"pareillement"* (same to you).

I have learned that greetings with shop clerks should be polite without being intimate. When I go to the village bakery, for example, I always begin with *"Bonjour, madame."* Not just *"bonjour,"* mind you, for that would be too abrupt. Although today's generation is more relaxed on that propriety, for most French there is something about a naked *"bonjour"* that makes their teeth itch.

Monique—always my teacher—taught me a variation on this pattern. She says the moment she enters a shop and sees more than one person present, her greeting is *"Bonjour à tous,"* meaning "Good day to every-one." I like the efficiency of that. All the politesse covered in one sweeping salutation.

However, you must *not* follow *bonjour* with *"Comment allez-vous?"* because asking how someone is would be too intimate. Remember, the French are very private and would never share the state of their personal wellbeing with a stranger—and a foreign stranger at that. Even to be asked is a curiosity to them. I know what I'm talking about. Before I understood this *faux pas*, I was routinely seared with censorious eyes when I gaily asked a store owner, "So how the hell are you anyway?"

What you can talk about after an exchange of *"bonjour madame, bonjour monsieur"* is the weather. This is acceptable small talk. In fact the French phrase for "small talk" is *parler de la pluie et du beau temps* (to talk about the rain and the beautiful weather). Monique explained all this to me one day as we were walking to the bank in Pérols. So, as soon as we stepped into the bank, I said to the bank clerk, *"Bonjour. Il fait beau."* (Good day. The weather is beautiful.) The clerk smiled nervously—not quite knowing what to make of me. Even I knew that my transition to small talk was too sudden, but sometimes I just have to poke fun at the French. (Not to worry. They get their licks in too.)

Sometimes it's fun to hear the French speak English. If they are fluent, I am always impressed. If they struggle, I struggle along with them, for I know the feeling. And, sometimes, they say things that are worth a chuckle—not unlike some of my lingual blunders.

One day, I went into a bicycle shop to buy an inner tube (*chambre à air*). The clerk recognized my accent after two words and said in halting English, "Ah, you are wanting a rubber."

There are a few precious moments in everyone's life when a straight line is just too beguiling to resist. This was one of those moments. "Are you thinking I might get lucky this evening?" I asked in French, which didn't translate well at all.

"Huh?"

I took pity on him and explained that "a rubber" was what you used for protection when you're having a good time. I wanted something for my bicycle tire.

He laughed nervously—either out of embarrassment or lack of understanding—I'm not sure which.

Learning a second language is never easy, but the road is made less torturous when you learn from the people you love. Why? Because your loved ones are forgiving; they are willing to stick with you through all the malapropisms and *faux pas*.

One of my favorite French teachers is Pascale Ducros, the daughter of our friends, Jean-Marie and Monique. Pascale is a beautiful young woman, who could charm the pants off of Ebenezer Scrooge. She is bright, animated, and, incidentally, deaf since birth. As a result of that challenge, Pascale's communication style is very straightforward. She doesn't have time for fawning fanfare or diplomatic correctness. Next to me, she's the most direct person I know, and I love her for it. I tell her parents that she's the only person in the entire country who understands me.

Pascale has taught me a great deal. First, she has reminded me that the art of conversation is a rarity—in any country. Whether French or American, only a few have the skill of looking someone in the eyes and posing a thoughtful question. Nor do they know how to listen—not really.

During my stay in France, I was rarely asked about my American heritage—other than the obligatory "What part of the United States do you come from?" And when I responded, I was seldom heard and hardly ever asked a follow-up question.

That is not a French fault; it is a *human* fault. Americans do no better on that score. Very few Americans know what it means to enter the skin of another person and explore his or her experience. What Americans call conversation regarding our French adventure could be captured in one sentence. "Oh, you were in France for a year. That's nice." Period. End of discussion. Then, in the time it takes to inhale, "So how about those Seattle Seahawks?"

In contrast, the most intimate conversations I have had in France have been with Pascale. She looks straight into my eyes when she asks questions—and she asks plenty, which I adore. And when she listens, she is, of course, riveted to my lips. And then, to make sure that she understands, she follows up with a question for clarity.

When in discussion with the family around the dinner table, I always know when Pascale wants to say something to me. I can see her in the corner of my eye, her entire face turned toward me. I love that feeling.

"How do you like France?" Pascale asks, looking so intently at me that I feel like a newborn baby seen for the first time by adoring parents.

"There is so much to say," I begin.

"I'm listening," Pascale says.

"First there is the history: the centuries of kings and kingdoms."

"What is it about our history that you find so intriguing?" Pascale asks.

Now that's a question—a question that demonstrates a true interest in my experience, a question that requires some effort on my part to respond. That is the art of conversation, which, of course, is only complete when I return the favor and ask about her experience.

Isn't it ironic that a deaf girl would teach me what it means to be truly engaged and truly heard? Both Americans and French have much to learn from Pascale about the gift of intimate conversation.

"Do I have an accent when I speak to you in French?" I once asked Pascale.

"Yes," she said. "You speak like this." Pascale mimicked my fashion of speaking French: mouth wide open with teeth and tongue flapping in the wind. Then I remembered something I had read: The French hardly move their lips! It was something I needed to learn: to allow the words to flow naturally, without tension or grimace. That was a challenge for me because at that time some combinations of French sounds—like the curious cacophony of "s's" in the French pronunciation of the word *association* (ah-so-si-ah-si-on)—are like trying to deliver a Shakespearian soliloquy with a mouthful of escargots, shells and all.

Now when I speak French, I pretend to be Jean Gabin, a famous white-haired French actor (the French equivalent of Spencer Tracy), who was so laid back in his delivery that his lips hardly moved.

So, I am most grateful to Pascale for helping me with my French diction, but, even more, for being an ideal model in the art of attending to another person.

Learning a second language as an adult can be infuriating. How can I describe the feeling? It's opening night at the theater, and no one comes. No, that's not right. It's opening night; the house is packed; you have the lead and can't remember a single line. No, no, that's not it either. It's opening night; the house is packed; you have the lead and know all your lines, and the reviews are unanimously unkind. Worse than unkind. They are brutal. That's the feeling I had my first two months in France. I had practiced my lines for over two years, and I still was not understood.

One day, a French tourist was driving slowly down the street, in the way people do when they are completely lost. He pulled off to the side of the road where Jean-Marie and I were standing. The driver had that where-the-hell-am-I look in his eyes, so I said, "*Bonjour.*"

That's all I said, one perky "*bonjour.*"

And, immediately, the driver turned to Jean-Marie and asked for directions.

Mon Dieu! My American accent could be detected in one lousy word. Jean-Marie and I laughed about it later.

"Is my accent that strong?" I asked Jean-Marie.

"I don't know," Jean-Marie said. "Say *'bonjour.'*"

"*Bonjour.*"

"Yep, it's that strong."

That's frustrating. For two years, I had studied French every morning for two hours. I used every method conceivable: textbooks, literature, audiotapes, videotapes, and a weekly French club meeting. I really did work at it. But there is no textbook written, no videotape recorded that can replace the power of living in the country.

But being in the country is no piece of cake. My first two months in France were particularly humbling. In addition to dealing with French traffic, bureaucracy, and nonexistent housing, every sentence I spoke was peppered with errors. I was corrected moment by moment. Sometimes, with the best of intentions, the French would try to rescue me by offering a word or phrase in English. And sometimes . . . oh, baby, sometimes my wife would correct me. After sixty days of French immersion, I was feeling a little undone.

And on top of that—although I knew better—I was feeling a bit competitive. Nita had not studied a lick and never bothered with the oddities of French grammar. But, having grown up in Guatemala, she spoke Spanish like a native, and that base gave her a huge head start. She rattled along in French without thinking once about verb tenses or the antecedents of personal pronouns. And she was terrific! So, when she (like the well-meaning French), chose to help me by providing a word when I was stuck mid-sentence, I wanted to leave her barefoot and penniless in a tiny village in the Pyrenees and let her find her way home on her own.

Finally, one morning when we were both in the bathroom getting ready for the day, I rehearsed my speech in my head. When I was satisfied with my choice of words, I looked at Nita.

"Honey," I said. "I'm really frustrated. And I'm hoping that you'll be able to help me out. I don't get it. I've studied French so hard these last couple of years, and yet I'm still struggling. Whereas, you seem to have no problem whatsoever. This will probably sound dumb, but it would really help me out if you did a couple of things for me. First, please don't correct me unless I look to you for help. Let me work it out myself."

Nita continued brushing her hair without comment. I couldn't read how she was taking my plea.

"And, second, please let me tell my own stories." For whatever reason—perhaps out of pity for the listeners—Nita had started to finish, or at least embellish, my plodding narratives.

Nita stopped brushing her hair and said in her Mary-sunshine way, "I can do that, honey. But, gee, I think you are doing just great."

You gotta love the girl.

* * *

WITH THE POSSIBLE EXCEPTION OF THE ITALIANS, I don't know any other people who have a greater repertoire of gestures than the French. They have gestures from everything from "cuckold" (pointed index fingers over their ears) to "magnificent" (kissing their fingertips). Knowing the gestures should be a required survival strategy for any foreigner serious about learning the language. I'll share with you the most common and useful gestures to add to your kinesthetic lexicon.

Learning how to count

Ask Americans to count on their fingers, and their index finger will snap to attention on number one. That doesn't make sense to the French. For them, number one is the thumb, followed by the index finger and so on down the line. I have to admit, I think the French have something there. Why start counting in the middle of the hand?

He is drunk

Is there someone in the group who is a little tipsy? It happens. I was on a New Year's Day trek with about thirty French hikers. When we got to our turnaround point, we stopped for lunch, and the French started unpacking bread, cheese, and bottles of wine and cognac from their backpacks. I have no idea how they bore the weight, but the French never whine about porting wine.

There was a great deal of laughter, and the wine was being poured with enthusiasm. Now, I don't want to suggest that the French are any more intemperate than a randomly selected sample of Americans. They do like a good glass of wine (as do Americans), but that's about as far as it goes. However, on this day, a tall, athletic man had too much to drink. I only noticed because a friend pointed an ear in his direction.

"What?" I asked.

Now his eyebrows were raised as the head pointing became even more insistent, as if he were trying to shake water out of his ear.

"What are you talking about?"

That's when I was introduced to the "he's drunk" gesture. My friend made a loose fist, raised his fist to his nose, placed his nose in the tube formed by his hand, and twisted back and forth, much like you would turn a doorknob left and right and left again.

I got it. Now I could see that the tall man was happily soused.

I know that sort of overindulgence is frowned upon by the French because the man's impropriety was the topic of conversation all the way back to the head of the trail. They were concerned for two reasons. First, because he misjudged his limits, and, second, because they wanted to make sure that he was not behind the wheel on his way home. He was not; they made sure of that.

My eye

Both French and Americans share the same expression, "my eye," which is to say, "That's a whopper if I've ever heard one." The only difference is that the French employ a gesture that can express the sentiment without words. Place the tip of your index finger about a half inch under your lower eyelid and lightly pull down.

Jean-Marie introduced the gesture to me one day when I had launched into a story about a leisurely walk through the backstreets of Montpellier. I had just breathed in the delectable scent from a small bakery—the flour and sugar wafting onto the narrow cobblestone street. My eyes closed to languish in the heavenly perfume of freshly baked bread. When I opened my eyes again, there was a beautiful young woman in a black summer dress strolling my way. No, not strolling, *sashaying*—not in a provocative way but in a confident, graceful manner that said, "I am a Mediterranean beauty. Watch me if you wish, catch me if you dare."

I wished, but I daren't.

"But that was not the best part," I said to Jean-Marie, my eyes narrowing to build the suspense and draw my listener into the story.

"What was the best part?" he asked, with what I thought was just a hint of incredulity.

The best part, I explained, was in the next moment. Just an instant before she swished by me, she looked straight into my eyes and smiled a soft and wonderful flirtatious smile.

"That was it?" he asked.

"That was enough," I said, knowing that I had set the scene for my last line. "At that moment, she and I had an affair, as good as any steamy rendezvous in a secret hotel overlooking the Mediterranean."

It was then that Jean-Marie tugged on his lower eyelid and said, "I have some bills to pay."

I have some bills to pay! How rude! The French are supposed to be the ultimate Latin lovers. Well, I'm here to tell you that nothing can match the imagination of a healthy American libido.

Just for the record, that intimate moment with the woman in the black dress did happen (all the stories in this book are true). Whether you are a man or a woman, do not be surprised if you experience an equally delicious moment when you are walking the backstreets of a French city center. If it can happen to me, it can happen to you.

Damn, that's irritating

I have to admit that I am easily annoyed by the abundance of human tomfoolery: parents who fetter their children with names like Notorious, Corleone, and Sha-Dynasty; a preacher who uses the pulpit for personal gain; a CEO who makes 380 times the company's *average* salary. I could go on, but you get the idea. But despite all the irritations that assail me, I don't have a gesture to express my annoyance.

The French do. Their gesture is called *la barbe* (the beard) and is made by stroking the side of your jaw with the backside of your fingers. I imagine that the metaphor has something to do with the prickliness of a three-day-old beard.

I've seen the gesture used typically in a family setting.

"I couldn't get the car out of the garage this morning."

"Why not?"

"Because all your stuff was in the way."

"Why didn't you move it?"

"Because it's not my stuff," and, just like that, the hand caresses the jawline as if to say, "Damn, that's irritating."

Fear

Americans don't have a universal gesture for expressing fear. I recently did a survey of a few American friends to prove my point.

"If you could not use words, how would you express fear?" I asked.

One friend flared his nostrils, turned the corners of his mouth down, and opened his eyes wide. For my money, he looked less fearful and more zombie-like.

Another extroverted friend framed his face with both hands and then shook his open palms, which made me think of jangling tambourines. He reminded me of a stiff-legged Jimmy Durante shuffling off stage while waggling his fedora and saying, "Ha-cha-cha-cha."

When I asked my wife to give me her rendition of a moment in fear, she looked, quite frankly, as if she had just been electrocuted.

No, we Americans don't have a definitive gesture for fear, but the French have come to the rescue to fill that deficiency. The gesture is simple. They invert their hand as if they were suggesting the petals of a flower and then tap their pressed fingers against the thumb. The gesture is similar to an expressive Italian compressing his fingers and shaking his hand: "'Atsa onea gooda meataball." Only the French don't shake their hands, they tap their fingers. And if we are talking scared-out-of-their-pants kind of fear, they would make the gesture with both hands. At that point, you know the story is going to be Stephen-King scary.

The first time I saw the gesture was in a backyard swimming pool. My friend, Marie, was learning to scuba dive. She had her tank strapped on, and she was attempting to remove, replace, and clear her mask underwater for the first time. I was in the pool with her, standing directly in front of her giving directions.

"To clear your mask," I said, "just press the top rim of the mask, tip your head back, and exhale through your nose."

Marie was staring intently at me as if I were reciting my wedding vows to her. "Okay," she said. "Let's try it."

We were only standing in four feet of water, so we sank to the bottom of the pool and rested on our knees. Marie was able to take off and reset her mask with ease, but when she tried to clear her mask, she inhaled instead of exhaled, which fired a draft of water up her nose. Her eyes flew open, and she popped to the surface like a submarine missile, coughing up pool water. There was no thumbs-up sign. What she gave me was the tapping-fingers fear sign—not with one, but with both hands.

In Marie's defense, I have to say that she is an undaunted trooper. "I can do this," she said with determination.

"Just *exhale*," I said.

"*Oui,* exhale, exhale," she chanted like an incantation. In the next instant, we were both on our knees again, and she doffed, donned, and drained her mask like a champ. We celebrated with a thumbs-up sign.

As a footnote, Marie took to diving like a fish. In fact, she is now the owner of a dive shop in the South Pacific. Not bad for a girl whose first mask-clearing attempt resulted in a snout full of water.

When you are really inflamed

I probably should not teach this to you. Maybe this is a good time for the children to leave the room. But those of us with a more sturdy constitution should probably be familiar with the French gesture for "you can take your *#!%^ and shove it." Personally, I've never used the gesture—I wouldn't want to be kicked out of the country—but I have seen it used on occasion.

Here's how the gesture is made. Turn the palm of your right hand over as if you were carrying your dinner plate to the kitchen table. Then, with your left hand tap your right wrist and allow the right hand to flip up to the sun. It is the French equivalent to the American one-finger salute. I told you it wasn't pretty.

Now the French can be very inventive with variations of this gesture. I once witnessed a car accident at a busy intersection. Before checking for injuries and before writing down license plate numbers, one driver flew out of his car and started screaming a string of invectives that were not included in my glossary of *French Phrases for Tourists*.

Not to be outdone, the other driver bailed out of his car and gave his astringent assailant a nasty three-tiered rejoinder. He first slapped his wrist, then his elbow, and finished with a whack across his shoulder—his right fisted arm poking a hole in the sky over his head. I think it's safe to say, I was witnessing a boiling point of rage.

To be clear, I have never seen one of my French friends use this salacious gesture—I tended to mix with a rather polished league of people—but if you are in France for any stretch of time, you will eventually see the obscenity flashed in the heat of battle when the Latin blood is sizzling. I just thought you should know.

A few other favorites

I'm just scratching the surface when it comes to French gestural ingenuity. They were coming at me so frequently in le Midi that I began making a list. Here are a few more of my favorites.

1. *J'en ai ras le bol.* I've had it up to here. Shade your eyes with your right hand and "slice" across your forehead.
2. *À peu près.* It's just an estimate. Place your hand in front of you as if to shake hands and rotate your hand back and forth.
3. *Que dalle!* The expression means "absolutely nothing." You might use it when someone asks you what you have been doing lately. Close your hand, but stick out the thumb in typical hitchhiking form. Then place the nail of your thumb behind your front teeth. Finally, snap your hand forward, allowing the nail to make a clicking sound against the teeth.
4. *Alors là.* This has many nuances: There's nothing I can do about it. It's not my fault. I don't know. Raise both hands to shoulder height, palms open. You know the gesture: "Stick 'em up."
5. *Il a un poil dans la main.* He has a hair in his hand, meaning "he is lazy." Open your hand and pull an imaginary hair from the middle of your palm.
6. *Aïe, aïe, aïe!* Someone is in trouble. Hold your hand in front of your stomach, allowing your fingers to be loose, and then quickly shake your hand.

7. *Il est cinglé.* He is crazy. There are two ways to express this sentiment: (a) Tap your temple with your index finger or (b) "screw" your index finger into your temple.

8. *Passer sous le nez.* The literal translation is "it passed under my nose" but means, "it slipped through my fingers." Slide your index finger under your nose.

Passer sous le nez

9. *C'est facile.* It's easy. We say, "It's so easy, I could do it with one arm tied behind my back." The French say, "It's so easy, I could do it with two fingers up my nose." (I know, it's strange, but there you have it. But, just to be fair, the French rightly think it's pretty weird when we say, "It's raining cats and dogs.") Directions: Place your index and middle finger in the opening of your nostrils.

10. *On s'en va.* Let's go. This is a great gesture when you want to indicate to your wife across the room that it's time to leave the party. Place your hand in front of you as if you were going to shake hands and tap your wrist bone. Be careful with this one. Remember, your hand is vertical with the floor, not horizontal. If it were horizontal, palm down, and you tapped the inside of your wrist, you would be telling your wife across the room to *#!%^ off, which is never a good choice.

* * *

AFTER THE FIRST TWO MONTHS, I began to notice small changes. First, I noticed I was comprehending more—reading the paper, listening to the radio, talking to friends. Suddenly, I could take in an entire French movie and actually understand! It was amazing. Then, I noticed I had more phrases in my repertoire—a lot more. I knew how to comment on the weather, my health, or even the state of human affairs. And then, little by little, I was aligning these phrases into full sentences. Sure, I was still making mistakes, but I was being understood. The language was coming along after all.

Some of the most dramatic improvements came in understanding and respecting the rules of language that have been embedded in the culture for hundreds of years. For example, I no longer used the informal "you" for everyone—from the youngest child to the oldest grandparent. I've learned my lesson on that score.

In 1971 Nita and I made friends with Pierre Michel, who at that time was a fifty-five-year-old educational supplies salesman. Monsieur Michel was a very proper and traditional Frenchman. He was well educated and very articulate. His home was cluttered with stacks of books, including all the classics, and fine traditional paintings, particularly an astonishing self-portrait by his grandfather. The French have the interesting term "BCBG," meaning *bon chic bon genre* (chic and conservative). It is a term that refers to a particular French stereotype: one who is upper middle class, well dressed, well mannered, well heeled, and somewhat bourgeois. Pierre Michel was definitely BCBG.

During our one-year stay in Grenoble, we had the Michels over for dinner, and they returned the favor. We truly enjoyed each other's company although I think that Pierre was particularly smitten with Nita, who has always been a beautiful and charming woman.

Over the years, we corresponded with Monsieur Michel, sending him a card or letter at least once a year. His letters were always warm and very newsy.

On our reentry into the country in 2002, Nita and I revisited our old friend in his Grenoble apartment. Pierre, now an unusually spry eighty-six-year-old, served a wonderful five-course dinner. We talked animatedly for hours around the formal dining table. I used the informal you—*tutoyer*—from the start. I figured that thirty years was long enough to be on a casual playing field. Later in the evening, Pierre said with a wry smile, "I am a little surprised that you are using the informal you with me."

He caught me off guard. "Why, yes," I said haltingly. "I think of you as a dear friend, and I *tutoie* out of genuine affection."

Pierre smiled. "But, my American friend," he said, "it is not a question of affection. It is a question of respect. To *vouvoyer* (formal you) does not mean that you feel less affectionate toward another. In fact, in some old families, spouses will often *vouvoyer* each other. To use the formal you is to hold the other in high regard."

"*Vraiment, je suis désolé.* Truly, I am sorry," I said sincerely. "I would never want to be disrespectful, and, of course, I hold you in high regard—the highest. From this point on, I will use the formal you."

"No," he said with a smile, "it is too late now."

It is true that once the *informal* "you" is employed, using the *formal* "you" is a little like calling your best friend Ziggy "my dear Mr. Finkel." But it can happen. Monique gave me an example. She and Jean-Marie became friends with a man who later became her boss. As a friend, she used the informal *tutoiement*. But when she became his employee, she suggested—and he agreed—that she should revert to the formal you. Still, there was a twinkle in Monique's eye each time she used the more formal pronoun with her old chum.

For me, I now follow two simple rules.

1. *Tutoyer* children, cats, and dogs.
2. *Vouvoyer* the rest of the world unless (or until) they invite me to *tutoyer* them.

That way, I am never wrong.

As the months rolled by, there were other signs of improvement. I didn't fake understanding nearly as much. In those early days I could be caught grinning like a golden retriever, nodding my head in agreement when, in fact, I didn't understand a word. Nor did I have to control the conversation with a constant stream of questions (a trick I learned to assure tracking a topic).

I even learned to detect the broadest French accents, like French with an Italian or Spanish inflection. Of course, as usual, I became cocky with my newfound skill.

One day, I was writing a letter at the dinner table while Nita was watching a sci-fi movie on television. Someone was speaking with an unusual accent.

"That person is not French," I pronounced to Nita proudly.

"You're right," Nita said, "it's a robot."

"There you go," I said. "I'm getting better. I can now tell the difference between a Frenchman and a robot."

So yes, there is much work to be done, but I finally see some progress, and that's encouraging. And maybe, just maybe one day, when I least expect it, speaking French will read more like the following headline:

Opening Night
Standing Room Only
Johnson's Performance Flawless
Rave Reviews
Bof.

CHAPTER 4

Finding Lodging

THIS WAS MY VISION FOR A HOME IN FRANCE.

A stone farmhouse nestled in the countryside with a fireplace big enough to stand in. The farmhouse floor would be a burnt golden tile, and in the kitchen there would stand an enormous stone oven for baking bread. In the master bedroom I would sleep in a four-poster canopied feathered bed, and at the foot of that bed would repose a brindle Great Dane, his head on his paws, his eyes following me, his imperious master, as I pulled on my Italian-leather knee-high boots.

Outside, a courtyard would be shaded by a grand oak tree—planted during the Crusades in commemoration of the boys who died on pagan shores.

The house would be surrounded by five-hundred-year-old vineyards. And within the split-rail fenced pasture, a few shaggy white goats would munch on their breakfast, their kids frolicking in the morning sun. Along the side of the house would be a cavernous wine cellar, stocked with lightly dusted bottles whose labels sang out like a love song: Riesling, Chardonnay, Sauvignon, Merlot, and Pinot Noir—wines so exquisite that Bacchus himself would recite rapturous odes of joy.

Walking distance from the home—across the arched Roman bridge and down the cobblestoned road rutted by ancient chariots—would be a *boulangerie* stocked with baguettes and brioches and croissants and a myriad of fruit tarts.

The baker would greet me with a warm Mediterranean smile. "Ah, Monsieur Johnson," he would say, "Johnson" sounding more like *Jah-soh*, which would make me smile. "I am so happy you have come this morning. I have created something especially for you. *Regardez*, a chocolate crisp with layers of a flaky crust and a strawberry center that whispers, 'Let me be your temptress *ce soir*.' I have named it 'Monsieur Johnson' in honor of my great American friend."

* * *

THAT WAS MY FANTASY. There must be a hideaway like that somewhere in France, but I have not found it. Sure, there are thousands of picturesque villages and hamlets scattered across the mountainsides and valleys of France. But finding one with a house or apartment available for rent is another story.

Our search for lodging took a little over a month—thirty-six days of scouring the cities, villages, and countryside. Admittedly, a major setback was our timing. We arrived in Montpellier on the fourth of August, the absolute worst time to be looking for a rental in southern France. Why? Because all of France is on vacation in August—in le Midi. If you can find a villa, a *maison*, an apartment—shoot, if you can find a boxboard lean-to—in southern France in August, you have either phenomenal good luck or, more likely, inside connections. We had neither.

However, we did have a lifeline: our trusted friends, Jean-Marie and Monique, who were gracious enough, courageous enough, to find room for us in their lovely home in Pérols. Without them I would have been strumming my guitar in the town square with a sign that read WILL WORK FOR SHELTER.

The Ducros are a kind and generous family, no question, but even saints have their limits. We figured a one- or two-week stay would be the very most we could impose on our dear friends. So we immediately began our search for a place of our own. It was our single mission in life.

Very quickly, we learned that there were three traditional housing resources: real estate agents, *gîtes*, and the offices of tourism. We assaulted all three. Not since the D-Day invasion have Americans been so committed.

Our search began by visiting the local estate agents—*agences immobilières,* they are called. Each new exchange was like the last.

"*Bonjour, madame.*"

"*Bonjour, monsieur.*"

Their eyes begin to gloss over before I finish my opening sentence. "I am looking for a house or apartment to rent."

That's when they would hit me with that uniquely French way of expressing either disdain or impossibility: a little puff of air exploding from the side of the mouth. (Yes, it's a distant cousin of the "phutt" sound described in Chapter 3.) My wife makes that sound when she is sleeping. Her lips, perfectly sealed, cause her breath to build up in her mouth until her lips can no longer contain the pressure and—poof—the air bubble bursts from the corner of her mouth. It's cute when she does it. But coming from an *agent immobilier*, it is crushing: the terrible French air puff.

"Puff. There is nothing," the agent would say.

"Nothing?" I would repeat morosely.

"Nothing, nothing. *Rien, rien.*"

"But if something becomes available, you will call me," I pleaded.

"*Ben, mais oui,*" they would say, visibly placating me. (I knew when I was being placated. Their baby browns transformed into drooping dead-fish eyes drifting over the Mediterranean.) Still, they would deferentially take down my name and phone number.

That conversation was repeated dozens of times—little puffs of air exploding all over southern France.

There were other variations:

"*Désolé.* I'm sorry, we only sell."

"We only have studios."

"We only rent for three years at a time."

"It is the high season, you know."

When it comes to lodging, it is definitely a seller's market in le Midi. As one agent explained to me, "Everyone is looking for the sun."

Because the demand is so high, agents have the upper hand. Writing three-year contracts for rentals is not uncommon. Nor is it uncommon to demand hefty fees. The apartment we finally landed was a one-bedroom, sparsely furnished 460-square-foot, third-story apartment (no elevator). The price was $568 a month, and we were delighted with the bargain. That is the off-season price, from September to June (often May). The price for the same apartment in July and August is a whopping $3,200 a month—or more.

To find a furnished apartment in southern France, you must go to the resort towns—Grand Motte, Carnon, Palavas, Frontignan—and eighty percent of these are studios or one-bedroom apartments. Finding a furnished, two-bedroom apartment—especially one with a decent view—is a rarity. Most of them have been tied up for years. The small apartments are popular because they are easily sold to vacationers during the summer and to university students during the school year—yielding a good return on a reasonable investment.

A second option is *gîtes*, country farmhouses that have been converted into furnished holiday apartments, but the tariff can be steep: four hundred to seven hundred dollars per week for a two-bedroom. And, more often than not, you will find that *gîtes* are only available during the summer months. The locations are often lovely, but you must be willing to adjust to a very quiet rural setting.

A third option—after estate agents and *gîtes*—is to go to the Office du Tourisme that is located in almost any town with over ten thousand inhabitants. These offices are always helpful, and, more importantly, they offer a list of studios, apartments, and occasionally villas that are rented directly by the proprietor—avoiding the *agences immobilières* altogether.

This is my preferred way of looking for lodging. You sidestep many of the problems that accompany a transaction with an agent (more about that in a moment). Usually owners are very anxious to show you their apartments. The downside is proprietors can sometimes overstate their property's appeal. Nita and I were once lured into driving thirty miles to see an apartment with "a direct view of the sea," only to discover that "a direct view" required hanging over a balcony (Nita holding on to my legs) to get a glimpse of blue the size of my fist at arm's length. Still, I have had better luck with individual owners than with agents.

* * *

IN ONE MONTH I was let down a half-dozen times by French estate agents. My first disappointment was with an agency in Carnon, which I will call Seaside Rentals. The first time I walked into Seaside Rentals, it was mid-August, the high season. I was directed to a young lady who, as I was to discover in a moment, spoke English. To protect the names of the innocent agents (there must be someone somewhere), I'll call her Annette.

"I'm looking for an apartment with two bedrooms," I told Annette in French.

Annette recognized my American accent immediately. "Would you prefer that we speak in English?" she asked in French.

I smiled. "No," I said, "I really prefer to speak in French. It is good practice for me. Thank you for asking for my preference."

"It is only natural," Annette said. "I think we may have just the right apartment for you. It is *en première ligne* (first line, meaning directly on the beach). There are two bedrooms, a washing machine, a dishwasher, a television, a telephone, a balcony, and a garage."

Annette had just rattled off my list of requirements. *"Parfait,"* I said. "When can we see it?"

"Not for two weeks," Annette said. "Renters are there until the end of the month. But I think you will like it very much. It is very bright and airy."

"I'm sure we'll love it," I said. "Now, we are first in line to see it, right?"

"Absolutely."

"That's good," I said, "because, as you know, finding an apartment is next to impossible."

"Oh, yes, I know," Annette said.

So we shook hands, and I left with the promise that we would have the first chance to see and rent the apartment on the beach. But, just to be sure, I would call Annette every four or five days to confirm our understanding.

"Oh, yes," she would say. "You are first in line. Don't worry. I will see you at the end of the month."

In the two weeks that followed my visit with Annette, Nita and I combed the beach and countryside for apartments—just as a backup precaution. There was nothing. "It is very difficult to find an apartment these days," they would say, stating the obvious. And then they would add, "Did you know that the price of apartments has doubled in the last two years?"

"Really?" I would say.

"Oh, yes. *C'est comme ça.* That's the way it is."

So when the end of the month finally arrived, Nita and I were very anxious to see "the airy and bright two-bedroom apartment on the beach."

I practically danced into Seaside Rentals. *"Bonjour à tous,"* I called out.

Annette came to the front desk to greet me. *"Bonjour* Monsieur Johnson," she said. "May I help you?"

May she help me? Of course, she could help me. Why was she talking to me like I was a stranger off the street? I was ready to move into what I considered to be *our* apartment; the current residents were merely squatters.

"I'm here to see the apartment," I sang out.

"Oh, I'm sorry Monsieur Johnson . . ."

The room went dark for a moment. I saw myself on the beach, a bony derelict with a scruffy beard, leathery sunbaked skin, and sandals carved out of driftwood. Nita was cooking hermit crabs for the third time this week over an open fire. But tonight was a special night. Tonight, we would invite Annette for dinner, and I would take her out to the water's edge and strangle her in the surf!

"The apartment is already rented. Someone took it sight unseen. You didn't have it reserved."

"What do you mean, 'I didn't have it reserved'? I had it reserved, I had it reserved." Turning to Nita, "Didn't I have it reserved? Tell me I had it reserved!"

"What does having a reservation mean?" Nita asked calmly. (I hate it when my wife is calm in the middle of a disaster.)

"You must pay the agent's fee in advance," Annette said coolly.

"But you said *nothing about that!*" I howled, the blue veins in my neck throbbing. "You said that we would have first rights to seeing the apartment. Remember!"

"And, yes, you would have had first rights," Annette said. "Only, the people who took the apartment did not *see* the apartment. They took it sight unseen."

"But, but, but . . . why didn't you tell us it had been rented? We have been waiting for two weeks for this apartment."

Annette's smile was a slit of bewilderment. "We are very busy here, Monsieur Johnson," she said in a tone that made me want to smack her.

"Let's go," Nita said in English, recognizing my symptoms for internal hemorrhaging.

I looked at Nita as she guided me to the door. "I'm not happy," I whimpered. "I'm not happy at all. That was our apartment."

"I know dear."

"I *really* wanted that apartment."

"Yes, sweetheart."

"But she gave it to someone else."

"Yes, dear."

"After she promised that she would give it to us."

"That's right, honey."

"I . . . I can't believe she did that. That wasn't very nice."

"No, it wasn't. She's not a nice woman."

So the search continued. Day after day, one agent after the other told us that nothing was available. Then, on a whispered lead from a friend, we called Marlon Apartments.

"Oh yes," a woman said. "Your friend called us, and we do have an apartment for you. It's a two-floor apartment overlooking the port on one side and the sea on the other. Would you like to see it?"

I practically leapt through the phone line. "Yes, we would like to see it! We would like to see it very much. When can we see it?"

"Right away," the woman said.

"Great," I said. "We can be there in five minutes. You won't rent it between now and then, right?"

"No, we won't rent it in the next five minutes."

"Promise?"

"Yes, I promise," the woman said.

In five minutes we were in the Marlon Apartments office, both of us panting like a pair of Labrador retrievers. Ten minutes later, we were walking through the apartment. There were a few problems. The front door was swollen with moisture and would only open to a forty-five-degree angle; the television didn't work; and the awning over the terrace was broken. But it was roomy, and the view was terrific. I immediately put on my "close-the-deal" face while Nita was skipping from room to room, singing, "I love it, I absolutely love it."

I pulled Nita off to the side. "Try to control your enthusiasm for a minute," I whispered, "so I can close this deal within our budget."

That's one of the differences between Nita and me. When Nita sees something she likes, she makes puppy squealing noises. She may as well open up her purse and say, "Take whatever you want. Would you like my car keys? How about my 401(k) account number? My shoes are brand new; they'd be lovely with your dress; would you like them?"

I, on the other hand, look for leverage: little faults that I can use during negotiation. There were the problems with the front door, the television, and the awning. All that was immediately evident. But there was also no garage and no private parking. I would have to fend for myself on the bustling narrow streets of Carnon—a real problem in a French resort town during the high season.

As I wandered through the apartment, I started to chronicle the litany of problems. "Hmmm, the elevator is a little small, don't you think; the wallpaper in the bathroom is rather garish, wouldn't you agree; the sun will probably wake me up in the morning. There's that to think about, you know."

Finally, I turned to the agent with my hard-boiled business face attached. As a seasoned and wily negotiator, this would be my *pièce de résistance*. All I had to do was make sure my voice would not crack like a kazoo out of sheer excitement. "So, there are the problems with the door, the television, and the awning," I began.

"I can't imagine that the proprietor would want to do anything about that," the agent said.

"But surely we should be able to open the front door," I said, already mentally giving in on the television and the awning.

"I don't know," the agent said.

"Okay, okay," I said, my voice becoming more kazoo-like by the minute. "Could we do this? Could you call the proprietor and see what he is willing to do? But while we are waiting for his response, you must promise not to rent the apartment. Agreed?"

"Agreed."

"Say, 'I promise.'"

"Pardon?"

"Say, 'I promise I won't rent the apartment to anyone else.'"

The agent looked at me strangely and then smiled. *"Bon,"* she said, "I promise."

"Will you call today?" I asked.

"Yes."

"When will I hear from you?"

The French hate this kind of pressure, but I was in no mood to be culturally sensitive. I wanted the apartment—even with a front door that only opened halfway.

"You will hear from me tonight or tomorrow at the latest," the agent said. "Okay?"

"Okay."

The agent did not call of course. Not that night, not the next morning, not the next day. So I called.

"The proprietor is not in," the agent said.

"Can you call again?" I insisted.

"No, we have already left a message."

"But if you called again . . ."

Suddenly the agent's voice had the nip of dry ice. "No, Monsieur Johnson. We will let you know as soon as we hear from him."

"But you will not rent out the apartment in the meantime."

"No, we will not rent the apartment."

A day later, still no call. Two days later Nita and I decided to revisit Marlon Apartments in person.

"Ah, Monsieur Johnson," the agent said. "We have bad news."

The room went dark. It is morning on the beach. We are recovering from a torrential midnight thunderstorm. Nita is drying out our sleeping bags over a skein of driftwood. I notice something out of place washed ashore and walk to the water's edge to investigate. It is the front page of Le Monde. *There is a hint of a smile on my lips as my eyes narrow to read the headline:* MYSTERIOUS SERIAL KILLER SLAYS ANOTHER REAL ESTATE AGENT.

"You see, the proprietor has decided to give the apartment to his son for the year while he is at the university. Sorry."

Aaarrrgg.

Nita and I step out into the sunshine.

"I don't know what to do at this point," I said truthfully. "We have stayed with the Ducros for a month. They've been wonderful, but we can't abuse their kindness for much longer. It's just not fair to them."

"I know," Nita said quietly.

I said nothing for a long moment. "All right, this is a long shot, but what if we went back to Seaside Rentals. Maybe something has opened up in the last week."

"You mean Annette?" Nita asked.

"Uh-huh."

"I didn't think you would ever go back there again."

"At this point I don't have a choice. I'll do whatever it takes to find an apartment."

Nita and I got in the car and drove to Seaside Rentals.

Annette greeted us the moment we stepped into the agency. "*Bonjour* Madame Johnson, Monsieur Johnson."

Contrary to French protocol, I launched right into business. I was still angry with Annette but decided to marshal my rancor—anything for an apartment.

"Annette, we still have not found an apartment," I said, with just a *soupçon* of wretchedness in my voice. "We have looked everywhere. There is nothing. Has anything opened up since we last saw you?"

"As a matter of fact," Annette said, "something has become available. It was originally reserved for another couple, but they have had some difficulty with financing."

I didn't have the slightest sympathy for the economically challenged renters. At this point, *sauve-qui-peut* (every man for himself) was my motto.

"It is small," Annette said. "Only one bedroom, but it is directly on the beach."

A soft zephyr of hope caressed the back of my neck. "Could we see it?" I asked timidly, sure that the apartment must be either underwater or overrun by a band of drug addicts with untidy bathroom etiquette.

"Absolutely," she said.

Ten minutes later, Annette opened the door to a third-floor apartment. It was indeed small, just 460 square feet. There are men in New York City, who wear lavender suits and pinky rings, who have cars with more square footage. But the walls were white, the terra-cotta tile smooth and clean, the draperies, tablecloth, and bedspread *Provençal*. There was a good-sized bedroom with room enough to make the bed—no gymnastic maneuvering required. The room had a wall-to-wall window that offered a view of two-story holiday apartments across the street, a canal, and the 2,100-foot mountain, Pic Saint Loup, on the horizon.

The bathroom was small with poor lighting and no drawers or cabinets for storage, but the tub doubled as a shower, which is critical for me. (There is something about sitting in a porcelain tub of dirty water that gives me the creepy-crawlies.) The kitchen was compact but had cabinets replete with three frying pans, white dishes, and aluminum silverware. A range, an oven, and a half-fridge completed the kitchen.

The living room featured a generous day bed, a fourteen-inch television (important for learning French), a telephone jack (indispensable for chatting with French friends and communicating with folks back home via email), a round pine dining room table, and three French impressionistic prints.

All that was fine, even admirable, but the crowning feature was the balcony, a six-by-ten-foot surface that overlooked the beach, sunbathers, and the Mediterranean Sea. The sky was cloudless, the sea turquoise blue, interrupted only by the distant crescent sheets of canvas of a hundred sailing boats. And then there was the sound—the waves breaking softly on the shore, like the sound of lovers whispering tenderly in the night.

Nita and I looked at each other and smiled. "We'll take it," we said in one voice, not thinking once about the price ($568 a month, including garage).

It was then that the French bureaucracy kicked in with a vengeance.

We drove back to the agency, sat down, and started the paperwork. Annette clicked off the documents that were required:

- Formal application
- Confirmation of apartment insurance
- A canceled bank check
- Two photocopies of two separate identification cards
- Marriage certificate
- Salary pay stubs for the last three months
- Most recent tax statement
- A letter from my employer confirming my employment

Daunting, to say the least. I took in a deep breath, opened a two-inch portfolio of certificates, licenses, and applications reserved for just this kind of French torture and unleashed the longest French sentence of my career as a francophone. "I am self-employed," I said, "but I do have an attestation from my American bank—translated into French by an approved embassy translator and stamped by the French Consulate in San Francisco—confirming that no less than eighteen hundred dollars will be deposited into my French bank account each month, the exact sum required by the Consulate to obtain a long-stay visa. Will that be sufficient for proof of income?" Breath.

Annette narrowed her eyes, looked at me, looked at the stack of documents, and said, "*Oui*, that will be sufficient, but you must have the rest of the documents."

"Oh, I do," I said, maybe a little too anxiously. "I do, I do. There is this and this and this too," I said, peeling out the required documents. I was beginning to feel a bit smug.

"*But . . .*"

I knew it, I just knew it. Of course our papers were not in order. I could see it coming. "You think you can get away with this?" she would say, the ashes tumbling from a cigarette stub at the corner of her mouth. "Ha, and again, ha! Maybe you would like me to get the directrice, Madame Paininzeebutt, and have her work you over. She knows how to deal with people like you. She can do things with ordinary kitchen utensils that will make you wish you had been born a lizard."

"But," Annette said, "you must pay now for the agency fee, the first month rent, and an additional two months security deposit. That comes to, let me see . . ." Annette began mumbling to herself as she worked the calculations, converting from francs to euros. "Yes," she finally said, "that will be two thousand and sixty euros, eighty centimes."

"Fine," I said in an instant, unfolding a wad of traveler's checks.

"Mais non," Annette said, with an apologetic smile, "we do not accept traveler's checks."

"Mais non," I said, hinging on sarcasm. "Then, here is my Visa card. You do accept Visa?"

"Ah ça, je ne sais pas—that, I don't know," Annette said. "I will have to ask Madame la Directrice Paininzeebutt."

Annette rose slowly from her chair and moved to a hidden office in the back of the building, visibly reluctant to disturb the *directrice*. I gave Nita a crooked smile—an I-don't-know-if-this-is-going-to-fly kind of a look.

A moment later, less than a moment later, Annette was back. "Sorry," she said, settling into her chair. "We cannot accept Visa cards from foreigners. If you were French, yes, but you are American, of course."

"Of course," I said, looking at my watch. "Fine, I will go to the bank and get the money."

"I will stay here," my wife volunteered.

I looked Annette straight in the eyes. "But you must promise not to rent the apartment to someone else while I'm gone."

"Bien sûr," Annette said. "Certainly. After all, your wife will be here to protect your interests."

"Yes she will. Please remember that," I said with the sinister tone of Vinnie the Fish, the mob bookie, citing the consequences of a late payment.

With that I swept out of the agency and rushed off to the bank in Pérols, which was just a few minutes away.

"*Bonjour*, monsieur," I said to the bank clerk, remembering my French manners. I waited obediently for him to return the greeting while the clock took on the tempo of the slowest adagio imaginable.

"*Bonjour*, monsieur," he finally said.

Okay, I thought, that's done. Now let's do some business. "I need to cash two thousand euros in traveler's checks," I said. "Today, right now," I added for emphasis.

"Impossible," the bank clerk said. "Tomorrow, perhaps, but not today."

Okay, okay, okay. I'm all right. I'm calm. I'm in control. This is not going to be a problem for me. Every day in every way, I'm getting better and better. I love myself. I love the French. We are all God's children, one with the universe, and at peace with the world.

"And why the *hell* not?" I demanded.

"Because," the bank clerk said, infuriatingly calm, "we have insufficient funds. I can give you five hundred euros, but that is all."

"But I need two thousand euros."

"*Eh oui,*" the bank clerk said, throwing up both hands.

Yeah, I've got your "*Eh oui*" right here buster. Fine, I thought to myself, as I spun on my heels and barreled out the door. I'll go to the cash machine and draw out enough for the agent's fee and then pay off the rest the next day. There was an ATM right around the corner. I put in my card and punched in my code.

INCORRECT CODE the machine flashed back.

What do you mean "incorrect code"? I punched in my numbers again. Okay, I'm in. I tapped in the sum, €500. The machine instructed me to validate the request, but which button was the arrow pointing to? I wasn't sure. The letters on the buttons were worn off. So, I guessed.

INVALID TRANSACTION the machine shouted back at me in big impertinent block letters. PLEASE CONTACT YOUR BANK ADMINISTRATOR.

Somewhere, in a place far away, the setting sun turns the sky an evanescent golden hue. Bluebirds sing "tweet, tweet, tweet" as they glide in a synchronized ballet across God's canopy. The children are laughing. Little girls in pink dresses play double Dutch while boys in striped T-shirts and worn high-top tennis shoes draw a circle in the soft blanket of sand for a friendly game of marbles.

There is a place like that somewhere in the universe. As for me, I was a breath away from doing battle with an ATM. The only thing that stopped me was the image of me sharing a French prison cell with Jean-Luke DuScarface, the serial mother rapist.

Reluctantly—agonizingly reluctantly—I returned to the bank. Three women with big purses were ahead of me. The second hand on the big clock on the wall clicked my life away. Then, a mind-bending eternity later, it was finally my turn.

"I'll take your offer to exchange five hundred euros in traveler's checks," I said immediately.

"*Bonjour*, monsieur," the bank clerk said.

Right. "*Bonjour*, monsieur," I said. "I'll take the five hundred euros."

The bank clerk just smiled at me. What was going on here? Bank clerks never smile—certainly not French bank clerks. And then he said, "*Vous allez bien?*"

"Yeah, yeah, I'm doing just fine," I said. "About the five hundred euros?"

"*Oui*, but of course."

I few minutes later, five hundred euros richer, I headed back to the agent's office.

Nita was still there, waiting patiently, calmly. "Everything okay?" she asked.

"Don't ask."

"What's wrong?"

"I told you not to ask."

I turned to Annette. "I will not be able to have the entire sum until tomorrow," I said. "But I do have the agent's fee to reserve the apartment."

"There is no hurry," Annette said.

"Oh?"

"I have spoken to the proprietor, and he may want to give the apartment to his daughter for ten days before she goes back to the university. He will let us know for certain tomorrow."

"*Ce n'est pas possible,*" I said. "It's not possible. Tell me it's not true."

"*Si, c'est vrai,*" she said as cool as French yogurt. "Yes, it is true. So, perhaps you can collect the rest of the money, and I will call you as soon as I have news from the proprietor."

"You will call us as soon as you have news," I said in the form of a statement.

"Oh, yes," Annette said.

"And that will be today sometime," I said.

"Certainly," Annette assured me.

"Okay," I said getting up slowly. "I will talk to you later today."

"Yes, Monsieur Johnson. Later today."

"Okay, later today. I'm going now, but we'll talk later today."

Nita put her arm around my shoulder and led me out the door, little spit bubbles forming at the corners of my mouth.

"I don't like this," I said.

"I know, honey, I know."

"But I really wanted to move in today."

"And we will move in," Nita assured me. "Just not today."

The rest of the day, I sat by the phone and waited, but Annette did not call. I did not sleep very well that night. I kept dreaming about sleeping on the beach. French-speaking cooties worked their way under my blanket and gnawed on the back of my legs as if they were feasting on buttered corn on the cob.

But, in typical southern-France fashion, the next morning was sunny, and I was hopeful again.

I showered, had breakfast, and headed for the bank, delegating Nita to stand guard over the phone. I was able to exchange $1,500 in traveler's checks without a hitch. Already I was feeling better.

But when I returned from the bank, Annette had not yet called. In fact, two days passed without a word. Finally, I called Annette.

"*Bonjour* Monsieur Johnson," she said.

"*Bonjour* Annette," I said and then waited in silence for some news.

"How can I help you?" she said.

Huh? "The apartment," I said. "You have news about the apartment."

"Ah, yes," she said, "I have good news for you, Monsieur Johnson. The proprietor has decided to rent the apartment to you right away."

I turned to Nita, who was closely monitoring the conversation. She gave me one of her angelic looks: the isn't-life-a-glorious-thing look. I adopted the same expression. It was a religious moment for me.

"So, if you will come to the office in two days, we will have the paperwork ready," Annette said.

"Two days? What do you mean 'two days'? I can't wait two days."

"That is the best I can do," Annette said.

"But . . ."

"Two days, Monsieur Johnson."

One day later, I called Annette to confirm our meeting on the following day.

"Oh, yes," she said. "Everything is in order."

The following day, Nita and I had one item on our agenda: to see Annette. We arrived ten minutes early and waited fifteen minutes for Annette to greet us. But I was in control. I had adopted Nita's isn't-life-a-glorious-thing look, which is an expression I describe as half grinning, half stoned—a kind of creepy, peaceful look.

"*Bonjour* madame, monsieur," she said across the counter. Would you please sit down?"

I did not like her tone—one that was laced with peril. "Everything is in order. However, there is one little difficulty," Annette said. "You are a foreigner, you know."

"I know."

"And as such, you pose a risk. We have had problems with foreigners in the past."

The isn't-life-a-glorious-thing look was quickly draining from my face. "Uh-huh."

"So," Annette continued, "you have a choice. You can either have a French citizen sign a guarantee on your behalf, or you can pay the rent for the entire year in advance."

I stared numbly at Annette. If looks could kill, Annette would have been a lifeless meat loaf sandwich.

But I remembered the mantra that I had repeated to myself again and again when I was preparing for the French adventure back home: You are going for a cultural experience. Bureaucracy is part of the cultural experience. Embrace it as best you can. Still, the American in me could not help asking one question. "We have been waiting two days for this meeting. Why didn't you call me about this problem earlier?"

"Oh, you understand, Monsieur Johnson, we are very busy."

"Uh-huh."

There are times when it is a sweet luxury to turn your back on poor service, to walk out the door, and with that defiant and noble gesture pronounce that you are "mad as hell and not going to take it anymore." Oh, that is a splendid sensation, a moment to relish like the taste of a luscious dark chocolate truffle melting slowly in your mouth. It is a moment when your soul cries out in ecstasy, "Oh, oh, oh." This, however, was not one of those moments. This was a moment for eating humble pie.

I suddenly remembered something Monique had told us. She had to sign a guarantee for her daughter, who, ironically, was a doctor in residence and earned three times her mother's salary. "I might have to sign for you," Monique had cautioned. At the time I brushed off the idea as ridiculous. It was not ridiculous any longer.

"I will have a friend sign for us," I said flatly. "What is required?"

"We must recreate your dossier," Annette said, uncovering a stack of documents from her top desk drawer. "Perhaps, it is best to start with this."

Annette placed a single sheet of paper in front of me and then patted the paper. "In addition to the documents you have already provided," she said, "the guarantor must supply these." Annette patted the paper again.

- Application form
- Bank statement
- Two separate identification cards, with photos
- Vehicle registration
- Pay stubs for the last three months
- Tax statement
- Attestation of employment, signed by the employer
- The last three monthly mortgage receipts
- The last three monthly utilities receipts
- Statement guaranteeing payment of security deposit and monthly rent

I gaped at the application. It included a two-hundred-word statement of legalese that the guarantor was required to copy *by hand* and subsequently sign, "read and approved."

"And if we are able to collect all this by tomorrow, will you give us the keys to the apartment?" I asked, my face as expressionless as a death mask.

"In principle."

En principe are French wiggle words. I repeated more slowly. "If we are able to gather all documents, and if they are in order, will you give us the keys to the apartment?"

Annette stared at me for a moment. "Excuse me," she said, getting up from her chair. She escaped to the back of the office, knocked lightly on the door of La Directrice Paininzeebutt and, after a pause, stepped in.

While she was gone, Nita said, "Honey . . ."

Whatever it was—an appeal for self-control, caution, courtesy, or cultural diplomacy—I did not want to hear it. Without looking at her, I simply raised my right hand as a call for silence.

Annette returned. *"Oui,"* she said. "If all the documents are in order, you may have the apartment."

"That is all I needed," I said. "We will see you tomorrow."

"I am very busy tomorrow," Annette said.

I gave her a frostbite stare.

"Will ten-thirty in the morning be all right?" she asked.

"I will see you then."

That night I sat at the dinner table with Monique, and we gathered all the necessary documents. I was astounded by Monique's composure—completely unruffled, an undaunted veteran of French bureaucracy. Two hours later, all forms were completed, all documents photocopied. To this day, I am humbled by Monique's unconditional gesture of friendship.

At 10:30 a.m. sharp, I entered the agent's office. "May I speak to Annette," I said to the receptionist.

"She has stepped out," she said. "She will be with you in two seconds."

I sat down and waited. At 11:00 a.m. Annette walked through the door. She offered no apology for her tardiness—just the usual *"Bonjour, Monsieur Johnson."*

I offered her the stack of documents.

"Yes, yes, everything seems to be in order—*bien en règle*. Now, we will go to the apartment," Annette said. Strangely, she informed me that we would be driving in separate cars.

"Wouldn't it be easier to go in the same car?" I asked.

"Non. Cela ne se fait pas."

"That is not done?"

"Mais non, monsieur."

A few moments later, we were in the apartment. For the next hour and a half, Annette generated a list of all the damages to the apartment: a crack in the tile, a small depression in the wall, a section of scuffed-up wallpaper. Meanwhile, I generated my own list, scrutinizing every corner of the apartment. Finally, we consolidated our lists, and I signed yet another document, an attestation of the apartment's condition.

Then Annette gave me an inventory of all items in the apartment—I mean *everything*: one bed, four pillows, six spoons, one refrigerator, two ceiling light shades, and, not to be forgotten, a key ring with a flat rubber caricature of a dog—112 items in all. I was tasked with confirming the accuracy of the inventory.

"There is no hurry," Annette said. "You can bring your rectified list to the office anytime within the next week."

All I can say is that it was a good thing we double-checked the inventory because we were missing one dinner plate, one soup bowl, two steak knives, and a fork. The way I was feeling about Annette and Seaside Rentals, I was ready to take that fork and . . . ohmmmmm. Breathe in, breathe out.

The deal was finally sealed with the signing of a six-page contract—three copies—initialed on every page and signed *"lu et approuvé, bon pour accord"* (read and approved, good for agreement). The contract was official on September 9, one month and five days after our arrival in France. It was a long time in coming, but we were finally in our own apartment.

* * *

It is not uncommon for the French to admit that they cheat on taxes. Their reasoning is that they are so heavily taxed that it is only fair to recoup what they can on the sly. I have suggested earlier that the French like to keep their shutters closed to protect their privacy. Another reason may be to hide their assets from the taxman.

We occasionally saw evidence of this phenomenon during our year in France. For example, one fifty-five-year-old Frenchman admitted to me that although he had been working for a year, he was still collecting unemployment benefits.

"How have you managed that?" I asked.

"It's simple," he said. "My current employer pays me in cash."

"Ah, so your employer pays you no benefits, dodges any tax liabilities, and you walk away with a salary that is tax free."

"*Voilà.*"

"*And* to make the deal even sweeter, you continue to collect unemployment."

"*Oui.*"

"And you are all right with that?"

"Of course," my friend said, pursing his lips. "Everyone does it."

Here's another example. One fall day, when I was on an all-day hike, Nita decided to clean the sliding glass door that opened onto our apartment balcony. She stepped onto the balcony and closed the sliding door behind her. The door was heavy and cumbersome to close, requiring a firm tug. The impact of the door colliding into the doorjamb jostled the locking mechanism. In an instant, Nita was locked out of the apartment.

When a next-door neighbor stepped out on her balcony, Nita explained her dilemma and asked if she might use her phone to call Seaside Rentals. Of course, she could. The neighbor looked up the number and passed her mobile phone to Nita.

Nita dialed the number and asked for Annette.

"This is Annette."

"I have locked myself out of the apartment," Nita explained. "Do you have an extra key?"

"No, I'm sorry, we don't. But we will send a locksmith." (Given my experience with Annette, I suspect that she *did* have a key but preferred not to be inconvenienced. I have no proof, but that's my best bet.)

Thirty minutes later, a locksmith arrived, entered through the neighbor's apartment and stepped over the half-wall barrier that separated the two apartment balconies. With the help of two hefty suction cups, he was able to lift the door just enough to detach the lock. Nita was in the apartment in less than thirty seconds.

"That will be fifty euros," the locksmith said.

The price, about sixty-five dollars, seemed a little steep, but Nita was in no mood to quibble. "Okay, I'll write you a check."

"I don't take checks," the locksmith said.

"It's from a local bank," Nita said.

"I don't take checks," the locksmith repeated coldly.

"Well, I'm sorry; I'm afraid you'll have to take a check. I don't have enough cash with me."

"I will drive you to the bank," the locksmith said.

Now Nita is an agreeable, even-tempered woman, but this proposal seemed strange even to her. Still, she agreed to ride with the locksmith to the bank where she withdrew enough cash to pay her debt.

When Nita recounted her story to four French guests at the dinner table that night, they all nodded and said, almost simultaneously, *"Il voulait éviter les impôts."* That was my assessment too: He wanted to avoid paying taxes.

Of course, the French have been devising ways to avoid paying taxes for as long as taxes have been levied. For example, if you visit the seventeenth-century private homes in the beautiful medieval village of Pézanas, you will discover that many windows have been bricked up for over two hundred years. Why? Napoleon Bonaparte discovered that conquering Europe was an expensive proposition. To pay for his war machine, he levied taxes based on the number of windowpanes owned by the individual taxpayer. The French response to this onerous new law? Convert windows to brick walls.

Cheating the tax collector is not an unknown practice in the United States. No argument there. But I can't say that I have ever dealt with a locksmith, or any service provider for that matter, who has gone to such extents to hide sixty-five bucks from the taxman.

CHAPTER 5

The Curious Kingdom of Car and Driver

IF YOU GO TO SOUTHERN FRANCE IN AUGUST, you must be prepared to face bumper-to-bumper traffic—a Gallic caldron of speedway drivers. Everyone is on vacation in August, and it would seem all of them cluster on the French Mediterranean beaches. Oh, there must be a few people in Paris, but they are just the last holdouts who are packing their bags for next week's trip to le Midi.

One August weekend, Nita and I drove west from Montpellier, through Carcassonne, and on to the Pyrenees. We left on a Thursday, so the going was not too bad, but we came home on a Sunday, and that was another story.

At first we tried the narrow winding back roads. If time is not an issue, that is the best way to see the French countryside. But if you are on a schedule, it can nettle your backside. Most of the side roads cut directly through the villages that pepper the hills and valleys, many of which have one or two stoplights. The traffic was perpetually backed up beyond the city limits. Slowly, we would edge forward until we finally arrived at the town center, stalling at the stoplights. We were averaging twenty-five miles an hour—tops.

So we decided to try the national autoroute. On the downside, you pay a toll and lose the benefit of breathing in the authentic old world of France. On the upside, the travel is generally faster and more direct. But on that Sunday evening, even the autoroute was clogged. At that point, there was nothing to do but turn on the radio and sing along.

To make matters worse, with the adoption of the thirty-five hour workweek, many French employees manage their work schedule to accommodate three-day weekends. That means that traffic becomes noticeably heavier on Thursday night and through the weekend.

You cannot talk about the roads of France without mentioning the French fashion of driving. On second thought, I can't really define what the French do behind the wheel as *driving*. It is more like . . . well, *scurrying*— high-speed, frenetic scurrying. Think of mice on tiny roller-skates, darting helter-skelter in and out of harm's way with all the sensibilities of high school dropouts on three cups of French coffee. That's a Frenchman in the driver's seat.

I met a British gentleman in a supermarket checkout line my first week in France. He was carrying an armful of groceries while shuffling two liters of punch on the floor with his feet. I offered a portion of my cart to make the wait a little more bearable. He hesitated and then accepted.

As we waited in line, we started chatting, and the conversation eventually turned to French motoring skills. My new English friend politely assessed the phenomenon.

"To put it diplomatically," he said, "they have a rather *carefree* attitude about driving, wouldn't you say?"

Diplomatic is right. I tend to be less generous.

The French term for tailgating is *"coller au pare-chocs,"* meaning "to stick or glue to the bumpers." That's an appropriate expression because French drivers do, indeed, stick to you like glue. I was constantly exceeding the speed limit in France, not because I preferred speeding, but because I preferred staying alive. If I rolled at the designated speed limit, I backed up traffic in a Paris minute. When I looked in the rearview mirror and saw a caravan of cars strung out behind me, it was truly frightening—the driver directly behind clinging so closely to my rear bumper that I could actually make out the stubble on his chin. And when I came to a screaming halt at the first wide spot in the road to let the automobile equivalent of a bicycle peloton whiz by, I was usually compensated for my kindness with a look of disdain—or worse, the dreaded hand-flung-over-the-shoulder gesture.

This speedway method of driving is not limited to the occasional lead-footed teenage boy. This is a way of life for the French, regardless of age or gender. *Mon Dieu,* I have seen Frenchwomen tailgate police cars! I'm not talking about unmarked cars. These are full-fledged squad cars with POLICE MUNICIPALE in bold print across the trunk.

I once took a ride with an eighty-two-year-old Frenchman at the wheel on a serpentine stretch of road between Saint André-les-Alpes and Digne. I wasn't nervous, I was terrified! He was jamming gears and taking corners on two wheels, accelerating as he zoomed out of the curves.

Then this French senior citizen, this normally docile and gentle human being, decided to pass a slower, more sensible driver (he had to be British) on a blind corner. When another car emerged from around the mountainside, my elderly friend simply straddled the solid-white centerline while I noisily sucked wind. He seemed completely unruffled—as nonchalant as sitting on the edge of the bed and pulling up his socks.

The driver's wife looked over her shoulder at me. "Do you have fear?" she asked. (The French idiom is "to *have* fear," not "to *be* afraid or fearful.")

"Just a little," I gasped. I looked at my wife, who was sitting in the back seat beside me. "If I'm squashed like a bug, give my baseball cards to my brother," I whispered.

One of the first tasks of any American driver is to get the hang of the ever-present *ronds-points* (traffic circles). My friend, Jean-Marie, told me that these road managers were installed to help slow down traffic. The French took it as a direct challenge and turned the *ronds-points* into diabolical merry-go-rounds. In the States young adventurers satisfy their craving for adrenaline by bungee jumping and hang gliding. In France thrill seekers hit the traffic circles during rush hour. For me the secret to negotiating the *ronds-points* was to quickly find my slot and go for it with undaunted courage (to hesitate was death). Personally, I found that shouting "yahoo" in the process was helpful.

Despite my fortitude, I was still occasionally undone by a Frenchman behind the wheel of a four-cylinder compact. On one sunny afternoon, I was making my way on a side road to a nearby town. As I was approaching a traffic circle, I looked in my rearview mirror. A white Fiat with red racing stripes was speeding toward me at full throttle. I eased into the circle counterclockwise, in strict observance of international law, you understand. That's when the Fiat driver made his move, careening around the rond-point—*clockwise*—beating me to the exit at twelve o'clock high. For a moment, we looked like the Blue Angels cutting a Rorschach inkblot design in the sky.

I'm convinced that if you can manage the French surprises waiting for you at what should be a slumberous back road traffic circle, you can manage just about anything.

Except possibly the occasional low-flying *moto*. The motorcyclists in France are a different breed. They are on earth for one purpose: to trigger nervous ticks in American drivers. These are the twenty-year-olds in blackout full-face helmets for their heads and thongs for their feet (you figure it out). They ride Hondas, Kawasakis, Suzukis—all designed to peel the freckles off your face by sheer G-force.

Consider the sound of a Harley hog—the low rumble that you feel in the seat of your pants. Do you have that sound in your head? These super sport bikes do not sound anything like that. The monster *motos* do not rumble. They do not roar. They *scream*. The sound is unforgettable—like elephants in heat.

Even when driving ten miles per hour over the speed limit, I was repeatedly shaken when one of these crotch rockets blasted out of nowhere. Often riding the divider line through traffic at blistering speeds, I'm convinced that these young daredevils are responsible for reshuffling my DNA.

Are the *motos* dangerous? I'll just say this. In 2012, French motorcyclists accounted for less than two percent of all vehicles but eighteen percent of all fatalities.

I may not have the most objective evaluation of French motorcyclists, which I blame on "The Nimes Affair."

Nita and I were sharing a bit of the South of France with two American friends, Dave and Mary. A couple of decades earlier, Mary played Maria, and Dave and I played Jets in a community production of *West Side Story*, so it was great fun to see them again.

We were excited about taking in the sights at Nimes. We parked our car a few blocks away from the magnificent Roman arena, which is still the site of two annual bullfights. As always, the traffic was bumper-to-bumper, and the parking was at a premium. We were lucky to find a piece of curb the length of our Fiat on a narrow side street.

The four of us got out of our car, which halted the traffic for a split second. At that moment two impatient young motorcyclists, each with female companions hanging on for dear life, jumped the curb of the sidewalk and roared past us, leaning left and right as they skinned by Mary and Nita.

I was outraged. As they bounced back onto the street, I shook my fist at them and shouted, *"Vous . . . vous . . . vous . . ."* That was it. In the heat of the moment, that was all my brain could muster. "You . . . you . . . you . . ." I felt so inadequate. I wanted to blister their incivility with something elegantly pithy like, say, "How would you like me to reinstall your tailpipe, Buster?" But no—I had nothing.

To sour me even more, one of the bad boys looked over his shoulder at me and hollered, "Nice comeback, idiot!"

As they sped away, only their cackling muted the scream of their mighty two-stroke motors. There is no sound in the world more scornful, more contemptuous, more snarky than the sound of teenagers laughing their butts off.

I was still smoldering when Dave put his arm around me and said, "Easy, Allen, you're not a Jet anymore."

"That's not right," I said under my breath. "You know what I mean? That's just not right."

"Fuhgeddaboudit," Dave said in Brooklynese. "It ain't over yet, Action. We gonna rumble wid dem scumbags, an' dis time we gonna be packin' blades."

Dave always knew just the right thing to say to make me feel better.

The French have a relaxed regard for traffic regulations. At a dinner party one evening, I asked two French couples what registered in the brains of French drivers when they saw the speed limit of seventy kilometers per hour (forty-three miles per hour). Both men responded simultaneously. "One hundred and ten kilometers per hour (sixty-eight miles per hour)," they sang out.

"One hundred and ten kilometers!" I howled.

"Of course," one of the men said. "We add forty to the posted speed limit. If you are ticketed driving faster than that, the fine is much more severe."

My friends may have been exaggerating a bit to implant fear in the mind of their American cousin (they succeeded) but not by much. The French simply do not respect the speed limit or any other traffic regulation. I have seen them crash red lights, turn right on a red light (not legal in France), and consistently blow off yield signs.

That is why I define driving in France, not as getting from one destination to another, but as staying alive on the road.

Driving courtesy also comes in small doses in the land of the Gauls. One day I was taking care of some business in Montpellier. It was raining hard, so hard in fact that le Lez River overran its banks, shutting down two key bridges in and out of the city. The streets quickly jammed up. I found myself in the left lane of a four-lane thoroughfare, needing to turn right to work my way home via the back door. The traffic was bumper-to-bumper.

I looked at the man in the silver BMW to my right. He had a mobile phone in his right hand and a cigarette in his left (as far as I could tell, he had to be driving with his knees). His hair was midnight black and perfectly cut and shaped like cake icing—a fifty-dollar haircut if ever I saw one. His skin had a high-sheen, porcelain finish, which made him look more like a Renaissance sculpture than a human being. His window was rolled down, his left elbow resting on the sill.

I tried to catch his attention so that I could get passage to the right lane in front of him.

"Yo," I said. (How do you say "yo" in French anyway? I don't think the word translates into French, but I have heard the French say *"Ohé."* I know that because that's the expression they use to awaken me out of a daydream—something that happens more often than I would like to admit.)

In any case, my "yo" had no impact on the sculpted exfoliated Frenchman. I was getting closer to the intersection where I needed to make a right turn, so I started waving, first demurely and then with increasing frenzy as we approached the corner. Next, I was bouncing up and down in my seat, my arms flailing like a wounded chicken hawk. Still no response.

They tell me in France you only use your horn for true emergencies. The French would probably disagree, but by my account this situation more than qualified. I tapped a friendly toot on my horn. No response. I tapped two friendly toots. Toot-toot. Nothing. "Screw this," I said out loud and laid on my horn—one long, unbroken blast. Finally, the well-groomed man with the pudding hair and toilet-bowl complexion did a slow burn over his left shoulder.

"May I?" I asked, gesturing that I wanted to cross in front of him.

"Et pourquoi? Moi aussi, je veux y aller." And why should I? I, too, want to go there. To underscore his censure, he edged up a little closer to the car in front of him.

"Why should you?" I muttered to myself. "How about out of ordinary human kindness? Have you *heard of the concept?*"

As it turned out, the car ahead of me edged forward, and I was able to slip into the right-hand lane two cars beyond the BMW. Is gloating permitted?

The BMW affair was not the only evidence of the dearth of driving civility. One Sunday morning Nita and I decided to drive into Lattes to take advantage of their wonderful open-air market. We were in the right-hand lane coming off an overpass. Just behind us a subcompact truck came lickety-split from a merging road, two lanes to our left. He was either distracted or drunk (I'm guessing the latter) because he crossed a continuous white line (illegal even in France) and then crossed into our lane, running us off the road before crashing into us. None of us were hurt, but he pretty much turned my left door and front fender into papier-mâché.

The truck came to a stop thirty to forty yards ahead of us. I got out of the car to assess the damage and start the paperwork. A short man with a three-day beard charged out of the truck screaming something about my mental capacity.

"Wait a minute," I said. "Are you trying to tell me that this was *my* fault?"

The short man actually laughed in my face. "*Eh oui*—it's your fault," he said, raising his hand to his temple and turning his wrist as if he were unscrewing the bolt from an oil pan—the French gesture for "are you crazy or what?"

I leaned toward Nita, who was sitting calmly in the car. "Are you getting this?" I asked in English. "This guy is precious."

"What?" the man asked. He was now hopping like a Kenyan Maasai warrior, his shabby black loafers clearing the asphalt by the height of a French cricket.

I thought it best not to aggravate the man any further. "Forget it," I said to the bouncing Gaul. "Look, you can say whatever you want. I'm taking pictures." (I usually carried my digital camera with me because I invariably saw something enchanting or, in this case, flat-out weird.) I started snapping pictures of my skid marks, the damage to my car, the damage to the truck—all with the choleric little man hopping up and down in the background of each frame.

When I shared this story via email with a French friend, who is now living in the United States, she offered this advice:

"Allen, what you experienced is typical. It is the Latin way. You must learn that in such cases, it is you who must jump out of the car and start insulting the other driver. It is the only way to be right! It is what we all do in such cases if the accident is not too severe."

I am not trying to suggest through these fleeting anecdotes that the French are crazy—just a little self-absorbed, particularly when under stress and in conflict with a faceless stranger. Their attitude is not really hostile, that's more American, but rather inconsiderate and self-serving. They are like the kid on the screaming motor scooter, sans muffler to gain that extra .01 boost in horsepower, who jolted me out of my dreams *every* morning at 5:35. If I were to ever catch that little scamp and question his civic sensibilities, I'm sure—as faceless as I would be and, what's more, an American—he would tell me in common street French, "*Ça, je m'en fous pas mal*—I couldn't give a damn," and I would believe him.

* * *

I've said it earlier and I'll say it again. I'm sorry, but the French don't have a clue about customer service. It's just not their style. I don't really blame them. After all, how can you expect them to emulate what has never been modeled?

The aftermath of our car accident proves my point. This is the story of how we dealt with the insurance company after the accident.

Day one: I called the insurance company. No one answered, of course; it was Sunday. But, in addition, there was no message machine and no number to call in case of an emergency. That night I transferred a copy of the accident photos to a CD.

Day two: I called the insurance company. Our agent, Jean-Paul, answered the phone.

"Jean-Paul, I've had an accident."

"Okay, come into the office."

"Can't I just give you the information over the phone?"

"You had better come into the office."

"Then that's what I'll do."

I hung up the telephone and headed for the door and then, on a hunch, I decided to pack up my laptop computer. Ten minutes later, I walked into the insurance office. The secretary, Jacqueline, intercepted me before walking into Jean-Paul's office.

"Jean-Paul told me you were coming in," she said. "Let me help you over here."

I pulled up a chair at Jacqueline's desk.

"Can you run this CD?" I asked, presenting the silver platter. "It has the photos of the accident."

"No, our computer system is not that sophisticated. Do you have the accident report?"

I ignored her question. "You don't have a CD player?"

"No. Do you have the accident report?"

"No CD player at all?"

"No. The accident report, *s'il vous plaît*."

"Fine," I said, setting up my laptop. "Here are the pictures of the accident. See this?" I asked, pointing at the photo on the screen. "These are my skid marks. You can see where he ran me off the road."

"Did you have a witness?"

"Yes, my wife was with me."

"I see. No witness then."

"All right, no one other than my wife, but as you can clearly see in the photo . . ."

"Photos are not admissible as evidence."

"Huh?"

"Could I see the accident report now?"

I reluctantly fished out the accident report.

"The other driver didn't sign the report," Jacqueline said.

"No, he said he would not sign because he was not in agreement with my description of the incident."

"Then it's his word against yours."

"But the photos . . ."

"Not admissible."

I was starting to pant. I looked over my shoulder into Jean-Paul's office. He was hunched over a stack of papers. "Could I speak to Jean-Paul, please?"

"He will tell you the same thing. Listen, Mr. Johnson, we will see what we can do, and we'll call you back."

I funereally walked out of the insurance office, my laptop in one hand, my besmirched CD in the other.

Two hours later, Jacqueline telephoned.

"Could you make color prints of your photos?" she asked.

"I don't have a color printer. I don't have *any* printer, for that matter."

An audible sigh. "No color printer?"

"No, do you have access to a color printer?"

"No. Hang on a minute." Jacqueline put her hand over the receiver and shouted something to Jean-Paul. A moment later, she was on the line again. "Could you come back into the office again? Please bring the CD. I will also prepare a statement for you to sign."

"When would you like me to come?"

"After lunch, two thirty."

"Okay, two thirty."

When I walked into the office that afternoon, Jacqueline was working with another client.

"Ah, Mr. Johnson. Did you bring the CD?"

"Yes. Did you find a way of making prints?"

"No, I'm afraid not," Jacqueline said. "Not yet."

"I can make prints," the man at Jacqueline's desk said. "I have a Macintosh." Then, switching to English, he said, "It is zee best."

"But my disc is in Microsoft Windows format."

"It does not matter," the proud Macintosh owner said, "I can do anyting."

The Macintosh guy smiled. Jacqueline smiled. I smiled. We were all smiling.

"Great," I said. "That's awfully kind."

When the Macintosh guy had finished his business, I thanked him again and walked over to Jacqueline's station.

"I haven't finished the report yet," Jacqueline said. "Could you come back in a couple of hours?"

"Uh, no," I said, feeling myself getting huffy. "Let's do this. I'll sign at the bottom of a blank piece of paper. You write out the report, and then email it to me. You can email right?" Jacqueline nodded that she could. "Good. I'll read your report. If it sounds good to me, you can transfer the text to the sheet of paper I signed. Okay?"

"Okay."

"Now, where do I go to have the damage assessed?"

"That's only done from 8:00 to 10:00 a.m."

Not surprising. "Where do I go tomorrow?"

Jacqueline drew the directions on a business envelope.

"And where do I go to get the car repaired?"

"We can talk about that later."

"No, let's talk about it now."

Jacqueline sketched the directions on a second business envelope.

Day three: When I arrived at the adjuster's office at 8:00 a.m., a man in a blue smock was noting the damage to another car. I waited fifteen minutes, during which time the adjuster walked around the car, into the office, and out again. When he was finally finished, I directed the man to my car.

"Go into the office," he said, "and speak to the receptionist."

Okay, I'm going into the receptionist's office now.

I stepped up to a counter. The receptionist was transferring papers from one stack to the other. Five minutes later, she got up and walked to the counter where I was tapping out Calypso rhythms. I noticed that the adjuster was now standing next to me, his chin in his hand.

The receptionist gave me a form to fill out—including my name, address, and, just in case the question should come up, my place and date of birth. Meanwhile, she made photocopies of my car registration.

A few minutes later, I handed the form to the receptionist, who handed it to the adjuster, who was still standing beside me with his chin in his hand.

The adjuster and I walked outside. He made a few notes on the form, gave me a copy, and said I was now authorized to take the car to a garage for repair.

That sounded good to me, *but just to be safe*, I returned to the counter in the office and asked the receptionist if I might use the phone to contact my insurance company.

"You don't have a mobile phone?" the receptionist said.

I wanted to say, "Yes, I do, but my real goal in life is to irritate the French." Instead, I bit my lip and said, "Unfortunately, no."

"*D'accord,*" she said, clenching one side of her mouth in irritation.

She dialed the number for me. The line was busy. She returned to her work. Fifteen minutes later, I asked if she could call again.

"Oh, are you still here?" she asked.

"Yep, I'm still here."

She dialed the number again and this time got through. I stepped behind the counter to take the call.

Jacqueline was on the line.

"I've had the car assessed for damage," I explained. "They tell me I can go to the garage now to have the car repaired. Are you in agreement with that?"

"Yes, I will call the garage to tell them you are on the way."

"Great."

"But you will have to pay a two hundred and seventy-euro deductible until the office in Paris determines who was at fault."

"He was at fault. That is the only judgment that can be made."

"We will see."

I gave the receiver back to the receptionist, thanked her, and started to leave. Then, a question occurred to me about something the adjuster had written on the damage report.

"May I have a quick word with the adjuster?" I asked.

The receptionist let out a gasp of air. "What for?"

Not the response I was looking for. "I have a question for him."

"He's in a meeting," she said. "You'll have to wait."

In fact, I had seen the adjuster light up a cigarette and walk into the office of the *patron*, the boss.

I waited. Twenty minutes later, I was still waiting. Now, I'm thinking there's no telling how long this meeting will take. I decided to knock on the door. I heard the receptionist protest, but I pretended not to hear her. The adjuster opened the door, allowing a billow of cigarette smoke to escape the sealed office.

"Yes?" the adjuster said.

I voiced my concern, was told not to worry, made an about-face and left—at no time making eye contact with the "protector of the gate."

I drove to the garage and spoke to the receptionist, who took another photocopy of my car registration and set a date for repair in one week.

Day ten: I drove the car to the garage. It was a happy day. I was growing weary of squeezing in and out of the caved-in door on the driver's side.

"When will the car be ready for pick up?" I asked.

"In about three days. Just call to check up on the status."

"Could you call me when it is finished?" I asked, already knowing the answer.

"We're very busy. It would be better if you called."

"Right."

Day fifteen: I called the garage in the morning. No, the car was not ready. They had to order a new headlight. I wondered why the headlight hadn't been ordered five days earlier but said nothing. The job would take a couple of extra days. When I asked if they could call, I was told that they were awfully busy and that it would be best if I called them.

Right.

Day seventeen: I called the garage. Yes, the car was ready. I could pick it up at four o'clock that afternoon. I arrived on the hour.

"I'm sorry," the car is not quite ready, the receptionist said, "but we're on it."

"Fine."

An hour later, just at closing time, I was given the keys to my car.

Day nineteen: The garage called and said that the mechanic who had worked on my car thought that the horn might not be attached. He was right; the horn didn't make a peep. I returned the car to the garage, and the horn was rewired.

Day thirty: I still had not heard from the insurance company regarding a judgment of who was at fault. I called Jacqueline.

"Oh, yes," she said. "The other driver was found to be at fault."

"Great. When do I get my two hundred and seventy euros?"

"We are processing that now."

"So, what should I expect? A week or two?"

"Oh, no, it will be a tiny bit longer than that."

"Just how much of 'a tiny bit'?"

"A tiny bit."

One hundred and eighty-two tiny-bit days later, I received my check for 270 euros. Arrrg.

CHAPTER 6

Libertè, Ègalitè, Fraternitè

I KNOW I HAVE BEEN WHINING. And, as often is the case, I have to remind myself that living in another country should not be a lesson in comparative cultures. It should be a lesson in understanding a *single* culture. But that's not always easy for me. My brain has been well schooled to compare new and novel encounters with my past experiences. And, naturally, when I do that, there is the risk of becoming grumpy.

I hope my French friends will accept that as an apology and grant me one more indulgence—to take a shot at explaining what makes the French so, well, French.

Why are real estate agents insensitive? Why are French drivers often frenetic and rude? Why are insurance companies long on their own personal conveniences and short on customer service? In a word, I think it is linked to the French concept of liberty.

The French are passionate about their personal liberty, which I am defining as "doing what I damn well please." It is seen in every segment of French culture: education, politics, mass media, social behavior.

Unfortunately, that freedom often results in the violation of the rights of others.

On the beaches of Carnon, there are numerous signs that forbid the presence of dogs. Yet, those signs are constantly ignored. The French allow their dogs to run free and leave their deposits on the popular beaches.

I remember overhearing an angry conversation from the terrace of my apartment one sunny afternoon. A Frenchman, who lived on the first floor of our complex, was shouting at a countryman whose golden retriever was scampering along the beach.

"Don't you see the sign?" the angry resident asked.

"Yes, I see the sign."

"Well then?"

"*Je m'en fous*—I could care less," the dog owner said.

In the last ten years, every major city of France has been defaced with what the French call *des tags* (graffiti). Jacque Lang, who at that time was the Minister of Culture, called the practice "art" and used tax resources to set up expositions for the artisans. Now, there is hardly a building that is held sacred in France. I have seen grand seventeenth-century doors desecrated with *tags* that are nothing more than initials scrawled in black spray paint.

On the car ride back from a day hike, the conversation turned to abortion.

"It is clear," the French driver said, "we must protect the rights of the woman."

"Yes, I agree," his wife added. "A woman should be the ruler of her own body."

At no time was there any mention of the rights of the unborn child.

I asked a former high school principal what is was like to be an educator in France.

"It is very hard," he said. "There is no respect for the teacher any longer. They are ridiculed, shouted at, even spat upon."

"Is it really that bad?" I asked.

"Not in all neighborhoods but in too many—particularly in larger cities."

"Do you think it will improve?"

"I don't see how."

"Are you glad to be out of it?" I asked.

"Oh yes. I just wish I had left sooner."

One day on the radio, I listened to an interview with a Frenchman who had just won five million dollars in the lottery.

"What is the absolute greatest satisfaction in having won so much money?" the interviewer asked.

What would the man say? To start a business? To take a world cruise? To help his family and friends? No, no, and no. His response was *"Maintenant je peux dire 'zut' à tout le monde."* Now I can say "get lost" to everyone.

One day, in a small French Mediterranean village, I was stuck in traffic on a narrow street. Not atypically, a truck driver had stopped in the middle of the road to unload his cargo. For no particular reason, I looked in my rearview mirror. In defiance of French law, a businessman in an upper-end Renault was expounding into his mobile phone—curious, I thought, given that a police officer was standing on the corner, literally within arm's reach of the driver. Two minutes later, the businessman grew impatient and decided to back up—*through the intersection*—and make a right-hand turn.

I looked at the policeman. He was chatting with a villager, clearly unconcerned about the flagrant traffic violation.

When I asked a French friend how that could happen, he just smiled. "You're in le Midi," he said. "We are relaxed here."

A conversation with a twenty-five-year veteran of the Montpellier police helped clarify the phenomenon.

"What is it like to be a policeman?" I asked.

"It is very difficult. The spirit of the French is to break the law, particularly in southern France. That spirit is really more Latin than French. You will find the same attitude in Italy and Spain."

"So, how are police officers viewed?"

"We are the enemy. Have you ever noticed oncoming cars flashing their lights at you as a warning that the police are down the road?"

"Yes, I have noticed that."

"That is an example of what I mean. A police officer is not seen as a friend—someone who can help, someone who can protect—but rather as someone to trick or avoid. And the people will join forces to defeat us. As soon as we become more diligent in enforcing a law, the people will protest. They will strike or demonstrate to challenge our duty to protect them. *C'est dingue*—It's crazy."

That lack of respect for policemen is even typified in the French language. For example, the slang word for a "speed bump" in France is *"un gendarme couché"* or "a sleeping policeman." In other words, the police are something to be run over.

* * *

MIDWAY THROUGH OUR FIRST YEAR IN FRANCE, I decided to join a singing class led by an operatic soprano, Marie-Françoise. I knew that the students were asked to sing a solo at each session, so I strapped my guitar to my back and bicycled to the small community center.

There were six students, three men and three woman. In French fashion they kept pretty much to themselves, so in American fashion I introduced myself to each student.

"Hi, I'm Allen. What's that? Yes, I'm American. And don't you think this should be fun?"

Marie-Françoise arrived a few minutes late and was visibly winded. *"Oh là là,"* she said. "I'm so sorry to be late. You cannot believe my life right now. But let's not talk about that. Let's sing."

We formed a circle and started vocalizing, modulating a half step with each scale. La-la-la-la-la-la-la-la-la.

After the warm-ups, the first student, Chantal, was asked to sing. She was an attractive thirty-something woman with black cropped hair and long eyelashes. When she was in position behind the microphone, she put her weight over her left hip and kicked her right foot out to the side. She was a beguiling siren in her black miniskirt and textured leotards— a French version of Liza Minnelli in *All That Jazz*. All she needed was a black bowler hat to complete the picture.

She sang Charles Trenet's classic, "La Mer." Her voice was pleasant enough, but she sang without expression while totally ignoring the audience. She made a fist around the microphone and sang in a somewhat breathy tone with her eyes closed from beginning to end.

When she had finished, we politely applauded.

"I love that song," I said. "And you have a lovely voice."

"Thank you," she said.

"Although I would have liked to have seen your eyes."

"I beg your pardon."

"And I wonder if you were paying attention to the lyrics."

"Of course, I was paying attention."

By now I could tell I had already gotten under Chantal's skin. And I had promised myself that I would not be a bigmouth, which is hard for me. So I just smiled.

"Very nice," I said, trying in vain to repair the damage.

I was up next. I had prepared an arrangement of "A Day in the Life of a Fool," accompanying myself on guitar. It was a song I used to sing in Seattle nightclubs when I was in my early twenties. I knew the tune inside out, so I sold it as if I were playing to a full house.

When I had finished, the applause was enthusiastic, and Marie-Françoise said, "*Et voilà*, an American who knows how to present a song."

I sneaked at peak at Chantal, who was chattering about something to her neighbor—something derogatory I imagined. Marie-Françoise was now coaching me about the quality of my voice. "Consider opening your throat even more," she said. "Allow the resonance to vibrate from your head and chest."

"How exactly should I do that?"

"It's easy. What you need to do is . . ."

About then I was having trouble hearing Marie-Françoise. Chantal was still leaning into her neighbor, her voice picking up a couple of decibels.

I held my hand out to Marie-Françoise. "I'm sorry," I said. "I really want to understand your suggestions, but I'm having a hard time hearing."

Then I turned to Chantal, who was still oblivious to the world outside of her own leotards. "Chantal, excuse me."

She didn't register anything.

"Oh, Chantal," I said, fully open-throated, my voice vibrating in my head and chest, "I wonder if you would be willing to be quiet for a moment. I'm trying to hear what Marie-Françoise has to say."

Oh my. That request—sensible and quite dignified, I thought—was the beginning of a Greek drama. Chantal's eyes were on fire. "How dare you! We are Latin here! We are not in the United States. We are in France. Please don't tell us how to behave. You do not have the right."

I could feel my blood start to rise. "Do I have the right to honor the words of our instructor?" I looked at Marie-Françoise. She was silent, clearly out of her comfort zone.

"You have the right to respect our culture," Chantal said. "If you can't do that, perhaps you should leave."

"I see." I looked at Marie-Françoise. She was actually picking at a piece of lint on her blouse.

Although tempted, I did not leave. If for no other reason, I chose to stay for the remainder of the session out of respect for our instructor. At the end of the class, I did not dare look in Chantal's direction, and she did not dare look in mine. I waited for the room to empty so that I could speak with Marie-Françoise alone.

"I am sorry for that," I said.

"Don't worry about it," Marie-Françoise said. "I think it is just a question of jealousy."

"Perhaps. It is a shame because I know that I could learn from you. But I think it would disrupt the class for me to continue."

"I understand."

"But I am not willing to give you up."

"That's kind."

I had been asked by the president of the local community center to give a concert for the village. I thought it would be wonderful to have Marie-Françoise join me as a special artist. "Would you be willing to sing with me?" I asked.

She did not hesitate. "Absolutely."

That was the beginning of another beautiful friendship. First we sang for Pérols. Then we were asked to sing for a nearby gospel choir. Then we sang a third time for a choral competition.

"I love singing with you," I once told Marie-Françoise. "You are such a gifted musician."

"I feel the same about you. I know how to be a singer, but you have taught me how to be an entertainer."

Making music with Marie-Françoise was always a snap. Becoming her friend was as easy as Do-Re-Mi. We are still the best of pals.

Wherever you go, there will always be a few people with an attitude or a grudge or, in this case, a misguided understanding of personal freedom. Chantal believed that her liberty entitled her to fawning adoration. The slightest criticism was a violation of her noblesse. To quote from the Bard, she expected the world to speak to her with "bated breath and whispering humbleness." (No country has a monopoly on that. In the States, teenage girls wear T-shirts that read, "Not everyone can be a princess. Someone has to applaud when I walk by.")

On this point my philosophy was resolute. I would not allow a single, unhappy encounter to color my perception of an entire nation. And besides, there were always those very special people who made everything worthwhile—people like Marie-Françoise.

* * *

How does one calculate the cost of absolute liberty? What is the cost of all the lost workdays accumulated each week across the nation by striking workers? What price do you attach to the thousands of French men, women, and children who lose their lives on the roads and highways of France each year? What is the price of entitlement and narcissism masquerading as liberty?

I don't know the answers to these questions. They are too expansive and impersonal to comprehend. I can tell you from a *personal* perspective that absolute liberty—liberty without the temperance of equality and fraternity—will destroy a relationship.

I want to share a story about a Frenchwoman I met in France—how I fell in love with her, not in a romantic sense, but as any compassionate man or woman cares deeply about the spiritual and intellectual well-being of another human being. I will call the woman Sharice.

I met her at a Christmas party at the home of a friend in Pérols. The woman was standing alone in the kitchen, sipping from a flute of champagne. She was lean, with thick dark-brown hair that was cut short and close to her face—a style that accented her high cheekbones and hazel eyes. I placed her in her mid-forties. Standing there alone, holding the stem of the champagne flute with the fingertips of both hands, she looked pensive and a little sad. I decided to speak to her.

"I was hoping to find someone who was not engaged in conversation," I said. "May I speak with you?"

Shaken from her reverie, the woman looked at me and smiled. "Of course," she said.

"My name is Allen."

"I'm Sharice."

I really don't enjoy cocktail parties where the conversation revolves around weather, sports, or politics. So I sidestepped all of that and asked a personal question—a practice that most French (and many Americans for that matter) find surprising, if not intimidating. On the other hand, there are a precious few who consider the tactic refreshing. Sharice fell into the latter camp. "Tell me, Sharice, you look a little sad tonight. Do you have the blues?" She knew the meaning of the word "blues"; the French have adopted the American word into their vocabulary.

Sharice looked into my eyes to gauge my sincerity. I held her gaze.

"Perhaps a little," she admitted.

"Tell me about it."

"Oh, there is not much to tell." Then, after a pause, "No, that's not true. There is a lot to tell, but you seem like a nice man, and I really don't want to trouble you with my little problems."

"It's no trouble," I said truthfully.

She must have believed me because she began speaking softly and slowly about her three children, whom she adored, and her husband, an alcoholic, whom she could not abide. In fact, she was in the process of filing for a divorce. Our conversation lasted close to an hour. When we said goodbye, I told her I hoped that I would see her again one day.

That wish came true. In fact, we saw quite a bit of each other. I told Nita about Sharice, and we had her over for dinner. Later, I went on a couple of hikes with her in the Cévennes mountain range. I enjoyed her company. I always felt that I did not need to censor my thoughts with her. I could be silly or profound and never feel misunderstood or criticized, even when my French was labored. It was a good feeling, and I told her so.

After I have spent some time with someone, I always wonder if the person could be one of my "golden friends." To explain, a "golden friend" is a lifelong companion, someone with whom I can be transparent and nonjudgmental and expect the same in return. They are hard to find—I have maybe a dozen at the most—but when found, they are invaluable.

I do not blithely ask someone if he or she would like to join my very exclusive club. I must see something in them that is magical. They must be perceptive, curious, and intellectually alive. They should also be playful, funny, unmannered, and a little irreverent. Most importantly, they must know how to listen, not to problem-solve, but to understand. They do not turn what someone else has said from the heart into a springboard for their own monologue. They seek to better understand. The job requirements are tough. I figure that only one in a thousand can pass muster. But I thought that Sharice had the right stuff.

"I'd like to be your friend for a lifetime," I finally told her one day.

"But why?" she asked. "I have so many problems."

"Who doesn't? It's called living."

"But why me?"

"Well, for starters you are charming and intelligent and funny. Will that do?"

Sharice looked down and smiled, a timorous look of self-satisfaction. "I don't know if I deserve you," she said wistfully.

"Yeah, you're right," I said, feigning resignation, "you don't deserve me."

She gave me a rabbit punch to the arm.

One weekend, we had planned to take in an early movie and then dinner. She was to meet Nita and me at our apartment at five o'clock that evening. She didn't show. There was no phone call, no email message— nothing. She didn't answer her phone. When I did finally manage to reach her three days later, she seemed very cavalier.

"Oh, yeah, I'm sorry about that," she said. "I was feeling pretty depressed, I guess."

"Well, come on over," I said. "Let's talk about it."

"No, not today."

That was not the last time Sharice blew off a rendezvous. A few weeks later, she missed a meeting for a luncheon and then, a month after that, a half-day hike along the seashore. And in each case, there was no warning and no apology.

Two days after the last rebuff, I saw her walking away from me in the parking lot at Carrefour. Although I called her by name, she did not stop. I called louder. Still no response. I was not going to let her get away with that. I chased her down, grabbed her by the arm, and swung her around.

"Hey, Sharice. Hold on a minute."

"Allen! How are you?" she said, kissing me on both cheeks.

"Well, okay, but I'm a little confused about you."

"What do you mean?"

"I mean our rendezvous two days ago. That's what I mean."

She said nothing.

"What's going on?"

"Oh, my life is a mess," she said.

"Okay, I understand. Maybe I can help you with that, but not if you're going to continue standing me up."

Sharice was now looking at the ground.

"I love you," I continued. "I meant it when I said I wanted to be a friend for a lifetime, but *je ne peux pas compter sur toi*, I can't count on you. I will always be your friend, but I will not allow you to abuse me."

I could see Sharice recoil on those words. "I'm sorry," she said. She put her arms around me and gave me a long, hard hug, kissing me on the neck before releasing me. I knew at that moment that I had lost her.

After that Sharice would not respond to any of my email messages. She never spoke to me again. I still miss her, and I still love her. I have not given up on her. I still send her an email message from time to time to wish her a happy birthday or to let her know that the door is always open. She continues to be silent.

When liberty becomes a pass to ignore a friend, when liberty becomes an excuse to wallow in depression, the strain on a friendship is unsupportable. I probably should add a few other job requirements for "golden friendship": self-confidence, optimism, and trustworthiness.

What cost is absolute liberty? For me the toll is impossible to calculate. What price should I place on friendship? What value should I ascribe to human intimacy? That is the cost—and not one heartache less.

What is the source of French indulgence?

In a discussion with Gérald, a retired French special forces colonel, I wanted to understand what he saw as the source of his country's unbridled personal freedom.

"Our motto—*Liberté, Égalité, Fraternité*—born out of the French Revolution, is an important part of our national heritage."

"Especially *liberté*," I offered.

"Yes, especially *liberté*. In fact, I am afraid that *égalité* is less important, and *fraternité* is nearly extinct. We seem to only remember *liberté*."

"But liberty without equality or fraternity is empty, wouldn't you agree?"

"Yes. And that's the problem. Are you familiar with the events of May 1968?"

I was. It was a massive revolt—nearly a revolution—that was in part fueled by the anti-Vietnam War protests in the United States. It was not long before the movement crossed the Atlantic. Beginning with anti-war demonstrations at Nanterre and Sorbonne Universities, the student revolt quickly captured the attention of underpaid union workers. At one point thousands of students battled the police in the streets. One hundred and twenty-two factories were occupied, and ten million workers, comprising two-thirds of the workforce, were on strike.

As quickly as the revolt had ignited, it was as quickly extinguished when the French government drew up an agreement with the largest Communist-backed union that was occupying the factories. The laborers returned to work, leaving the students isolated in their revolt, which in any case was abating with the approach of summer vacation.

"That revolt," Gérald explained, "brought about some good. For example, it helped women enter the workforce. But it also did a great deal of harm."

"How so?"

"In education the adherence to hierarchy was broken down. Before 1968 the professor had complete power. After 1968 that power was shared with the students. Don't get me wrong. Education was in need of reform. In the old system the student was not allowed to interact with the professor. The students' education was built almost entirely on memorization. Education was too rigid. But the changes that came out of 1968 have gone too far. Today high school and college professors have little control over their students. Many consider it to be the decline of French education."

"Were there other changes?" I asked.

"We changed in the same way the United States evolved after the 1960s. Morally, culturally, sexually, intellectually. It was a different world—a more indulgent world. We became *trop égoïstes*, too selfish. Parents became overly permissive, ultimately losing control of their children. Sexual mores became more relaxed. Street demonstrations and strikes became the weapons of political change and, all too often, frivolous gripes."

Gérald's observations reminded me of just how nonsensical strikes had become in France. One day I discovered to my consternation that the Montpellier tram was shut down because a teenager in a rough neighborhood had tossed a brick at a streetcar. The response from the tram conductors was to go on strike for increased security—abandoning thousands of Montpellier residents who depended on the tram for daily transportation.

Gérald continued. "After the 1960s work was seen as an evil necessity or, at best, an institution to serve the pleasures of the employee and not the interests of the employer."

I had certainly seen evidence of Gérald's last point. Each year French federal workers enjoy a thirty-five hour workweek and twenty-five days of vacation (thirteen more days than American workers). Despite that schedule, the French routinely told me that work was something to be endured, not enjoyed.

One French electrical engineer told me that the French live for vacation. He theorized that the decline in work satisfaction occurred in the early 1990s when the workforce was increasingly absorbed by the age of information and technology. "As a nation, we stopped creating a product and, instead, started transferring data. It is difficult for an employee to become passionate about his work when his only source of communication is a machine. It became natural to crave the human contact that is now absent from the workplace. The solution? More vacation."

Several French executives told me that they actually preferred working with their American colleagues. When I asked why, I was told that Americans enjoyed work. They were serious, diligent, punctual, and goal oriented. "It was always a pleasure to collaborate with my American friends," one IBM manager told me. "They appreciate hard work."

The French are well aware of their more relaxed attitude toward work. They even make jokes about it, as made evident in a full-page cartoon in the September 14, 2002 issue of *Madame Figaro*. The drawing depicted a male candidate for employment sitting across the desk from a bank executive. The caption read, "I have chosen to orientate myself toward the banking sector because someone told me that you have lots of tall single blonds with great bodies."

I described the cartoon to Gérald.

"Yes," he said, "humor is often very close to the truth."

I wanted to go deeper. "Can you give me a specific example of a cultural change in France?"

"It used to be that lessons on morality were presented several days a week in our elementary schools. That ended after 1968. It was as though morality suddenly became old-fashioned. There is some talk about reinstituting lessons on morality, but it hasn't happened yet." (Gérald lent me a copy of a morality text designed for high school students—a 1920 publication entitled *Morale: Instruction Civique—Droit Privé, Économie, Politique.* It included such staples as courage, goodness, integrity, and civility.)

"What do you see for the future?"

Gérald shook his head. "I tend to be a positive kind of person. But frankly, I don't see positive changes happening quickly. Today's young people are the children and grandchildren of those who protested in the streets in 1968. Those children have grown accustomed to a liberal lifestyle. Every political administration talks about reform, but the problem is this: Cultural changes always run deeper than political referendums.

"But I will say this," Gérald continued. "We know that we have a problem, and we are concerned. That awareness is the beginning of change. It will not happen in my lifetime. It may not happen in my children's lifetime. But I think that the French people will grow so weary of the current state of chaos that change will inevitably occur. It may not swing back to the way it was before 1968—we wouldn't want that anyway because life was too rigid—but some order has to return. I have some faith—well, call it more a wish than faith—that things will change someday."

When I first spoke to Gérald, I wondered if his observations were unique. But the more I spoke to the French, the more I realized that his thoughts were a reflection of the general population, at least the mature population. The reaction of youth is predictable. Young people will always call for greater freedom with less responsibility, but French adults are ready for the trinity of *liberté*, *égalité*, and *fraternité* to be equally balanced. They know that *liberté* without *égalité* is injustice and that *liberté* without *fraternité* is narcissism.

One evening I had a quiet conversation with a French couple with whom I had been a friend for thirty years. I will call them Antoine and Sandrine. At one point, we began talking about our future goals.

"I will not be here that long," Sandrine said.

"What do you mean?" I asked.

"When I am fifty-five, I will commit suicide," she said in a steady voice.

I stared in disbelief at my friend. Sandrine was then fifty-two years old, an avid cyclist, and in perfect health. I could see in her eyes that she was serious.

"My God, Sandrine, why would you even say such a thing?" I asked.

"It is simple," she said. "After fifty-five your health begins to deteriorate. Your body becomes soft and your mind addled. You have done everything you are going to do. There is no sense in continuing."

I looked at Antoine, who was sitting quietly next to his wife. I asked him what he thought of Sandrine's statement.

"Yes, she has said that before," Antoine said matter-of-factly with a faint smile that suggested it was out of his control.

When I asked Sandrine about her responsibility to family and friends, she responded, "They have their lives to live, and I have mine. I have a perfect right to end my life as I choose."

As of this writing, Sandrine is now fifty-four years old.

Interestingly, according to the 2013 United Nations Human Development Report, male suicides are forty percent more frequent in France than in the United States. And Frenchwomen commit suicide eighty-nine percent more frequently than American women.

Unbridled liberty has its toll. When any nation—France and, yes, the United States—is more concerned with liberty over equality and fraternity, the richness and sacredness of the community is placed at risk. Is any social erosion more dangerous than that?

CHAPTER 7

Making Friends

BEFORE LEAVING THE STATES, I worried about making friends in France. "Maybe they won't like me," I said to my French friend, Nathalie, shamelessly fishing for a compliment.

"Oh, not to worry," Nathalie said to me in French. "There are over sixty million people in France; you're sure to find someone who likes you. I suggest you start in Lille and work your way south."

Happily, making friends was not a problem, notably due to a wonderful and relatively new French tradition, *la foire des associations* (the fair of associations).

One weekend in September, all the clubs and associations within a community set up booths in a central square. In Montpellier, a city of 250,000 inhabitants, there were nearly 1,100 booths scattered throughout a one-hundred acre neighborhood called Antigone. Built in the 1970s to accommodate thousands of French citizens who left Algeria during the Algerian War of Independence, Antigone is a magnificent community of apartments, business offices, shops, and four central squares. Designed by Catalan architect Ricardo Bofill, this massive neo-classical housing project was constructed with prestressed concrete that has the look and feel of stone. The four in-line squares run the length of the development and are so expansive and uncluttered that I felt as though I were strolling from one massive acropolis to the next.

But on the day of the fair, Antigone was drenched in a torrential rain that, as we would learn later, claimed twenty-three lives further inland. Still, the French were not deterred. Thousands of people strolled from booth to booth—some protected by umbrellas, most impervious to the rainfall—and soaked up the virtues of each club.

Every association imaginable was represented, all vying for the visitors' patronage. The exchange at the first booth I stopped at was typical.

"*Bonjour* mesdames, messieurs," I said, quickly slipping under the plastic tarp for protection from the rain.

I was immediately greeted by two men and two women, all with grand smiles. "You are brave to visit us in this inundation," one woman said, her eyes shining with hospitality.

"Oh, not really," I said. "It seems that everyone is having a good time. Why shouldn't I?"

"*Et voilà,*" one of the men said.

"Please tell me something about your association," I said.

A woman handed me a tri-fold brochure. It read "Choeurs de L'Enclos, Montpellier." It was one of a dozen classical city choirs that I would visit that morning.

"We are a choir of one hundred and fifty voices," the woman volunteered. "We perform large pieces: masses, requiems, and cantatas from the masters."

"For example."

"In past years we have sung *The Planets* by Holst, *The Requiem* by Mozart, *The Creation* by Haydn."

"Impressive."

"Yes," the woman with shining eyes said. "Would you like to hear a recording?"

"Yes, I would."

I sat down on a chair next to a portable CD player and listened to a few measures of Bach's *Saint Mathew's Passion*. It was glorious. "That's exciting," I said, taking off the headphones. "Are you sure you can use a baritone with an awful American accent?"

"Oh, but you speak French very well," one woman said. "We are already an international choir. Two of our members are English and one is German. It would be wonderful to have an American. Besides, this year we are doing *The Mass* by Handel."

"In English?" I asked.

"But, of course," shining eyes said. "You could help us with our diction. Please come. We rehearse every Friday evening from eight-thirty to eleven."

"Perhaps I will see you soon," I said

"I hope so," shining eyes said.

I waved goodbye and moved to another booth—and another and another. There were sections of booths dedicated to the arts, others to athletics, still others to social and environmental issues. There were individual booths on French patchwork, African dance, photography, theater, politics, scouting, mountain climbing, scuba diving, and gardening. There were associations devoted to Zen, Buddhism, Pentecostal evangelism, and free thought. There were historians, archeologists, biologists, and astronomers. It was a sea of passion—for knowledge, for experience, for sharing ideas that had made a difference in the life of every association advocate.

At the end of a soggy day, I walked away with my head reeling with the possibilities. I could live a hundred lifetimes in France and not have enough time to explore all the interest groups. Then, as though we did not have enough options, Nita and I attended the fairs in Carnon and Pérols on the following weekend. At the end, I had a stack of brochures two inches thick. Finally, I sat down at the round dining room table in our little apartment and sorted through the staggering surfeit of alternatives.

Ultimately, I decided against the clubs from Montpellier, reasoning that it would be easier to form lasting relationships with people closer to home. That considerably lowered the stack of brochures. Then I created a matrix of activities, locations, meeting days, and expenses. In the end, I had chosen two activities for every weekday.

Monday
AM-PM: Hiking club
Late PM: Jazz course

Tuesday
AM: Tennis
PM: Basketball

Wednesday
AM: Hiking club
PM: Qigong

Thursday
Early PM: Painting
Late PM: Orchestra

Friday
AM: Hiking club
PM: Jazz club

It was a schedule that proved to be a bit ambitious. Indeed, there were a few natural eliminations—one of which was demanded by my fifty-six-year-old knees.

* * *

I HAVE PLAYED BASKETBALL MY ENTIRE LIFE. My brother, Ray, and I used to battle it out in the backyard almost every night after dinner. We would practice dribbling between our legs and launching left-handed hook shots from fifteen feet out (not a practical shot, but impressive if you sink it). I was never quite good enough to make the team in high school—a blow to my ego to this day—but I played innumerable pickup games in the park until my knees started talking to me in my early fifties.

The point is I knew basketball. And I figured I would teach the French a thing or two about how Americans play hoops. I didn't think my fantasies were in the least bit outlandish. I would saunter into the gym, an official NBA authorized roundball on my hip. I would affectionately tap the short-legged Frenchmen on their heads and say, "Let me show you how to shoot a running jump shot." And then, prefaced with a head fake and a perfunctory dribble between my legs, I would release a perfect on-the-go jumper from the top of the key. *Swish.* The sound of ball and net would echo in the halls and pirouette in the minds of adoring Frenchmen.

"Oh là là," they would whisper to each other, "did you see that?" And then they would shake away their disbelief and scramble to my side where I would be standing with one arm akimbo and the other leisurely spinning a basketball on the tip of my index finger. *"Monsieur, monsieur,"* they would cry, "pleez show us 'ow you making zee basket."

What really happened was nothing like that.

After finding the *gymnase* in Pérols, I got out of the car and walked over to two men in their early twenties who, from my five-foot-ten-inch perspective, measured well over six feet. That was my first misjudgment. There were no "diminutive" French basketball players. In fact, of the twenty players that showed up that first night, I was easily the runt. No, I take that back. There was a fourteen-year-old boy who was a bit shorter than I, but he was in a growth spurt, and I figured he would pass me up by the end of the week.

"I understand that you play basketball here tonight," I said to the lanky Frenchmen.

"Well, I don't know if you can call what we do basketball," one of them said in typical French humility.

"Whatever it is that you do, can I join you?"

"Sure," they said in unison. *"Allez-y."* Let's go.

The court was regulation size with portable glass-backboard hoops, not unlike what you would find in any well-equipped American high school or college gym. On the downside, the floor was linoleum on concrete. That was going to be hard on the knees, I thought.

There were no old men on the court that night, that is to say no old *Frenchmen.* Just one somewhat rickety American. With the exception of the fourteen-year-old boy (who had a fake pass move reminiscent of Pistol Pete Maravich), the entire squad was comprised of young men from eighteen to twenty-three. They all were lean athletes with defined guts and muscular shoulders. I unconsciously gave my love handles a tender squeeze.

We formed four teams in typical American schoolyard fashion: The first ten to hit free throws made up the first two teams. It's a screwy method—stacking the first two teams with the best shooters—but there are some traditions you just don't mess with.

Amazingly, I made my free throw and was teamed up with four horses led by a six-foot two-inch guard called Julien. I rated Julien a Division I university-level player, able to fast break in traffic, shoot from either hand, and surgically thread precise no-look passes in any direction. Julien could do all that and more. He was twenty-one and wore a Chicago Bulls uniform, replete with a Bulls baseball cap that sat backward on his head the entire evening. His shorts were baggy, just touching the top of his knees, and when he drove for a lay-up, his shorts slipped off his hips, revealing the top half of his bare buttocks. You've heard of plumber's butt? Julien had basketball player's butt.

The game started, and the four horses blasted up and down the court, a run-and-shoot game that is designed for players with young legs. I lumbered up the court on offense, arriving just in time to reverse directions and lumber up the court on defense. Eventually, I spent a lot of time meandering around the half-court line. I took one shot that bounced off the rim like a brick. Then, after a few more sluggish trips up and down the court, Julien shot me one of his no-look passes that slipped through my fingers like a fish. I looked at my hands and thought, how the hell did that happen? Julien had the same expression. It was the last pass I got from the talented point guard.

Our team, that is the four horsemen and one wrung-out American bar mop, collected fifteen points before the opposition, which gave us the right to take on the fresh challengers. That was not a happy moment for me. I stood there numbly, all my muscle fibers puddling into my tennis shoes. This was not being tired. I've been tired before. This was more like death. I wondered if anyone could administer last rites.

We lost the second game—thank all the heavenly hosts—and sat down on the bleachers at mid-court. I started talking to Julien, which was not easy. He spoke so quickly and with so much slang and so many contractions that it sounded more like Hebrew than French. Still, I got the gist of the conversation.

"Are you English?" Julien asked.

"No, American," I said, "My name is Allen."

Julien's eyes brightened. "Oh, like Allen Iverson."

I was stunned at how quickly Julien rattled off the name of the gifted NBA guard. "Yes," I said, "just like Allen Iverson. What's your name?"

"Julien."

"Ah, like Julius . . ."

"Right. Like Julius Irving. Dr. J."

Now, how is that possible? Julius Irving's last season as an NBA player was in 1987. Julien would have been six years old at the time. In contrast, I couldn't think of a single French athlete. I scanned my brain and all I could produce was Maurice Chevalier—not really known for his basketball skills. (Remember, this was before the French native Tony Parker was a household name with the San Antonio Spurs.)

"What NBA team is your favorite?" Julien asked.

"That would have to be the Seattle Sonics," I said, trying to sound as authoritative as possible.

"*Eh oui,*" Julien said, "Gary Payton. A good player, but a little temperamental."

"Uh-huh," I said profoundly, having already exhausted everything I knew about the Seattle Sonics.

"The Sonics are a good team, but San Antonio kicked their butts in the playoffs." I don't think the French say "kicked their butts," but that was the sense of Julien's commentary.

"*Bof,*" I said.

Just then, the team on the floor scored its winning point, and Julien leapt from the bleachers. "Let's choose up teams," he shouted. "Fabrice, Roland, Jean, and I will be captains."

It was interesting to me how all the players deferred to Julien's command—perhaps a privilege granted to the best player on the floor.

The four captains stood on the sidelines while the rest of us looked at our shoes at center court. The names were clicked off.

"I'll take Henri."

"David."

"Michel."

"*Viens,* Jean-Claude."

In less than two minutes, the sides were nearly chosen. Only two other players and I remained. And then the process of selection became slower—painfully slower—as the captains agonized, not over who would be the greatest asset, but who would cause the least damage.

"Eh bien," a captain said mournfully, "I'll take Gérard."

Now, it was between me, the former Emerson Elementary School standout, and the fourteen-year-old French version of Pistol Pete. As I stood there, hands on my hips, I realized that in all the schoolyard pickup games I had ever played, I had never been chosen last. *Never.* I lifted my head slowly and looked at Julien. It was his choice. I tried to send a telepathic message to Julien. "Choose me, Julien. Please choose me."

Julien looked at me for a moment, and my heart leapt. He would certainly call my name. We had a connection. We both knew Julius Irving by name—and Allen Iverson and Gary Payton.

And then I thought Julien's eyes became sad and apologetic like the eyes of a poetic hangman. *"Le petit gars,"* Julien said. The little guy.

For a moment I thought that Julien meant me, but then I looked at the French Pistol Pete and saw that, despite his growth spurt, he was still a couple of inches shorter than I. The fourteen-year-old leapt to Julien's side. And there I stood, the dregs of basketball manhood, the last player chosen in the sport of my choice.

"Come on, Allen," my captain said, followed by the awful French phrase spoken under his breath to no one in particular. *"Je suppose que tu es avec nous."* I suppose that you're with us.

I suppose that you're with us! Oh my God. Has there ever been a more cruel and shattering string of words? Why not just say, "What the hell, we'll take the crumbling fossil with the scrawny legs."

At the end of the evening, after three hours of full-court basketball, I was reduced to a few strands of kelp washed ashore on the beach. I had a calf muscle that was tightening up, and when I walked, my knee snapped and my groin popped. I limped over to Julien. Snap-pop-snap-pop.

"You have a great team," I said.

"Yes, like the Chicago Bulls," Julien said in English.

"Yes, like the Chicago Bulls," I said. "You are too strong for me. I'm afraid I would do more damage than good—to the team for sure, but especially to me."

"I understand," Julien said, returning to French. "But if you ever change your mind, you can come and play with us anytime. If you would like to run."

"Thank you, Julien. You are a good guy and a terrific player. Really sensational."

"*Bof.* I miss a lot of shots."

"Not so many," I said, turning away.

I was halfway to the door when Julien called out. "*Hé!* Allen." He trotted over to me and shook my hand. "I am sorry I did not choose you."

"*Merci*, Julien."

"*De rien.*"

I walked out into the warm Mediterranean night, got into my car, and for a moment overheard the wind chimes of time and remembrances that dance over the graves of old athletes. It is a sad feeling of loss when you realize for the very first time that you will never again be the first man chosen on the field of battle. Although he may never speak of it, it is an inscrutable surprise that eventually shakes every man to the core.

If that man is strong enough, centered enough, wise enough, he will surrender to the third act of his life. He will say, "So this is what it means to grow old." Then, if he is one of the lucky ones, he will in a moment, a day, a year seize the dignity to disabuse himself of his own immortality. He will come to embrace the grand and *almost* unlimited promises that await his discovery. There are ten thousand possibilities, only one of which is the exploration of a foreign land, including, not insignificantly, its epicurean delights.

CHAPTER 8

Bon Appètit

THE FRENCH DON'T EAT, THEY DINE. They don't lunge at food, they savor it. There is a word that they often use to describe themselves. *Gourmand.* It means "one who loves food and eats with great pleasure." (We have the same word in English, although, at least in my circles, it is seldom used. Moreover, it has a more negative sense in English: a person who is fond of good eating, often indiscriminatingly and to excess.)

I suppose that somewhere in the hills or back roads of France, there is someone who is not gourmand. Perhaps he is a shepherd who has never left his flock and has grown accustomed to eating berries and mutton chops. I suppose that man exists, but I have not met him yet.

The French I know make dining an event. In the States, eating (I will not call it dining) is more like an interruption. I have had meals stateside that have taken five minutes to prepare and three minutes to devour. In fact, as far as I know, we are the only country in the world that microwaves five-minute rice.

The French, on the other hand, will spend two or three hours at the table with guests—drinking, eating, and conversing about world affairs, current styles, and the neighbor's five yapping shih tzus.

My wife and I grew attached to the leisurely three-hour dinners in France. It was so much fun to eat like royalty and needle the French as if they were old college chums. A week after our return to the States, we tried to replicate the experience. We invited two couples—both close and longtime friends—for a dinner at our home. We sat down at the table at 7:30. One hour later, one of our guests said, "Well, this has been very nice, but we need to call it a night. Lots to do tomorrow, you know." And with that both couples whisked out of our home like swirling dust devils.

When they had left, Nita and I sat slack-jawed at the dining table.

"What the hell just happened?" I asked.

Nita shook her head. "It's just another culture, sweetheart. You can't expect them to be like the French."

"I don't like this culture."

"I'm afraid you'll have to get used to it. It's who we are."

"I'll never get used to it."

"Then prepare to be miserable."

That sentence pulled me up short. As usual, I realized that Nita was right. Both people, French and Americans, have qualities that are endearing. However, they are not always the *same* qualities. The trick is to love what is lovable, tolerate what is not, and stop insisting on cultural blending.

Nita and I got a flavor of the French flare for cuisine the first full day we were in the country. I awoke with the sun and walked out onto the Ducros' terrace. Even at six-thirty in the morning, the sun was warm and bright. Just another day in paradise, I said to myself. I noticed that Jean-Marie was in the open field across the street. He was doubled over, meticulously searching the ground . . . for what?

I crossed the street. "Hey, Jean-Marie, what are you looking for?"

Jean-Marie kept his eyes downcast. "It rained last night," he said. "That always brings out the escargots. Look at this."

Jean-Marie was now bent over an iron fence post. A half-dozen small snails were clinging to the rail. "Wow," I said, more out of respect for my French host than genuine admiration. Snails are not really my favorite culinary delicacy. In fact, I'd say on the scale of tasty delights, I'd rate escargots right up there with grasshoppers and earthworms. There is something about their little slimy faces with their tiny eyes and those miniature antennas with the balls on top (what's with that?) that makes me want to look in another direction like, say, directly into the noonday sun.

That said, I was in France, and, after all, I had made a sacred vow to keep an open mind during our stay. So, I bent over and started dropping what I judged to be the more succulent snails into Jean-Marie's bucket.

"Whoa, look at this one!" I said, holding the granddaddy of them all between my thumb and forefinger. The snail's articulated antennas were flinging wildly in the air like the arms of a drowning man. It was a monster, a gastropod with a coiled shell the diameter of a silver dollar.

"Size is not always synonymous with quality," Jean-Marie said, uncharacteristically cryptic.

I wondered for a moment if he was referring to Americans' penchant for all things enormous: five-carat diamonds, foot-long hot dogs, and Herculean football players, to name a few. "Oh, I see," I said, dropping a more unpretentious snail into the bucket.

"*Ça suffit*—that's enough," Jean-Marie said. "Time for the next step."

We crossed the street to the house. Jean-Marie took the garden hose and covered the twenty or thirty snails with an inch of water. "I'll be right back," he said, making his way into the house. While he was gone, some of the snails started inching their way up the side of the bucket. I imagined that they were instinctively aware that they were in mortal danger. A moment later Jean-Marie was back with a bottle of vinegar and a box of salt.

"What are you going to do?" I asked.

"I'm going to make them *baver*," he said. The first meaning of the word *baver* is "to slobber or dribble." I don't know the English equivalent for the second sense, but in French to *"faire baver"* is to cause the snails to discharge whatever slimy gunk is in their system. For Americans it is not a particularly pretty picture, but the French don't seem to cringe at the thought.

Jean-Marie dumped a half-cup of vinegar and an equal dose of salt into the green plastic bucket. Now the snails stampeded up the side of the pail. Jean-Marie scraped them off with the flick of his hand and the hapless fugitives plunged into the fatal brine, traces of *bave* floating to the surface.

That was hard. I was starting to feel connected to a few of them—one in particular reminding me of a cocky Steve McQueen on a Triumph, leaping fences in *The Great Escape*. I couldn't help rooting for the little guys.

* * *

THAT EVENING FRIENDS OF THE DUCROS INVITED THE FOUR OF US—Jean-Marie, Monique, Nita, and me—to a traditional five-course French dinner. The escargots served as our contribution to the affair. Our hosts were André and Nicole. They lived in a lovely stucco villa with a swimming pool in the front yard just inside a six-foot-high walled enclosure. As in most of the fine homes in le Midi, the floor was tile. You hardly ever saw hardwood floors—and never wall-to-wall carpet. French homes are built to last. At one time stone was the preferred masonry. Now concrete block is the material of choice.

Whenever I commented on the tile floors, I was always told that they were easier to keep clean. I'm sure that is true, but I think a more fundamental allure for the French is that tile will stand the test of time. The French I know do not think like Americans. Americans think a home should be built for a lifetime. The French think a home should be built for posterity, for the next generation and all the generations to come. That is something I found endearing about the French. I think their protracted sense of time and allegiance to unborn descendants encourages a society that is less disposable.

We were greeted like family, Nicole kissing me on both cheeks and André following suit with Nita. Three is the prescribed number of kisses in the Montpellier region (two in Marseille and an interminable string of four in Paris). However, at the end of the evening, when we were doing our kissing again, I noticed that Nicole only kissed Jean-Marie twice.

"Why was that?" I asked.

"Well, in principle, there should be three kisses, but sometimes Nicole gets impatient," Jean-Marie explained.

"Oh."

We were guided to the living room where we sat down around a large coffee table. André deployed an assortment of bottles on the table like tin soldiers in an imaginary theater of war: wine, whiskey, and liqueur. Serving alcohol was clearly the man's role. Meanwhile, Nicole offered two bowls, one with pistachio nuts and the other with Jean-Marie's escargots, toothpicks included.

Before going to France, I did not drink alcohol. It was a choice I had made as a boy after witnessing the devastation of alcoholism. But explaining that preference to the French—who per capita consume five times as much wine as Americans—can be a bit of a trial. They can't seem to imagine a grown man choosing not to drink, especially wine. So, to avoid the drama, I decided on this trip that I would enjoy what was offered. At first I took to bubbly champagne and the sweetness of white wine. But by the end of our first year in France, red wine was my beverage of choice. Unfortunately, at this first dinner, I had not yet developed a taste for wine.

"What will you have?" André asked me.

I tried to make my tone as casual as possible. "Some orange juice would be terrific," I said.

"With what?" André said.

"Just straight," I said.

"Ah, mais non," André said. *"Ce n'est pas possible."* It's not possible.

I glanced at Jean-Marie, who knew my drinking preferences at the time. "There is no need to insist," Jean-Marie said to André.

"Quand même," André said. "You must at least have some pastis. It's from the region."

"Some pastis, then," I said, reaching the limit of my resistance.

André poured an inch of the yellow liqueur into my glass, topping it off with water. Made from the licorice-flavored seeds of anise, the sweet-tasting pastis is a favorite aperitif among the people of Provence and Languedoc. As for me, I have always liked the flavor of licorice, so pastis was a good choice.

The escargots were passed around. I noticed that Nita took one and hid it among the pistachio nuts on her napkin, where it stayed undisturbed for the rest of the night. I took three—a tidy sum, I thought. I bayoneted the first one with a toothpick and, trying not to visualize the face of Steve McQueen, popped it into my mouth. It was a little chewy, I thought, with an aftertaste of parsley—not bad but not something I would order in a restaurant.

After the aperitifs, we were led to an enclosed glass terrace that looked out on a flourishing Mediterranean garden. We sat down around a solid oak dining table where we would stay, eating and chatting, for the next three hours. In typical French fashion, there were five courses.

First course: Bite-size segments of octopus, coupled with a fresh salad composed of skinned tomatoes, onions, and green peppers lightly bathed in vinegar and olive oil.

Octopus is not my favorite starter—a little too much like eating windshield-wiper blades for my money—but I accepted a second helping, if nothing else but to prove that Americans were not *total* barbarians.

"*Pas mal,*" I said.

"This one is a little tough," Nicole admitted.

"Oh, not at all," I lied, my tongue working overtime on a piece of octopus gristle lodged between a pair of molars.

The French are big on fish. The annual per capita consumption of fish and shellfish in France is seventy pounds, compared to just under forty-seven pounds in the United States. So it is no surprise that fish is often the first course after the hors d'oeuvres.

In other homes I have been regaled with shrimp, mussels wrapped in bacon (very tasty), crayfish (not much to talk about there), lobster, and, a personal favorite, stingray. *Une raie,* one of Monique's specialties, is a flaky and tender white meat that melts in your mouth. Had Monique not told me, I never would have guessed I was eating stingray.

It was not my first experience with the winged fish. I once went scuba diving among a school of stingrays in a bay off of Grand Cayman (the dive promoters have called the spot "Stingray City"). The fish were like puppies gliding overhead and through my legs in search of a handful of squid.

They were sandpaper rough on the slate-gray topside, and silky smooth, some might say slimy, on the snow-white bottom. Now, did I ever consider throwing one of those puppies in the frying pan for dinner? No way. Would I eat one now? In a minute!

While we are on the subject of seafood, it's not a big leap to amphibians and the French delicacy of frog legs. My friend Armelle once served them as an entrée. (I had told her it was something I wanted to try before leaving France. Lesson: Be careful what you ask for.) It is true what they say about frog legs. They taste like chicken, although a little more fatty by my palate. If you can get past the idea of eating a toad, they're really not that bad, although I prefer lamb chops or just about anything else that doesn't croak.

Second course: Stewed rabbit and a side dish of egg noodles.

The rabbit was tasty, not unlike chicken but a little wilder. The flavor reminded me of pheasant, a bird that my dad used to hunt when I was a boy.

"What are these kidney-shaped things?" I chirped, trying to make my question more of a children's game than an accusation.

"They're, well . . . kidneys," André said.

"Of course they are, I knew that," I laughed.

Monique turned to me. "You haven't had rabbit kidneys before, have you?"

"Well, let's see. Not for a long time. Not since . . . well, ever."

"How do you like them?" André asked.

"They have a kind of organ taste," I said authoritatively.

"Well, if you like that," André said, "you have to try something really special."

Actually, I had not claimed I actually *liked* them, but I let the assumption pass.

André leapt from his chair and disappeared into the kitchen. In a moment, I heard the rattling of what I imagined to be carving knives.

"What is he doing in there?" I asked Nicole.

"Oh, a little *bricolage*," Nicole said, impishly sidestepping the question.

Bricolage is a word that is often used in French. It means tinkering or doing odd jobs. The word is so rooted in the culture that there is even a chain of hardware stores called Monsieur Bricolage. However, if you live in France long enough, you will learn that there is another nuance of the word: slapdash or jerry-rigged. Jerry-rigging—like attaching electrical wires or plumbing to the *outside* surface of a wall—is a rooted Gallic tradition, as entrenched as vacation in August. The French make no apologies about the custom. If anything, they are amused. I once spoke to a seventy-year-old French Catholic priest who defined *bricolage* as "the art of taking bedsprings and making a bookcase."

So, when Nicole said that her husband was engaged in a little *bricolage*, I was not sure what adventure to expect.

"Et voilà," André said, emerging from the kitchen with a butcher knife in one hand and a mysterious, leathery creature in the other.

"Uh, what is it?" I asked, making no effort to disguise my apprehension.

"It's a *violet*," André announced proudly, separating the two halves of the organism as if opening a clam.

"And what in the world is a *violet*?" I asked.

For the next five minutes, the native francophones exchanged impassioned definitions of the sea creature, none of which made much sense to me. A few days later, I referred to an encyclopedia of sea life in Jean-Marie's library and discovered that a *violet* was, in layman's terms, a sea squirt. As it turns out, it is a rather advanced animal because, like humans, it has a spine (and, unlike humans, both sex organs, which I thought could be pleasantly diverting).

"Look how clean the inside of the bladder is," André said, standing over me with sea squirt and blade.

Sure enough, that was one clean bladder—like a sparkling white porcelain bidet.

"Here, it's for you," André said merrily, presenting the rubbery blob on the end of the butcher knife.

"Oh, I couldn't. It's too much," I said, surveying the table for someone—anyone—who wanted the sea biscuit more than I.

Everyone sat stock-still, arms folded, grinning back at me like a chorus of Stan Laurels.

"I insist," André said.

"*Merci,*" I said, giving up hope of rescue from the beaming quintet of diners. "Somewhere, I'm sure there are just the right French words to properly thank you."

"No thanks are necessary," André said. "It is given with *grand plaisir.*"

Grand pleasure, indeed. André's rascally side-glance to Jean-Marie recalled the day my brother offered me a jumbo jalapeño pepper that barbecued the inside of my mouth for a week. "Eat the whole thing at once," my brother had advised. "It's mild. You'll like it."

I sucked the sea squirt into my mouth and began chewing . . . and chewing. There are Michelin tires that are more tender. Finally, when no one was looking, I cupped my mouth and slipped out a sliver of bone that, as far as I knew, may have been the tadpole's backbone. "Yum," I said. "Now, that's eating."

There are worse things to eat than sea squirts. I know; I've eaten the worst thing. At a dinner with the Ducros later in the year, the main dish was duck. Now, I'm not particularly beguiled by duck, but it's not bad, and the French certainly know how to prepare it. So when the dish was served, I was content. But, I have to admit, I was somewhat surprised to see, in the center of the serving platter, the scalped head of the duck staring up at me with empty eye sockets. It was a sad expression, as though the duck were saying, "Gee-whiz, now I'll never fly south again."

"*C'est la tête?*" I asked, pointing with my dinner knife at the sorrowful duck head. As soon as the words were out of my mouth, I knew it was the wrong thing to have said. A question like that, and it's open season on naïve Americans.

"Of course," Monique said. "It's the best part."

Jean-Marie swooped in for the kill. "Oh, yes, *la cervelle de canard*—it is a rare delicacy."

"Duck brains?" I asked haltingly.

"*Mais oui,*" Jean-Marie said, stabbing the head of the duck with his fork. "Let me show you." With that, he started slicing into the duck's skull with his steak knife. "You're going to love this."

"You betcha."

The skull cracked open, and Jean-Marie scooped out the bird's brains with his spoon. "Here," he said, tapping the morsel onto my plate.

Everyone was looking at me, waiting to see what I would do. I really had no choice. I rinsed out my mouth with a sip of red wine, took a couple of short Lamaze breaths, and eased the ganglion into my mouth.

I let my tongue and palette savor the tiny organ. It was squishy, rather like goose liver (another Gallic favorite that I have actually come to enjoy, although not nearly as enthusiastically as the French). I just couldn't help thinking that I was devouring all the memories and aspirations of a feathered traveler: the hatching, the splashing around the pond with the other guys, and that *interminable* flight from Finland to the Mediterranean, year in and year out. ("Whose daffy idea was that?" my duck brain must have thought.)

"How do you like it?" Monique asked.

"Well . . . it's not my favorite," I said smiling, "but I suddenly have this irresistible urge to arrange all my peas in the shape of a 'V.'"

Third course: The cheese platter comprised of blue cheese, goat cheese, Camembert, and Cantal (a hard, sharp cheese).

In an election speech General De Gaulle reasoned that no one could unite a country that has 265 kinds of cheese. In the American movie *French Kiss*, the character played by Meg Ryan grumbled that only France could produce 452 varieties of cheese. That's a lot of curdled milk, but the largest count I'm aware of comes from Patrick Rance, author of *The French Cheese Book*, who placed the number at 750. Whatever the exact count, you can be sure that when in France, cheese will always be on the menu.

I do not know how the passion for cheese began in France, but I will tell you it is real. One of the hikes I took with the Pérols hiking club terminated at a farm that produced goat cheese. There were twenty-five hikers in the group and nearly all of them stood in line at the barn door to buy cylinders of goat cheese the size of a hockey puck for the bargain price of one euro a puck.

"When was the cheese made?" one of the hikers asked.

"This morning," the farmer said.

"Ooh," the hikers sang out, like a sacred incantation to the munificent god of the goat cheeses.

Nicole's offering was a typical French cheese course. When the platter came around, I took a wedge of two or three varieties, along with a couple slices of bread—my standard routine. And then everyone froze for a moment. I sensed the silence and stopped dead, my mouth wide open, a chunk of bread and cheese at half-mast.

"What?" I said, looking around the table.

"That is not *correct*," André said.

Now the adjective *correct* carries an impact in French that is missing in English. The first sense—as in English—means "without errors." The second sense means "acceptable," which is also shared in English. But the third sense of the word only exists in French: decent, moral, and just. When André told me that what I had done was "not *correct*," I knew I had crossed the line into cultural impropriety—that what I had done was somehow "indecent."

I smiled weakly. "What is not correct?" I asked.

"You cut a wedge of the blue cheese from the wrong end," André said.

"Huh?"

Then André explained in vivid detail the proper way of cutting a slice of blue cheese. Picture a wedge of *fromage bleu*. If you look carefully, you will see that the blue flecks—mold actually—are all congregated at the slender front tip of the wedge. Therefore, any cultivated human being (I think that most French believe that "a cultivated American" is an oxymoron) knows that one slices blue cheese from the side, thereby leaving an equal amount of blue mold for all to enjoy. I had committed the barbarous faux pas (*une gaffe* in French slang) of cutting from the tip of the block of cheese. How wicked is the act? Have you heard in the States that some cities are installing smart parking meters that reset to zero when a vehicle leaves the space? It's that wicked.

Naturally, I apologized all over the place. I even offered to paste the dishonorable wedge back in place. No, it was too late for that kind of nonsense. I poured a little more wine, more out of unstrung shame than thirst.

"Ah, I see you are enjoying the wine," André said.

"Yes, it is very good," I said, too embarrassed at the moment to confess that my palate was completely untrained. "I would say fruity without being ostentatious," having no notion of what the devil I was talking about.

"That's good," André said. If you like that, you are sure to enjoy some cider from Normandy.

"*Merci*," I said. A word of explanation here. With the right intonation, the word *merci* in such a situation is used to say, "no, thank you"—just the reverse of the American custom. To say "yes" in French—that you would indeed like something more to drink—it is more conventional to say "*volontiers,*" "*avec plaisir,*" or even "*je ne dirais pas 'non.'*" Voluntarily. With pleasure. I would not say "no."

"*Mais si,*" André said.

Happy to distance myself from the besmirched blue-cheese debacle and not wanting to offend my host again, I said, "Well, then, in that case, *avec plaisir.*"

André escaped into the kitchen and reappeared with a decanter of cider—"the real thing," I was assured.

André filled my glass, despite my supplications of "*merci . . . ça suffit . . . arrêtez!*" Thank you . . . that's enough . . . *stop!*

I took a long sip of the Normandy specialty. It was indeed tasty, rather light compared to the red wine—cider being four percent alcohol, one-third the alcoholic jolt of wine. Still, after the pastis and the wine, my head was beginning to say, "This is strange, and why does my wife have two sets of eyes, one set stacked over the other?" So I found myself reaching for my glass of water the rest of the evening.

One last personal footnote before leaving this section on cheese. My personal favorite is Camembert. I know it is the most pervasive, but there is a reason for that. It's good. I could eat it every day with a fresh *baguette* and during my year in France came pretty close to fulfilling my wish.

Fourth course: Almond and pear tart.

The French *pâtisseries* (pastry shops) are a marvel. Although I'm certain the French would protest, I would sacrifice the Eiffel Tower before giving up one French pastry shop. Walking into a *pâtisserie* is like walking into a Lamborghini showroom. You wallow in the wicked decadence of the place, all the while knowing that if your wife caught you there, softly moaning in a waft of new car leather, she would wag her finger at you in wifely scorn. There is no argument for justifying your presence in a French pastry shop other than unbridled indulgence—and, for me, it was practically the only place I wanted to be. Only the horror of the bathroom scale slingshotting into new territory tempered my enthusiasm for the sugary snacks.

Although there are a few good imitations in the States, the wonders found in a *pâtisserie* have no rival: chocolate muffins (they actually use the word *muffin*), *mille-feuilles* (layers of custard and airy, razor-blade-thin wafers), and, my personal favorite, *tartelette à la fraise*, a three-inch diameter pie filled with pale yellow custard and topped with glazed strawberries. *Tartelette à la fraise* is a misnomer. It should be called "sixty seconds in heaven," which is exactly how long it takes me to scarf one down if I'm trying to prolong the pleasure.

Now, I am generally rather prudent with my money (I have friends who would argue that the word I'm looking for is "chintzy"). All right. I admit I faithfully check the price tags in American grocery stores to ferret out the can of tomato sauce that registers the fewest pennies per ounce. And I will drive on empty for thirty miles if I think there is a gas station with unleaded fuel for two cents less. So it is amazing to me that I feel no reservation in plunking down two bucks for an apple tart that is gone in four bites. The only thing I can figure is that the euro coins are just novel enough to look like play money to me—like gambling chips in Las Vegas.

Nicole's almond and pear tart was, naturally, delicious. I was glowing like a beautiful bride when she served me a generous portion.

"Do you always eat this well?" I asked André with a smile.

Before André could respond, Nicole said, "Not really. A dinner like this is usually reserved for guests or family on Sundays."

"And as far as desserts are concerned," André added, "we typically will have fruit."

"Or nothing at all," Monique said. *"Il faut garder la ligne."*

Watching one's figure, as Monique put it, is routine with the French. Conversely, they are dismayed by the extent of American obesity (their word choice). A French exchange student I met in the States put it tersely. "They're fat. It's the first thing I noticed getting off the plane."

"You have a problem in the United States," Nicole said. "Many Americans are obese." (No argument there. In 2014 thirty-five percent of American adults were obese.)

"Yes, that is true," Nita said. "It's a big problem."

"It is starting to become a problem here too," André said. "What you have now, we will have in ten years." (Although André's prediction was inflated, the trend was certainly on target. In 2001 only seven percent of the French population was obese. Ten years later that number had doubled.)

Indeed, France has integrated a host of American practices, many of which I can hardly tolerate in the States. To see them arrive in France is agonizing. The French know this is happening. They know that their culture is being stripped away and, all too often, replaced with galling American exports: mindless cinema, degrading television talk shows, rap music, graffiti, sugar cereal, and MacDo (the French abbreviation for MacDonald's). They know it is happening but feel helpless in fighting it off.

"Allen," André said, "you have come to France to see the last remnants."

"What do you mean?"

"We are the last of the true French. You will see our fossils in a museum someday. In two or three generations, we will be indistinguishable from Americans." He said it with a smile, but it was laced with sadness that made my heart ache. I hoped he was wrong, but mounting evidence supports his prophecy.

"Have you seen our supermarkets?" André asked.

I had. Indeed, one of the most disturbing American transplants has been what the French call *les grandes surfaces*, the fifty-thousand-square-foot department stores that have spread across France like locusts. These stores (Auchan and Carrefour are two of the biggest) are replicas of the American Walmart discount store—only somehow more frenetic. Stepping into the Lattes Carrefour in August is like stepping into a Tokyo subway during rush hour—hordes of French people filling their carts with electronics, hardware, cookware, clothing, and groceries. Arms, legs, and hips are flying in every direction—the picture of chaos (and, incidentally, a microcosm of French roadways).

The stores employ a half-dozen roller skaters who weave in and out of aisles, skimming customers, all the while talking on cellular telephones. I interviewed one of these skaters—a tall, slender woman in her early twenties.

"What is your job?" I asked.

"Solving problems," she said. "Chasing down prices, delivering products, cleaning up messes."

"Is it fun?"

"Not really. It's hard on your body. That's why we wear all these pads."

I looked at her knee and elbow pads. They were scuffed and dented, the scars from too many crashes. "How long have you been doing this?" I asked.

"Two years."

"And how long will you continue?"

"Not long, I hope. I'm looking for something now."

"Thanks," I said.

She looked at me with a smile of gratitude. "Thank you for taking the time to talk to me," she said.

For me, every French *grande surface* has a roller derby feel about it: noisy, pushy, and impersonal. It is clearly not my favorite hangout. But the prices are lower than in the smaller shops. Consequently, it is where most French go for their weekly shopping.

Even André, an old-school Frenchman who valued the intimacy of a mom-and-pop *épicerie,* conceded to shopping at Carrefour once a week for groceries. Why? To economize, of course.

I looked at André. His elbows were on the table, his fingers laced and pressed against his mouth. His eyes were downcast, staring at nothing.

"I hope you are wrong," I said truthfully.

"About what?" André asked, looking up at me.

"About the death of French culture as we know it."

"So do I," André said without conviction. "So do I."

Fifth course: Coffee.

The French do love their coffee, and it is almost always offered at the end of the meal. But *faites attention* (beware), what Americans call coffee is nothing like French *café*. American coffee is a beverage, and there are some Americans who drink it in liters. French coffee is not a beverage. It is an injection and is served in a tiny three-ounce *tasse à café* that is so dainty that the most diminutive of men look like professional wrestlers drinking from a child's tea set.

By the time the coffee is served, the conversation often becomes more profound and, if you are really lucky, more intimate. On this evening, our hosts began talking about their roots.

"I was a *pied-noir*," Nicole volunteered.

Pied-noir is a name applied to French citizens who settled in Algeria after the French invasion in 1830. The name means "black feet" and was coined by the Algerians, reputedly for the color of French army boots. In 1962 Algeria regained its independence, precipitating the exodus of 1.3 million French citizens, an influx that France was ill-equipped to manage.

"Our family left Algeria with two suitcases, nothing more," Nicole continued. "I was seventeen. We lived in a one-room apartment in Montpellier. It was awful. Water would run down the side of the wall. I was cold all the time. *All* the time."

The room was very quiet now, everyone listening intently to Nicole's story.

"I could never get warm," Nicole said. "I remember asking my teacher for permission to wrap myself in a blanket during class. 'Absolutely not,' I was told."

"Were the *pied-noir* badly treated in France?" Nita asked.

"Oui," Nicole said flatly. "I was treated better by the Arabs in Algeria than by my own countrymen. My father was a baker in Algeria, but he lost everything. In France there was no work—nothing. He died within two years, angry and penniless."

Nicole paused for a moment. No one spoke.

"I miss Algeria," Nicole finally said. "We were happy there. It did not have to end the way it did. De Gaulle was wrong to go to war with Algeria. Of course, Algerians wanted their independence. It was only natural."

In 2002 the topic of immigration was already a polemic issue. (That controversy has not changed. In 2013 alone there was an influx of forty thousand immigrants, the largest share coming from North Africa.) I wanted to get André's take on the subject.

"What do you think of the immigration problem now?" I asked.

"*Problem* is the right word," André said. "Unemployment is already high in France. And relaxed immigration makes it worse. We are a socialist country, and when foreigners do not find work, which is often the case, we pay the bill. And we're getting fed up with it."

"Are the French racist?" I asked.

"No," André said. "The French are not racist, but the Arabs are."

"How's that?" I asked.

"They will not integrate into our culture. They will not learn our language. They live in their own communities. The girls go to school wearing veils. That is not right."

I have heard similar examples from other Frenchwomen and men.

- One Frenchman criticized a fourteen-year-old Algerian for refusing to enter a Christian church on a historical field trip.
- A French science teacher complained that high school Arabs demand and are given a separate table in the cafeteria.
- A French parent was appalled that Arab students should be excused from reading the French nineteenth-century writer René Chateaubriand because his manner of describing the Orient was thought to be racist by the Muslim community.

Many French citizens complain that the Muslim refusal to be integrated into the French community is a violation of the Republic's declaration of fraternity and the principle of separation of church and state. Some even fear that acquiescing to Muslim demands could result in the disintegration of French society. (It was in part for these reasons that Islamic head scarves were banned in French public schools in 2004.)

One fifty-year-old Frenchwoman I spoke to said, "We have gone to war over the question of religion before. I think it is time we do it again." Later in the evening I spoke to another Frenchwoman who was present when the comment was made.

"Her words were a little severe, don't you think?" I asked.

"Perhaps," the woman said, "but one can understand. She is scared, just as I am scared."

The issues of immigration and cultural integration are complex, but I do believe that one thing is certain. Most French people wish to protect their unique identity. They have a healthy and warranted pride in their heritage: their history, their language, their mores, their contributions to science and art. Understandably, they do not want to see that legacy vanish. So, it is not surprising to me that immigrants, particularly Muslim immigrants, are often viewed as a threat.

When I asked my French friends in Languedoc what could be done, most shrugged their shoulders, a gesture of impotence. And then they would say, "I am not fearful for myself. My life will not change dramatically. But I am fearful for the lives of my grandchildren and great-grandchildren to come."

Not everyone in France shares André's perspective on immigration. Jean-Marie, for example, is confident that the Muslim population will be integrated into the French culture in two to three generations. I think the future will lie somewhere between the attitudes held by André and Jean-Marie. Although integration may come with time, it will not be easy, and it will not be reached without embittered battles along ethnic, economic, and religious lines.

By the time we left the dinner table, nearly four hours had elapsed since our 7:00 p.m. arrival. The evening was an unbelievably rich experience. We had been introduced to a variety of foods and beverages, but, more importantly, to an intriguing culture, which, like all cultures, is a complex tapestry of virtues and challenges, courage and fears. And in the midst of it all, this American felt humbled and immensely grateful. What a joy to step into such an amicable and unrestricted learning milieu—a kind of cultural graduate school with the added benefit of good bread, cheese, and wine.

CHAPTER 9

On the Trail

THE HIKING CLUB OF PÉROLS was an absolute marvel to us. It had 250 members, ranging in age from twenty to seventy-five, all of whom were avid hikers and, more importantly, world-class talkers. Nowhere else did we learn so much about the language and spirit of being French. At the same time, we were introduced to a hundred villages, limestone cliffs and grottos, and cloistered farmhouses with stone ovens for baking bread. These images will never fade from my memory.

The club offered two full-day and two half-day hikes each week. The hikes were color coded to designate level of difficulty.

Color Code	Time	Distance	Elevation Gain
Pastel Green	2–3 hours	Less than 5 miles	Less than 200 feet
Forest Green	4–8 hours	5–10 miles	1,000 feet
Blue	8 hours	11 miles	2,000 feet
Red	8 hours	12–13 miles	Up to 3,300 feet

In other words, there was a hike for everyone. Nita logged in the half-day hikes while I sampled both half- and full-day excursions—the opportunities were just too rich to ignore.

* * *

My introductory club hike was an easy pastel green stroll (the French use the word *balade*) along the beach from Carnon to La Grande Motte. The group was led by Henri, a tall and hardy man in his mid-fifties. There were a dozen hikers, mostly women, in their fifties and sixties.

"We have a newcomer," Henri announced to the group. "His name is Allen, and he is an American."

"Ah, an American," a petite woman with black hair said excitedly. "I have a daughter who lives in Boston. Do you know Boston?"

"Yes, I . . ."

"What region do you come from?" another woman interrupted.

"I come from the state of Washington."

"Oui," she said. "Zee White House."

"No," I said, knowing this conversation by heart, "that is the city, the capital of the United States. I live in the state of Washington—in the far northwest. Do you know Seattle?"

"Ah, Seattle. No, not really."

I found a stick and drew the outline of the Unites States in the sand. "This is the Unites States," I said. "This is Florida, here's Texas, and here is the state of Washington."

"And here is Boston," the woman with black hair said, poking her finger into the sand at the approximate location of Boston Harbor. "My daughter lives here. Her husband is American so that is where she lives, of course, but she really prefers France. She doesn't feel safe in Boston. Do you feel safe in Boston?"

"Well, I . . ."

"He doesn't live in Boston," another woman corrected. "He lives in the state of Washington," poking the tip of her bare toe into the side of Mount Rainier. "Right there. That's where he lives."

134

I looked at the geography teacher. She was taller than the rest of the ladies, about five feet eight with short cropped blond hair and a flash in her eyes. Although she was in her early sixties, she had a straight back and clear complexion.

"What is your name?" I asked.

"Odette," she said smiling broadly. "And your name is Alain?" she asked, using the French pronunciation.

"Yes."

"But this is a French name. You have a French name?"

"Well, actually, my name is 'Allen,' but I thought it would be easier to pronounce, if I . . ."

"*Mais non,*" Odette said. "You must not use the French 'Alain.' That is old fashioned. You must use your own name. Allen. That is much more exotic."

She smiled and then did something I seldom saw during our first year in France. She actually winked at me.

"*Et alors,*" Henri said. "Are we going to hike?"

"*Mais oui.* Of course. Let's go," the group sang out.

We started out east along the sandy shore, strewn with the discarded homes of scallops, cockles, and razor shell clams. It was mid-September. The sun was shining brightly in a cloudless sky, and fishermen with their long poles were scattered along the shoreline, angling for *daurade* (gilt-head bream) and *bar* or *loup* (sea bass). The hikers formed groups of two and three, chattering over the sound of the waves breaking lightly on the beach.

I naturally found myself drifting toward Odette who, at the time, was examining the shell of a sea snail.

"Isn't it marvelous?" Odette said without introduction.

"What do you mean?"

"Why, just look."

I noticed that Odette used the informal "you" when speaking to me, as if we were old-time schoolmates.

"See how symmetrical the rings are? And how the shell circles itself like a tiny French horn? It is incredible, don't you think?"

Odette placed the shell in my hand. "Yes, it is," I said, turning the small shell between my fingers. "It's extraordinary. It makes me wonder what kind of life he had in the sea."

Odette swung her body around to face me straight on. She took both of my hands in hers. "Yes, exactly! That was what I was wondering too."

I laughed, delighted by Odette's childlike spirit—as though she were seeing the world for the first time. I wondered if she was married, and if her husband shared her seemingly uncomplicated passion for life.

"Are you married?" I asked.

"*Oui,*" Odette said.

"Does your husband hike with you?"

"*Ça, non.* He's a bit of a *pantouflard.*"

The word *pantouflard* always strikes me as funny. The French say it is a little pejorative. It comes from the same root as *pantoufle,* which means "slipper." By extension a *pantouflard* is someone who likes to stay at home—literally translated, then, as "the slippered one."

"I see that doesn't stop you from doing what pleases you," I said.

"Not in the least. My husband and I have been married for forty years. That's how long Moses wandered in the desert looking for the Promised Land, you know." Then, with perfect timing, she added, "I'm still looking." Odette peered at me with a turned-down mouth and deadpan eyes, grabbed me by the arm, and then let out a hoot in tribute to her own whimsical wit.

At the turnaround point Henri circled up the group.

"We are going to stop here for twenty minutes," he announced. "There is a café by the road for those who would like something to drink. Or for those who are a little more daring, you can go for a swim."

Now I was torn. I liked the idea of sitting in a seaside café, prattling away from the rush of the rolling sea, but then again, the thought of taking my first dip in the Mediterranean was terribly seductive too.

"What are you going to do?" Odette asked.

"I'm going for a swim," I said, deciding on the spot.

"Me too."

Because it had been previewed that the hike might include an ocean dip, I had worn a pair of polyester boxer shorts that could double as swim trunks. All I had to do was to strip off my T-shirt and kick off my tennis shoes. In a moment I was wading into the surf.

"Isn't this wonderful," Odette said. Her voice came from behind me. I looked over my shoulder, and there she was, naked from the waist up, kicking at the waves that were lapping at her ankles.

I searched all my memories in a millisecond. Yep, this was definitely the first time I had gone for a swim in the Mediterranean with a topless French grandmother.

We waded chest high into the surf.

"Can you do this?" Odette asked. With that she tucked her head and dove for the sandy bottom. In an instant her feet pierced the water's surface. They were locked together, straight and pointed like the flawless entry of a champion springboard diver. Then her feet—still perfectly vertical—turned full circle and slowly disappeared into the sea.

"Pas mal, hein?" she said, resurfacing and wiping the water from her eyes.

"Not bad at all," I said.

"Et alors?" Well then?

I took that as my cue to match her underwater ballet. I took in a breath and upended myself, but I forgot to exhale through my nose and got a snout full of saltwater. I aborted my acrobatics and came up hacking like a three-pack-a-day smoker.

"Les Américains ne sont pas très doués," Odette said with a hearty laugh.

"We may not be talented," I argued, "but we never give up." With that I plunged for the bottom again—this time mindfully exhaling through my nose—and launched my feet into the air. Not wanting to be outdone, I arched my feet and pointed my toes at the sun. It was beautiful for two seconds, and then my right calf muscle cramped up, and my feet flopped over like two dead mackerels. I bobbed to the surface, madly massaging my calf.

Odette was laughing out of control now, not in mockery but in the way children laugh when they have learned how to whistle or do a cartwheel. It was a warm, Christmas-morning laugh—a laugh that I would come to know as well as my own, for Odette became a frequent hiking partner and a dear friend by year's end.

* * *

My second hike with the Pérols hiking club was on a Monday. That day was reserved for the blue *randonnées* (hikes), the eleven-mile treks with two thousand feet of elevation gain. These were hardy hikers, able to trudge through thickets and scramble up mountainsides with ease. Although there were a few youngsters, most were in their fifties.

The hike was scheduled for a loop in the hills near Montpeyroux, northwest of Montpellier. The hilly landscape—dry and dark green—was clearly Mediterranean, with outcroppings of limestone and clumps of holm oaks. The wild thyme and rosemary were plentiful along the trail like a carpet set out for royalty. Olive trees were scattered at random across the hillsides, and straight lines of grapevines etched the flatlands.

After a thirty-minute drive to the trailhead, I got out of the car and sat on a stump to lace up my boots.

"Those are serious hiking boots."

I looked up at a figure silhouetted in the sun. "I like them," I said, shading my eyes to see the man behind the voice.

Seeing my distress, the man sat down alongside me. He was a stocky fellow, about five feet six inches tall, I guessed, with an uncovered thicket of black hair. His face was darkly tanned, almost terracotta, with pronounced laugh lines and straight white teeth. I placed him in his early sixties. "You are new," he said extending his hand.

"Yes," I said. "My name is Allen."

"My name is Gaétan."

"Gaé . . ." I said laboring over the pronunciation.

"You can call me 'Tani.' It is what my family calls me."

"Okay," I said, standing up and putting on my pack. "You have an interesting French accent, Tani."

"I was born in Spain."

"Ah, I see."

By this time the group of thirty men and women were saddled up and starting down a section of road. Tani and I fell in toward the rear.

"I came to France when I was a teenager," Tani said, "and I still roll my 'r's' like a Spaniard."

"It's charming," I said.

"That's what I think."

We walked for a while in silence until we came to a vineyard bursting with ripe dark-purple grapes.

"They look good, don't they?" Tani said, pulling out his pocketknife.

"Yes," I admitted, "but the proprietor won't appreciate you stealing them."

"That's true," Tani said, slicing off a clump of the fruit, "but then again, the proprietor isn't here. And, besides, you must taste them."

Tani placed a cluster of grapes in my hand. I ate them one by one, spitting out the seeds along the side of the road. They were sweet, very sweet. I nursed each grape, savoring the succulent meat under the thin purple skin. When I finished, I was tempted to go back and slice off a clump myself but had visions of an angry vigneron sweeping down on me with his wild-pig shotgun cocked, ready to pepper the succulent meat under my *own* thin skin.

Now we were on a narrow dirt road, winding our way into the hills.

"Wait a minute," Tani said, veering off to the side of the road. He snapped off a branch from a bush that looked a little like the sagebrush we find in southeastern Washington. He rolled the sprig between his hands for a moment. "Smell this," he said, cupping his hands under my nose.

I have to admit, I don't know my herbs. To me, oregano sounds like an Italian sports car—the Oregano X9-1000—and the only basil I know is my Greek cousin from Denver. As far as I could tell, the plant smelled like green tea. "What is it?" I asked.

"Guess," Tani said.

"I don't know."

"No, I insist. Guess."

"Uh . . . green tea?"

"Mais non, mon drôle d'Américain. C'est du thym." But no, my funny American. It's thyme.

"Hummm, thyme," I said, plunging my nose into his hands again. "So that's thyme, huh? *Ça sent bon.*" That smells good.

On the morning of that hike, Tani and others would call out my name each time they discovered another fruit. "Allen, Allen, you must taste this," they would shout. Within four hours, I was introduced to wild figs, apples, mulberries, blackberries, and sweet chestnuts that the French greedily gathered and stuffed into pockets and backpacks. "The chestnuts make a fine confiture," Tani assured me.

We stopped for lunch at a wide spot on the trail that offered a cluster of boulders as tables and chairs. Tani sat down beside me. I started to open my backpack to fish out my lunch when Tani grabbed my shoulder and tipped me to one side. As I balanced myself on half a buttock, Tani snapped off a branch that was wedged under my britches. Then he gave me a tug, which plunked me down squarely on both cheeks again.

"What in the . . ."

Tani smiled with all his teeth. "Do you know what this is?" he asked, waving a piece of shrubbery in my face.

You had to hand it to him. Tani was not giving up on the herbs and fruits of Languedoc.

"I don't have the slightest idea," I said honestly.

"Yes, you do," Tani said with a chuckle.

"No, really I don't. It would just be a guess."

"Then guess."

"Okay. Thyme?"

"*Ah, ça non*. It's rosemary!"

"Rosemary! I knew that. I was just about ready to say rosemary. One more second, and that's what I would have said. Rosemary."

"Are you making fun of me?" Tani said with a smile.

"*Moi?* Never."

"Are you sure?"

"Well, maybe just a little."

I plucked the lunch bag out of my backpack: a cheese sandwich, an apple, an energy bar, and a half-liter of water.

"What is that?" Tani asked.

"What?"

"That!" Tani said, waving a hand over my scanty picnic.

"That's my lunch," I said, a little sheepishly.

"No, that's not a lunch," Tani boomed. "This is a lunch."

With that Tani began to pull a five-course feast out of his backpack. He looked like a magician pulling rabbits and doves out of a top hat. He started with a full one-liter bottle of red wine. That was followed with a couscous and chicken casserole, pork sausage, dried apricots, and a box of chocolate-coated cookies.

I looked at Tani's buffet and then at my limp cheese sandwich. "That's incredible," I said.

"*C'est normal,*" he said.

I surveyed the other hikers who were scattered in twos and threes around us. It was a culinary orgy in full swing, right there in the backwoods of Languedoc. People were eating rabbit, artichokes, and pasta salads. They had apples and bananas and pears and, by my count, nine different types of cheeses. Then, every three or four minutes, one of the hikers would make the rounds to share a tasty delight.

"How about an aperitif," one trekker said, standing over me with a pint of yellow liquor in his hand.

"I'm sorry," I said, "I didn't bring a glass."

"Allen didn't bring a glass," the bartender announced to the other hikers.

"No glass?" Jean, the group leader said. "*Comment ça?* How is that possible? That is the first thing that goes into your pack, *Monsieur l'Américain.* You can leave your boots at home but never your glass."

In the next instant a hiker produced a short stack of plastic glasses, reserved, I assumed, for just this kind of setback: when an uncivilized American is caught in the woods without, heaven forbid, a proper vessel for a sweet aperitif.

"Thank you," I said, accepting the glass. I turned to the bartender. "Just a taste," I said.

"*Quand même,*" the bartender said, adroitly funneling two fingers of the liqueur into my cup.

"*Merci, merci, merci!*"

At that point, Tani leapt to his feet and hoisted himself onto a rounded boulder. Raising a glass of wine in perfect toasting form, he commanded the attention of the hikers. "Let's show Allen our hiking-club spirit!" he blustered. With that, all the trekkers lifted their glasses and in one voice, sang out, *"OooOOOH, santé!"* The wishes for good health echoed in the valley below.

Later, my cup was replenished with three types of regional wine—two reds and a rosé—all very good, of course, but I was getting dangerously close to my limit. Another glass and I would reenact Odette's underwater ballet by standing on my head and snapping my legs to attention. I was actually considering the idea when Tani placed his hand on the back of my neck and gave it two shakes. For a moment I felt as if he were a Latin percussionist and I the maracas.

"Allen, have you ever had a *canard*?" he asked.

"A duck?"

"Yes, but not that kind of duck."

"There's another kind of duck?"

Tani sneered at me sideways. He peered into his backpack and fished out a box of sugar cubes and a pint of liquor. "This is Calvados," Tani said, patting the flask. "It is an apple brandy, named after the department in Normandy. Ah, yes," Tani said, lovingly stroking the flask, *"l'eau-de-vie du Calvados."*

Tani offered me a cube of sugar, which I held between thumb and fore-finger. Then he poured the brandy over the sugar cube until it was fully saturated, the excess streaming from the bottom of the cube and forming a puddle between my boots.

"Bon appétit," Tani said, as I eased the soaked sugar cube into my mouth. "That is a *canard*!"

It was a strange sensation: a block of sugar in my mouth saturated with hot liquid—forty-five percent alcohol—setting my chest ablaze. (It is rather like a pancake recipe I invented, featuring a standard pancake mix—flour, milk, eggs, sugar, and butter—but peppered with my secret ingredient, the seeds from three or four dried red-hot chilies. Sweet, but with a zing.)

In between the wine and Calvados, I was offered slices of *saucisson* (large smoke-cured sausage), Cantal cheese, three types of cookies, and some homemade dark chocolate. It was a holiday feast.

Just as I thought it was time to pack up, Tani began to rummage in his backpack *again.*

"What are you looking for now?" I asked.

"My coffee," he said.

Of course! What would a French meal be without coffee?

Tani drew out a small camping cook stove and a miniature espresso machine. The appliance had a three-ounce aluminum cylinder for water and a tiny basket for ground coffee. The cylinder was topped with a miniscule shelf for the demitasse and a small shepherd's-hook spout that fed the cup. The whole thing was less than six inches tall.

Tani poured two to three ounces of water into the cylinder, filled the basket with coffee, and set the machine on the flaming camp cooker. In a few moments the water boiled over, rising up through the basket, through the spout, and into the tiny cup.

Tani turned off the stove and then delicately caressed the cup's handle with thumb and two fingers. He slowly drew the demitasse to his lips as if breathing in the scent of a beautiful woman. He blew lightly over the top of the brew and then sipped a drop—slowly as you would nurse a stiff jigger of whiskey.

"Ah, comme c'est bon!" he said with a smile that is normally withheld for hot baths, warm summer nights, and reading the Sunday paper in bed.

While Tani was communing with his coffee, I noticed that our leader, Jean, had a topographical map spread out over a rock. A couple of hikers were looking over his shoulder.

"This is how you locate yourself on the map using a compass," he explained.

"Of course, if that doesn't work," I said, "just holler out 'Would anyone like some wine?' and the French will come running from miles away."

The group laughed, and someone made a friendly wisecrack about savage Americans that I didn't quite catch.

The spirit of the group was warm and playful and generous, and I was feeling guilty that I had nothing tasty to contribute to the revelry.

"This has been a great experience for me," I said, "and I'm disappointed that I have nothing to share. But I can offer a song."

"That would be terrific," Jean said. "Attention, everyone, Allen is going to sing a song."

Now I felt a little embarrassed that I had offered. Would they think I was showing off? Of course I was showing off, but would they *think* it? That was the question.

Two years earlier, I had prepared a twenty-four-measure *a cappella* piece for a theatrical audition I did in Seattle. I thought, what the heck, maybe it'll work in the mountains of Languedoc. It starts off dramatically with the chorus of a 1929 Noel Coward tune "I'll See You Again." From there I coupled snippets of "I've Got You Under My Skin," and "I've Got a Crush on You." At the end, in honor of the French, I decided to add a few French lines of the Jacques Brel standard, *"Ne Me Quitte Pas"* ("If You Go Away").

I cleared my throat and belted out the first tune. When I got to *"Ne Me Quitte Pas,"* I suddenly forgot the lyrics midway through, and in unison the French hikers finished the phrase for me without losing a beat. That is one well-known tune in France.

There was a round of applause.

"Bravo," Tani said. "Now, this is a song that I like."

Tani stood up. Suddenly he looked much bigger than his five-foot-six-inch frame. His chest expanded, and he sang the first lines of a beautiful Spanish folk song—in Spanish, of course. His voice was stentorian—almost operatic—and as lush as summer at twilight. If we had been auditioning for the same part, he would have won hands down.

"That was wonderful," I said after he had acknowledged the applause with a deep bow from the waist.

"Eh oui," Tani said matter-of-factly.

Then with the concert over, we strapped on our backpacks and headed up the trail. An hour later all the aperitifs, wine, and coffee (with an occasional slug of water) were beginning to have their impact on all of us. We stopped near a grove of olive trees, and the hikers scattered. I paused for a moment, trying to calibrate the urgency of my bladder, and then, yes, decided I needed to find a rock or clump of brush after all. When I returned, adjusting my zipper, thirty smiling hikers were standing stock-still staring at me.

"What?" I said. *"On ne peut pas pisser en toute tranquillité ?"* Can't a guy take a whiz in peace?

"No," Jean said smiling, "not when you wait that long to find a bush."

"Geesh."

We adjusted our packs for the next stretch of the trail. But some of the women were happily chitchatting and, consequently, a little slow in slinging their packs over their shoulders. That was when Tani eased over to me.

"This reminds me of an expression that you should know."

"I'm always looking for new expressions."

"You'll like this one," he said with a nod and raised eyebrows. "If women are moving too slowly, say *'Allez les pisseuses!'*"

I tried it out in my mouth. *"Allez les pisseuses!* Is that right?"

"That's right," Tani said with a lopsided grin.

So, always one to incorporate new vocabulary, I cinched up my backpack and shouted, *"Allez les pisseuses!"*

It was not one of my finest moments. Claudine, a devout Catholic with doctrinaire notions about what is proper, whipped around and came within six inches of my face. "How dare you say that! That is a terrible thing to say, just terrible. And I thought you were a nice man."

"I am a nice man!" I pleaded, just as dismayed as she.

"Not when you talk like that."

"Yes, but Tani taught it to me."

The woman turned to Tani, which I confess was a relief to have the heat off of me. "Is that true Tani?"

Tani was the picture of innocence. "I'm sorry, what was the question?"

"Tani!" I roared.

What I learned later on the trail was that *pisseuses* had two meanings. The first was a reference to an individual with a weak bladder. That's bad enough. But the second meaning is a pejorative reference to a female. For most the word is only mildly offensive. But for a puritanical Catholic the expression must have had a wallop equivalent to saying, "Let's get going, you bitches."

Despite falling all over myself with apologies, I don't think Claudine ever forgave me. Even playing "the naïve-American card"—claiming I just didn't know any better—fell flat on its face.

And the rascal, Tani? I immediately forgave him. After all, he and I were much alike—each of us swimming in a gene pool of mischief. In fact, the incident became a running joke between us. Occasionally one of us would say to the other, "Are you ready to go, pisser?"—but *only* in private and especially far from the disapproving ears of Claudine.

After the *pisseuses* affair, we leaned into a steeper section of the trail. It culminated with a vista that stretched from Saint Guilhem-le-Désert to the north—with its magnificent eleventh-century abbey—and, if you looked hard enough, a sliver of the Mediterranean Sea to the south. Guarding the vista was a dolmen, a prehistoric stone tomb composed of two six-foot slabs of limestone still standing straight and tall like two primal centurions. A third slab had fallen from its perch, and was now wedged between the two weathered monoliths. We were suddenly silent. We all stood in wonder at how the massive stones could have been positioned by the ancient Languedoc mourners.

Twenty feet in front of the tomb was an engraved metal placard.

"Allen, look at this," Tani said.

I walked to where Tani was standing. He began reading the French text.

Every part of this soil is sacred in the estimation of my people. Every hillside, every valley, every plain and grove, has been hallowed by some sad or happy event in days long vanished.

Even the rocks, which seem to be dumb and dead as they swelter in the sun along the silent shore, thrill with memories of stirring events connected with the lives of my people, and the very dust upon which you now stand responds more lovingly to their footsteps than yours because it is rich with the blood of our ancestors, and our bare feet are conscious of the sympathetic touch.

Our departed braves, fond mothers, glad, happy hearted maidens, and even the little children who lived here and rejoiced here for a brief season, will love these somber solitudes and at eventide they greet shadowy returning spirits.

Chief Seattle, Duwamish
1884

I was so moved by the reading of the famous oratory that, in respect, I dropped to one knee and placed my hand over the noble words. At that moment Tani placed his own hand over mine. I turned and looked up at his face, obscured by the sun that was blazing overhead.

"We are all brothers, you know," Tani said.

I suddenly felt my eyes tearing up. "This is just so amazing to me," I said. "Here I am six thousand miles from home—hiking with you in this incredible French wilderness—only to be greeted by the sacred words of Chief Seattle. Can you imagine! Chief Seattle lived in my homeland—or rather I live in his. And now his spirit is here—a great Native American—right here in Languedoc."

"Then you are *chez toi*," Tani said, covering my hand with his own.

"Yes, I am. *Je suis chez moi.* " I am home.

CHAPTER 10

Song and Dance

FRED ASTAIRE has always been one of my all-time favorite actors. His screen character was always friendly, funny, and a little sassy—the kind of guy you would like to have as a best friend. As a singer he was honest and precise. The composers of the day loved to have their songs introduced by Mr. Astaire because he always remained true to the melody and lyrics. But when he put on his dancing shoes, he was magic. He could dance with a chair, a hat rack, or even a piano, and make it look like poetry. Why couldn't I be more like Fred Astaire?

So, it is no surprise that I should land on the idea of a dance course during my year in France. What better way to get to know the French?

But dance class was not my first idea. My first idea for Wednesday night was a course on Qigong. Right. I didn't know what it was either. The brochure I picked up at the association fair in Pérols described Qigong as an ancient Chinese discipline to clear the mind and release the hidden energy that lies beneath the stress of everyday life. The literature promised that I would become more relaxed, more creative, and more sexually vibrant. Okay, that worked for me. I could be more relaxed and creative, and as for sexual vibrancy, that had been on my wish list since 1957 when Elvis Presley swiveled his hips in *Jailhouse Rock*. So I decided to give Qigong a try.

I arrived five minutes early at the *salle de dance* where the course was being offered. About a dozen other Qigongers were already silently walking around the room in their bare feet, shaking their hands and rotating their heads like animate bobblehead toys. They were mostly women in their fifties, some a little pudgy, a few a little too thin. I took a closer look. Hmmm. On the surface none of them looked like they were particularly sexually vibrant. Frankly, they looked more sexually repressed, like old men on cruise ships or Catholic nuns in floor-length religious habits. But I decided that I might be wrong, that under their serene exterior—way under—they might all be flaming dominatrices, clawing to get out. Or not.

The instructor arrived on the hour. He was a short, middle-aged man with a flat stomach and a cropped receding hairline. He looked like a former wrestler—136-pound weight class I'd say. He walked directly to the cabinet that housed the music system and inserted a CD. Suddenly, the room was filled with the sound of tinkling bells, a lamenting sitar, and a couple of canaries on Valium.

The master walked to the center of the room in front of the wall-to-wall mirror while the students selected one of the two-by-five-foot foam mats draped over the banister by the door. We scattered throughout the room, placed our mats on the floor, and stood silently—reverently—on the pads.

Then the master said in a hushed, nearly imperceptible voice, "Let us visualize our breathing. Allow the air to flow leisurely and naturally into your mouth and deep into your body. Hold it, hold it. And now let your warm breath rise up, up ever so slowly and expel gently through your nose."

About this time I was wondering if it would be terribly impolite to pick up my mat and breathe my way out of the studio. In the end, I decided to stay—if nothing else but to see what we could possibly learn after breathing. How to unclutter the mind? Or, better yet, how to stop time? That could be useful.

After breathing for ten minutes, we imagined the stress evaporating from every geographical region of our bodies: head, neck, shoulders, chest, arms, legs, feet, fingers, and toes. I had to admit, I was definitely feeling pretty loose, all the way from my North Pole to my Tierra del Fuegos.

"This is really relaxing," I said to one of the pudgy ladies standing beside me.

The woman said nothing. She turned her head ever so slightly in my direction. Her eyelids were at near sunset. I think I saw the corner of her mouth turn up into what was either a smile, exasperation, or constipation.

At the end the *sensei* instructed us to lie on our backs, close our eyes, and allow our minds to drift. The master narrated a story in a velvety midnight-shift radio announcer's voice about a tropical forest with peaceable animals and a lazy butterfly that led us deeper into a land of power, serenity, and spiritual bliss. His last words were, "May you go in peace and rest in the knowledge that you are perfectly whole. You are who you are. You can be no other. For it is not in the knowing that you are one but in the unknowing. It is not in the sensing that you are reborn but in the unsensing. It is not in the being that you are found, but in the unbeing."

Okay. That must make sense to someone in the great somewhere who is either in the deepest state of nirvana or more heavily medicated than Cheech and Chong. But as for me, I was thinking, "It is not in the sleeping that we are made alive, but in the unsleeping." Maybe I was just feeling irritable because we had just spent an hour and a half on deep-muscle relaxation and quiescent butterflies, without one lousy word about sexual vibrancy.

The students, looking more sedated than ever, returned their mats to the banister and filed out of the studio in silence. Only one man spoke. "I'm going to sleep like a baby tonight," he said, his words sounding like an out-of-body prayer of thanksgiving.

I smiled and said, *"Faites de beaux rêves."* Sweet dreams.

* * *

On the way out of the studio, I noticed that there was a group of younger people waiting to come in. One among them was a man who looked like he might be in charge. He was a husky fellow with a shimmering red shirt unbuttoned to the sternum and a cowboy buckle that kept his black pants hoisted just below the shadow of a somewhat cantilevered paunch. His hair was midnight black and swept straight back, not unlike a flamenco dancer, I thought.

"Are you another class?" I asked.

The man squinted, his brain straining to decipher the words lost in the fog of an American accent. It was a reflex that would be repeated every time I spoke to him.

"You're not from here," the red-shirted man said.

"No."

"English?"

"No, American."

"Oh."

"So, are you another class?" I repeated.

"Yes, yes we are."

"What kind of class?"

"A dance class," the man said. "Would you like to join us?"

My brain ran a two-second movie of my future with the Qigong catatonic ward. "Yes, I would. I'd like to watch for a moment or two anyway if that's okay."

"Absolutely," the man said squinting.

I reentered the studio, along with a half dozen other aspiring dancers. They stood looking at their shoes in silence.

Oh, *quand même*, I thought, don't tell me these people are Trappist monks too. Although it violated French protocol, I decided to break the ice. I figured my nationality would pardon my gaucheness.

I walked over to a man in his mid-thirties. He had a slender body and a pleasant, boyish face. "My name is Allen," I said.

The young man smiled, a little nervously I thought, and extended his hand. "My name is Thierry."

"Jerry?" I asked. "You have an American name then?"

"No, I don't think so. I don't think Thierry is American."

"Oh, Terry!" I said. "Your name is Terry."

By this time, some of the other dancers were starting to circle around us, the way kids circle around a schoolyard fight.

"*Non*, THIERRY," he said correcting my pronunciation.

"Okay," I said, finally getting it, "Tee-air-ee."

Now that I had an audience, I continued to do introductions. There was Catherine (Thierry's wife), François and Brigitte (another couple, also in their thirties), and, finally, a single woman in spring-loaded blue jeans and short blond hair, cut and feathered to perfection.

"What is your name?" I asked the blond.

"Marie-France Sage," she said, her lips pursed and her eyes smiling.

When spoken in French, her name is lovely, the syllables mingling poetically in perfect harmony like the English word "sassafras." It is a name that feels good tumbling in your mouth. But the name struck me as funny. It tickled me that "France" was not only her middle name but also her country of origin, and that "Sage"—meaning "reasonable and well-behaved" in French—was not only her last name, but a description of her comportment.

So, I said, "I'm so pleased to meet you, Marie-France Sage. My name is 'Allen, *Les Etats-Unis, Mal Élevé,*'" meaning, "Allen, the United States, Ill-Mannered."

Marie got my little joke and laughed without restraint, which for me is always the first sign of a long friendship.

By this time the dance instructor had deciphered the mysteries of the studio CD player and turned around to face the class. "Our class is a little small," he said. "I was hoping for at least twelve dancers." Then after a pause he added, "There's a big soccer match tonight between Montpellier and Lyon on television. Perhaps more will come next week."

I immediately visualized the die-hard American football fan: a doughboy with a cheese-wedge cap, a bag of chips, and a bottle of Schlitz Malt Liquor. If the French soccer fans were anything like that, I thought it unlikely that they would be turning up anytime soon at a ballroom dance class.

"We'll start with *le rock,*" the instructor said, "and then the tango."

My heart leapt. The tango. Making love with your clothes on. Oh, yeah. I could see myself already: shoulders back, chest out, a raised eyebrow, and a sneer on my lips, gliding as one with my partner across the dance floor. At that instant, I decided to sign up for the year.

"Of course, the tango is very difficult to do," the instructor said. "Not everyone can do it."

I can do it, I can do it, I said to myself.

"It requires precision and perfect synchronization."

Not a problem. I'm a synch machine.

"The male dancer must be proud. He must think of himself as a god."

"Et voilà, c'est moi—that's me," I heard myself say.

The class laughed and I blushed—as people do whenever a secret fantasy slips from mind to tongue.

The dance instructor went on to talk about the course objectives, and I realized, true to French custom, he was not going to tell us his name. Well, that was something I just couldn't live with. I could not imagine myself calling him *"Monsieur le Professeur"* for the next year.

"Excuse me," I said.

The dance instructor squinted.

"My name is Allen. What is your name?" I asked bluntly.

The instructor smiled, perhaps thinking, What a curious, yet charming question to ask.

"My name is Marco."

"Marco," I said, "may I use the informal 'you?'"

Marco squinted, and when he was sure he understood, smiled the same smile. "Yes, you can *tutoyer* me."

"Good. Thank you."

Marco was now directing his discourse to me. "Should we start?" he asked.

I wasn't sure if he was waiting for my approval, so I said, *"Mais oui, allons-y"* Let's go. (I did not say, *"Allez les pisseuses,"* although it did occur to me. Occasionally, even I know when it's time to shut the hell up.)

Marco instructed the men to stand behind him, facing the women, who were positioned on the opposite side of the room against the mirror. "This is the basic step for *le rock*," he said. "One, two, three-and-four, five-and-six. And again: one, two, three-and-four, five-and-six."

I followed Marco's lead, my feet shuffling backward, forward, and side to side. The step was easy enough, and after a while I was beginning to feel a little smug. This dance thing is a snap, I said to myself. And then Marco said, "Let's try it with music." In a moment, Elvis Presley's "I'm All Shook Up" rattled the dance studio in Pérols, France.

It was a strange feeling. I felt like I was suddenly transported back to the USA. But it was also a *good* feeling. This is my music, I thought. I'll become a French legend before the night is through. I was singing along with Elvis. "Oh-oh, yeah, I'm all shook up." Marco paired us up. I was to dance with Marie-France, who was looking askance at my Elvis hip-swivel routine.

Come to the King, pretty mamma. Thank you very much.

Marco called out the cadence, and we started to dance to Elvis, and for a moment I was flying. And then, without warning, my feet defied me. Suddenly, I lost the beat, and before I knew what had happened, my left foot was where my right foot should have been.

Marco stopped the music. "Allen, what are you doing?" he asked politely.

"Well, everything was just fine for a minute, but then I got excited and more or less lost my way."

"*Ça se voit.*" One sees that, Marco said, squinting. "Shall we start again?"

"Please."

The second time around I was able to stay in rhythm, but without thinking my steps got progressively longer, which eventually forced Marie-France to take awkward giant steps to stay even remotely face-to-face. While the music continued to play, Marco walked over to me and tapped me on my shoulder. He had a pinched prune look about him as though I had just dropped my pants in public.

"Look, Allen," he said, "your partner, Marie-France, is the flower. She is what counts. You are of no importance."

Okey dokey, I'm glad we got that straightened out.

"Everything you do," Marco went on, "must glorify the flower. Do you know what you are doing to your flower?"

"Uh, glorifying her?" I said hopefully.

"*Mais non.* You are running her ragged. That is what you're doing. Do you understand?"

"I think so."

"It is very simple. Your job is to be a *charnière*. Do you know what a *charnière* is?"

I didn't. But whatever it was, I knew I wasn't it.

"Come with me," he said. Marco took me by the arm and led me to a three-foot gate that separated a small alcove from the studio. For a moment, I thought he was fed up with my clumsiness and was throwing me out for good.

"Look. This is a *charnière*," he said, pointing at the gate hinge.

"Oooh."

"You must be like a *charnière*. You pivot, but you do not move. Have you got it?"

"*J'y suis.*" I've got it.

Marco squinted. I could tell that he was not convinced that I had it at all. He smiled a tight-lipped smile and patted me on the shoulder. That's a good dog. "Go back to your partner," he said.

Marie-France was the perfect dance consort. Not only did she have good rhythm but abundant patience—a first-order job requirement when coupled with me. There was a delightful grace about her. She seemed to glide where I stomped.

"You're a wonderful dancer," I said after a pause in the music, knowing I couldn't risk talking and dancing at the same time.

"I like dancing very much," she said, ignoring the compliment. "And you dance very well yourself."

Now, I recognize condescension in any language, but my American bravado was quickly dwindling, so I accepted the compliment wholeheartedly.

"How are things going so far?" Marco asked.

"*Génial!*" Thierry said.

"Super!" Brigitte added.

"This is great," I said. "Marie-France and I are thinking about getting married."

After an hour of dancing *le rock*, Marco announced that we would now begin the tango.

Oh boy, oh boy, oh boy.

"Remember," Marco said, "eighty percent of the tango is the attitude. Men, you are the master, and she is your woman. Take command."

With that anthem, Marco demonstrated the initial step: two long slow steps, followed by two short quick steps, and so on. Each stride was a step of supreme authority—the foot slowly lifting off the ground with toes pointed downward; the leg, slightly flexed, thrusting forward from the hip; the open chest following in perfect alignment—like a proud matador, turning his back on the bull, his cape dragging behind in the arena dust. It was a work of art.

"And now you," Marco said to the men.

We awkwardly strode across the dance floor, as Marco called out the tempo. *"Lent-lent, vite-vite; lent-lent, vite-vite."* Slow-slow, quick-quick; slow-slow, quick-quick. I could not speak for the other men, but I was feeling less like a proud matador and more like the bull on roller skates.

After one trip across the room and back, Marco said, *"Ça ne va pas."* No good. "Allen, why are you looking at your feet?"

"I don't know," I said meekly, "to make sure they're still attached to my legs?"

"Mais non. Keep your head up and your eyes straight ahead. Now, take a deep breath."

I took what I thought was a respectable breath.

"No, no, not like that. Like this," Marco said, filling his lungs with air until his chest rolled out like a wine barrel. "You see? Now, let your shoulders drop. They must not be tense."

I let my shoulders drop.

"Oh là là. Impossible. Roll your shoulders back. Otherwise you will look like a country bumpkin."

The colloquial French word Marco used for "country bumpkin" was *"plouc."* It wasn't a word that I knew at the time, but I got its meaning.

"Un plouc," I repeated, pantomiming an oafish stride with knees bent, a protruding stomach, and arms hanging limply like ripe eggplants.

"Exactly," Marco said.

I struck my tango pose—chest out, shoulders back, chin up.

"Et voilà," Marie-France said.

"Bon," Marco said to the class. "Select a partner, and we will dance the tango as couples."

Marie-France gave me a nod. I was exceedingly thankful for that simple gesture, like a little proclamation of faith, despite my clunky dance skills.

I struck my tango pose again, and Marie-France took my hand and leaned into me like the perfect puzzle piece. The music started, and I took my first step forward—then my second and third. I knew almost immediately that something was wrong. The tango, as Marco explained to us, is a dance of contact—you feel the legs and hips of your partner—but when you move, you must move as one person. That was not happening. I was not *gliding* with Marie-France; I was *pushing*. After five minutes of plodding around the perimeter of the studio, we were both exhausted before the song was half done.

"Something is wrong," I said.

"Évidemment," Marie-France said.

Évidemment does not have the same sense as the English word "evidently," meaning "apparently." *Évidemment* is more definitive, more forceful, meaning "certainly" or "obviously." So, with a single word, Marie-France told me that she recognized there was a problem too.

"I feel like I am pushing you," I said.

"I feel like I'm being pushed."

"What do we do?"

Marie-France took my hand. "Let's try again."

We started to dance. Immediately, I could feel Marie-France flowing with my strides. "Yes," I said. "That is more like it." We continued to dance around the studio, becoming more and more in sync with every turn.

As we glided past Marco, he turned down the corners of his mouth and said, "Not bad. Not good, of course, but not bad," which, coming from Marco, was tantamount to being canonized by the Catholic Church.

At the end of the session, Marco taught us the Madison, a kind of line dance that can be seen in the 1988 movie *Hairspray*. It's a simple dance that features a ninety-degree right turn every four measures. By that time in the evening, all of us were fast friends. We laughed as we shuffled left and right to the two-beat western tune.

As we left the studio, I thanked Marco—a practice I would repeat at the end of each session all year long. He always appeared a little stunned when I thanked him, clearly unsure of how to accept my gratitude. In a way I thought of it as a kind of cultural exchange. This, my friend, is how Americans acknowledge a gracious and competent guide.

Walking across the courtyard to our cars, I started talking with Marie-France. I learned she had taken a new job as a supplier for a chain of gift shops and that her husband, Henri, was working in Lyon. Every Friday, Henri took the 200-mile train ride to Montpellier to join his wife for the weekend.

"I would like to meet him," I said.

"Èvidemment."

We continued talking, and Marie-France asked me what I did when I was not dancing.

"A little bit of everything," I said. "My wife and I like to hike, and I like to write in the morning."

"Do you write in French?"

"Are you serious? No, I write in English."

"What are you writing about?"

"Mostly my experiences here—especially the people I meet. One day I will probably write about you."

"Really?" Marie-France said, beaming. "And what will you say?"

"I'll say that you were the perfect dance partner."

Marie-France blushed. "Oh, you Americans know how to say the right things." And then, quickly changing the subject, "Is there anything in France that you want to do that you haven't done yet?"

I thought for a moment. "Yes. There is one thing. I'm an amateur jazz singer. I'd love to meet an authentic, old-time French jazz singer. Someone who knows the great old songs. That would be a dream come true."

"Hmm. That's interesting."

We said our goodbyes, and Marie-France leaned forward, offering her cheek as a signal for me to *faire la bise*—the kissing thing on each cheek.

* * *

ON THE FOLLOWING DAY, Marie-France gave me a call.

"Henri is coming into town late Friday night. I told him that I met an interesting American."

"*Merci.* That's kind of you."

"Actually, I told him I met a *rich* American."

"Not all Americans are rich, you know."

"*Bof.*"

"Don't say '*bof.*' There's no *bof* about it. I'm comfortable but by no means rich."

Marie-France said something that sounded like "Yeah, sure. Whatever."

I decided to let it go. Curiously, I could never change her mind about the modest heft of my wallet. In fact, it became an inside joke between us. Whenever she introduced me to someone new, I was always her "rich American friend."

"Saturday morning we would like to take you to the *abrivado* in Palavas."

"What's an *abrivado*?"

"You'll see," she said. "We'll pick you up at ten o'clock."

Saturday morning we spotted Marie-France and Henri from our bedroom window that overlooked the street. We hurried downstairs to spare them the three-flight ascent to our apartment.

Henri was a huge man with massive catcher-mitt hands. He was not fat—just big. He had a healthy shock of white hair and a broad, boyish smile. I liked him immediately.

"So you are the American who is dancing with my wife," he said, pretending to be menacing.

"Uh, *oui*, Monsieur Sage," I said in an exaggerated mousy voice. "But I don't enjoy it. She makes me do it."

"What do you mean you don't enjoy it?" he roared.

"I mean, I don't enjoy it . . . in *that way*," I said, shaking my hand the way the French do when they see a beautiful woman.

"I like this American," Henri said, laughing thunderously. He enveloped my hand in his and shook it like a pit bull going for the kill. When the handshake rocked me on my heels, he planted his left paw on my shoulder to keep me from tipping over.

We got into Henri's Renault—Nita in the back with Marie-France, I in the front with Henri. Nita and Marie-France started chatting immediately. I knew they would hit it off—everyone likes Nita.

Henri drove to Palavas, the seaside resort village a few miles west of our own village of Carnon. It's a pleasant town that features a canal—replete with fishing and sailing boats—that cuts through the center of the eighteenth-century village. On that day there was a riot of compact cars, motorcycles, and pedestrians. By a small miracle, Henry spotted a patch of sidewalk that matched the width of the Renault. He eased up to the six-inch curb and edged the car over the obstacle. It scraped bottom.

"Oh là là," Marie-France cried out.

"Ce n'est pas grave." It's not serious, Henri said calmly.

"Of course it's not serious," Marie-France protested. "It's not your car. It's *my* car."

The car stationed, we threaded our way through the festive crowd, finally stopping at a barricade that blocked a side street from the principal road. The four of us leaned side by side over the barricade that overlooked the main street.

"So, what is an *abrivado*?" I asked Henri.

"You will see," he said, echoing his wife's deferring tactic.

As we soaked in the warm Mediterranean sun, a brass and woodwind band—twenty to twenty-five musicians strong, none of whom were reading music—struck up a rousing march. Their tonality was accurate, bright, and well balanced.

The director, a tall, slender man with a sparkling gold cape and matching top hat danced in rhythm before the band. He kicked an imaginary ball over his head with his right foot and then with his left. Then he swooped down into a Cossack squat and launched himself straight into the air with legs straight and his top hat twirling in his hand over his head. It was an amazing workout. Whatever he earned, it was not enough.

I started chatting with Henri. In a few minutes, I discovered that he was the head chef for a high school in Lyon.

"What's the most difficult part of your job?" I asked.

"Trying to satisfy the wishes of all the students and, of course, their parents. The Arabs, for example, have very specific dietary requirements."

"Do you try to honor that?" I asked.

"No, that's something I'm resisting. I think it's important for all immigrants to be integrated into our culture. That includes eating the foods that we are accustomed to eating. Besides, it would be impossible for me to provide special menus for every ethnic preference. It just can't be done."

It was at that time that I heard the distinctive sound of galloping horse hooves. We leaned over the barricade to see what was happening. Then, from around the bend in the street appeared six stocky white horses—the kind that run wild in the Camargue, the nature reserve on the Mediterranean east of Montpellier. The horses were mounted by the *gardians*, the French cowboys, wearing white shirts and, for some, a black fedora.

The *gardians* formed a perfect V-shaped wedge as they galloped down the street. Within the wedge, partially hidden from view, were three black bulls. Adding to the excitement, a dozen teenage boys chased behind after the bulls, attempting to grab a *taureau* by the tail. Of course, the task of the *gardians* was to protect the bulls from the onslaught. With their honor at stake, they would occasionally swat the teenage runners with the traditional pronged cattle stick.

"So this is an *abrivado*," I said to Henri after the first of a half-dozen runs.

"Yes, this is an *abrivado*. Did you notice the pompoms on the horns of the bulls? The runners try to grab the bull by the tail and turn it around. Then they try to grab the pompoms. If they are successful, it is a great honor."

"How often are they successful?"

"Hardly ever. The *gardians* are very protective. Sometimes, you will see a *gardian* grab a bull by the horn to keep it moving forward."

Just then another team of white horses and *gardians* rounded the corner. This time, a boy had managed to snatch the tail of one of the bulls. He was half running, half stumbling until he lost his balance and tumbled to the ground. He quickly jumped to his feet, dusted himself off, and, with dancing eyes, recounted his exploits to his comrades.

With the last charge of horses and bulls, the crowd of spectators began to disperse. We worked our way back to the car. This time we stood to the side while Henri backed the Renault off the sidewalk, thereby avoiding a repetition of the awful grating sound of metal passing over concrete. We loaded into the car and headed north.

"We'd like to take you to a bar we know in Montpellier," Henri said. "The owner is a friend of mine, someone you should meet."

As we drove the short distance between Palavas and Montpellier, Henri volunteered that he was a national-level rugby player in his youth. Now he was a part-time referee.

Although I had never seen a professional rugby match (Henri would introduce me to my first game a month later), a vivid image sprang to mind: a throng of beefy men with tree stumps for legs colliding headlong into a brawny mass of equal power and girth.

"That makes sense," I said. "You look like someone who could be a rugby player."

"Oh, not everyone is my size," Henri said. "That's the nice thing about rugby. There is a position for every size."

"It seems like such a violent sport—and dangerous, given that you don't wear pads. Tell me, was your body covered with bruises at the end of a match?"

"Not really," Henri said modestly.

Henri spoke with such a soft, leisurely tone that it was hard to imagine him cracking heads with anyone.

By that time we had wound our way into the center of Montpellier. We turned down a narrow street framed with parked cars and *camionnettes* squatting over the sidewalks and pressed against the stone tenements like massive ornamental doorknockers. Anywhere in Montpellier (anywhere in France, for that matter) finding a parking spot is always a small wonder and an occasion for a little victory dance. As luck would have it, I spotted someone backing out down the street, and Henri gobbled up the space in an instant.

We got out of the car and rounded the corner where we were greeted by a typical French square. Shaded by towering sycamore trees over a cobblestone surface, the plaza was teeming with children, university students, and a few unshaven gentlemen in snap-down caps who exchanged handshakes at the corner café.

The morning market—with canopied carts of fruit, vegetables, and flowers—was in full swing. Money was exchanged, and apples and pears were dropped into the canvas shopping bags of sturdy women with floral-patterned dresses. Across the way was a small bar that belonged to Henri's friend, Philippe, the former rugby player. The bar was called LE BAR DES SUPER VEDETTES, The Bar of the Super Stars.

"Who are the super stars?" I asked Henri.

"Why Philippe and me, of course," Henri said with a laugh.

When we entered the bar, Henri kissed Philippe on both cheeks. "I would like you to meet my new American friends," Henri said.

"*Rich* American friends," Marie-France added with a grin.

Henri acknowledged his wife's addition with a nod. "This is Allen. He is a singer," he said, expanding his chest as if he were preparing to sing a line from a Wagnerian opera. "And this is his wife, Nita. She is . . . well, beautiful."

Philippe smiled a genuine smile and shook my hand. He, too, was a big man with broad, muscular shoulders and narrow hips. To me he looked more like a boxer than a rugby player. His hair was thick and coarse and dusted gray. *"Enchanté,"* he said. "Welcome to our little bar."

"Thank you. It's an honor to be here."

The pub was long and narrow, approximately twelve feet wide by forty-five feet long. The bar itself, a hefty hardwood counter with brass footrests, nearly spanned the entire length of the room. Although it was barely noon, the bar was already lined with clients, each nursing a bottle of beer or a glass of wine.

We were ushered to the back of the room and seated at two small tables that had been pushed together to accommodate the four of us. Then, hardly settled in our chairs, Philippe's wife, France, placed three-dozen open-shell oysters at the center of our table. I looked at the mountain of shellfish and then at France, who was smiling brightly, her hands resting lightly on her hips. She was a stunningly beautiful brunette, perfectly attired in blue jeans and a burnt umber sweater, unzipped at the neck by careful design.

I had always avoided fresh oysters in the past. They looked a little too much like fish bait for my taste. But, in the spirit of adventure, I cut the muscle from the shell, squeezed a little lemon over the shell and slurped the thing down, seawater and all.

"How do you like it?" Henri asked.

"A little salty," I admitted.

I selected a second shell from the tall stack while Nita sat back smugly in her chair and grinned. She has always alleged that she has an allergy to shellfish and that her eyes swell shut when she eats them. Understand, this is nothing I've seen firsthand, so I sometimes wonder if she uses the excuse as a deft ploy to avoid eating anything remotely strange.

I reached for a second oyster. This time I surreptitiously dumped out the seawater from the shell before swigging down the briny morsel.

"*Ça va pas,*" France said, catching my deception. "You must drink the water with the oyster. We say it makes a man virile."

"That has never been a problem in the past," I joked.

"Still, it is the way things are done," France said, clearly not budging on the time-honored protocol for feasting on oysters.

"Okay, okay," I said, giving up the fight.

As I was savoring my last oyster, I asked Henri how things were going in Lyon.

"Oh, nothing startling to report," he said. "No, wait, there was something that you might find interesting."

"What's that?"

"Well, I was the first person to come upon the scene of a car accident just outside of Lyon."

He had our full attention. Henri explained how he pulled his car off to the side of the road, called emergency on his mobile phone, and ran to where the victim was lying in a ditch, inextricably pinned under his overturned Renault Clio. By that time two other men scrambled down the embankment. Henri and the others lifted the subcompact off the chest of the victim and eased his limp body to a patch of level ground.

Henri desperately searched for a pulse; there was none. With no professional help yet in sight, he got on his knees beside the man. He pinched the victim's nostrils and breathed into his mouth. He checked for a pulse. Nothing. Henri cupped one hand over the other, pumped fifteen times over the heart of the victim, and then quickly breathed again into his mouth. Still there was no sign of life. Henri continued this procedure until firefighters arrived on the scene and pronounced the man dead.

"How did you know how to give mouth-to-mouth?" I asked.

"I took a class twenty years ago," he said with a shrug.

"Did it ever occur to you that you could be sued for your action?"

Henri smiled. "Not for a second. That's the difference between France and the United States. We don't have an army of lawyers waiting in hiding to take advantage of people's goodwill."

"Yeah, okay, but how do you *really* feel about it?"

"I hope I have not insulted you," Henri said.

"No, not at all. In fact, I can't argue with you. I remember reading somewhere that seventy percent of all lawyers on earth are Americans."

"That would not surprise me," Henri said.

I could see that Marie-France was getting a little fidgety. "Could we talk about something other than politics," she said.

"It's okay, Marie-France," I said. "It's interesting to get the French perspective on the States."

I turned back to Henri. "You're a good resource for me, Henri. Tell me more. How else would you describe Americans?"

Henri thought for a moment, and then he nodded as an idea came to his mind. "The French say that Americans are *de grands enfants*."

"Big kids? What do you mean by that?" I asked.

"Well, first, it's not a criticism—more of an observation."

"I understand."

"What I mean is you Americans are *naïfs*, as children are *naïfs*. This is very important. Do you understand the word '*naïfs*'?"

"Yes, we use your word in English. Naïve."

"Good. You see, Americans are quick to believe what they hear."

"You mean we are gullible."

"Yes, I suppose that is the word. For example, all of you seem to be behind your president. Everyone is waving flags and singing the national anthem."

"How do you know that?"

"It is what we read in the papers, what we see in the movies and on television. The French are not like that. If you have ten Frenchmen, you will have ten different opinions. We prize individualism. We hardly ever agree on anything."

"In what other ways are we naïve?"

"Americans are very Puritan."

"Meaning?"

"Meaning that you are very strict, very moral—also very *travailleurs*."

"We are hard workers?"

"Yes. You are very interested in making lots of money. We are interested in living."

Henri reminded me of something I had read once by the Italian scholar Umberto Eco. "In the United States there's a Puritan ethic and a mythology of success. He who is successful is good. In Latin countries, in Catholic countries, a successful person is a sinner."

"And that is what you mean by being children? We are naïve, Puritan, and hard-working?"

"Yes."

"Are you sure this is not a criticism?"

"Oh, maybe a little," Henri said smiling. "It is who you are."

Now Marie-France was really squirming. "Enough politics."

Henri raised his hands in surrender. "I'm done," he said.

It was then that I noticed a smallish, elderly man at the end of the bar. He had a glossy, unwrinkled face and wispy brown hair that he combed straight back. He wore a butterscotch corduroy sports jacket over a white open-collared dress shirt. At his feet was an unleashed ocher mop of a dog, a little terrier of questionable lineage. We exchanged glances, and the man smiled at me. I nodded, and the little man started to move toward me.

As the man was walking my way, Marie-France put her arm around my shoulder and whispered, "This is the real reason I wanted you to come. One of your dreams is about to come true."

I looked at Marie-France with curiosity in my eyes. "Really?"

She did not give away the surprise.

The man retrieved a chair from another table and sat next to me. "*Bonjour*, monsieur," the old man said.

"*Bonjour*, monsieur."

"I hope this is not an intrusion."

"Not at all."

"I am told that you are a singer."

"Yes," I said. "How did you know that?"

"Marie-France told me."

"Ah." I looked at Marie-France as she adopted a mischievous, quizzical look that said, "I wonder what this is all about?"

The old man smiled a soft, serene smile. "So, what kind of music do you like to sing?" he asked.

"Mostly jazz."

"Ah, yes. Ella Fitzgerald, Count Basie, Billie Holiday."

He already had my interest. "You know our American jazz musicians then."

The old man smiled again—humbly, knowingly. I was beginning to like that smile a lot. "But, of course. Do you know I once spoke to Bird in Paris? It was 1948 . . . no, 1949."

Bird was the nickname given to the famous alto saxophonist, Charlie Parker. "*Ce n'est pas vrai.*" No kidding. "Charlie Parker is a jazz legend."

"Yes, I know. He was a very nice man. And he loved to play. He would play all night long, just for the joy of playing."

"Charlie Parker," I said, pronouncing the words with reverence.

"Who do you like?"

"Oh, I'm kind of a crooner," I said. "So, I like Frank Sinatra and Sarah Vaughan and . . ."

"'How High the Moon.'"

"Yes, exactly. Are you a singer?"

He pursed his lips the way the French do to suggest a modest, qualified "yes." "Well, I do sing a bit. I like to scat," the old man said.

"So do I," I said. As I explored the old man's face, I thought a moment like this does not arrive every day: sitting in a bar in Montpellier and talking about jazz with a Frenchman with a little yellow dog at his feet. I looked at Marie-France again and gave her a smile of gratitude.

I turned back to the old man. "Follow me," I said. I snapped my fingers in time and sang the first four measures of "Fly Me to the Moon" in scat. "Bweep-bah-doo-be-doo, bah-doo-be-doo, bah-doo-be-dow."

And then, on cue, in tempo, and on pitch, the old man scat-sang the next four measures, the syllables tumbling out of his mouth with ease. He had an airy, slightly raspy voice, like the resonant overtones of a Coleman Hawkins tenor sax solo. It was magnificent. The people at the end of the bar stopped talking and turned around to hear what was going on. Henri started beating out the tempo on the table.

Sixteen measures into the song, I started singing the lyrics while the old man scatted fills at the end of each phrase. Our voices became louder, fuller, as a few people began to clap in syncopation on the second and fourth beat. We were swinging now. The old man had his eyes closed and his head tilted back. I imagined he was raising his voice to Charlie Parker within heaven's gate. His little yellow dog sat up and cocked his head to one side, puzzled by his master's strange behavior.

We were both singing freely now, reveling in that wonderful, ineffable steam that fills the chests of singers when they finally stop thinking about what note comes next. In a word, we were flying—just two grateful passengers going along for the ride. I looked at the old man. With his eyes still closed, his face was luminous as if he had entered another dimension, a dimension frequented only by dreamers, poets, and *les vieux chanteurs français*. I knew that he was singing, not from his brain but from his soul.

We finished with a scat free-for-all, our voices intertwined, building on the rhythmic and melodic ideas of the other.

When the last note drifted into space, we were both laughing, and the bar patrons were clapping and hooting. One man put two fingers to his mouth and let loose with a whistle blast. Henri slapped me on the back so hard he nearly buried my face in a plate of barren oyster shells.

The old man cupped my face in his hands and kissed me on both cheeks. *"Merveilleux, absolument merveilleux,"* he said, his eyes lustrous with pure joy.

"Marvelous indeed." I wrapped my arms around the French singer. "*Merci. Merci beaucoup.* You are the best."

Then I looked into the eyes of Marie-France, who was beaming. I did not have words. I just shook my head in thankfulness. And then, because sometimes a look is just not enough, I took her into my arms as well until Henri blustered, "Hey, that's enough, you American gigolo!"

I released Marie-France and turned to her burly husband. "I love you too, Henri."

"Not like that you won't," he said, expanding his enormous chest. "There are limits to international détente."

"But no limits to love," I said, which sparked a noisy outcry of approval from everyone sitting around the table.

I just smiled, for there is one thing I know for sure. Timing is everything.

CHAPTER 11

The Jazzmen of Montpellier

It was at Le Bar des Super Vedettes that I learned about a jazz club in the south end of Montpellier called Jam Action. On Thursday nights, after a concert by a professional combo, amateur singers and instrumentalist were invited to jam.

For readers who may be unfamiliar with the term, a "jam" is a gathering of musicians, often meeting for the first time, who improvise on well-known jazz standards. Typically, the musicians will begin a number by introducing the original melody of the tune, which is called "the head." Then, each musician will play his or her interpretation of the song, often straying from the melody while still adhering to the basic chord structure of the tune. Finally, after all have had a chance to solo, the musicians return to "the head" to bring the song to a close. The pattern is almost classical in its simplicity: presentation of theme, embellishment on theme, reprise of theme.

In French slang, a jam session is called "*un boeuf,*" meaning ox, steer, or beef. It is said that the expression derives from the famous Right-Bank cabaret in Paris, Le Boeuf sur le Toit (The Ox on the Roof), which became a center for American jazz in the 1930s.

After poring over a map of Montpellier to pinpoint the location of Jam Action—no easy task—I headed out the door with my cornet tucked under my arm.

Now, as a jazz singer, I'm not that bad—I made my living as a singer in my twenties for half a dozen years, and I've had my share of accolades— but I know my limitations. Let's just say that I'll never dethrone any of the truly great jazz singers like Mel Torme and, more recently, Kurt Elling. Still, I do like to sing, and if the voice is in good form, and the gods are with me, I can swing. So it was with mixed emotions that I got on the Palavas freeway to Montpellier—the emotional goulash of anticipation, excitement, and nervousness, like the feeling of asking the pretty popular girl out on a date. You *really* want to, but you just know she speaks a different language or has read all the Russian novels or has caviar and champagne for breakfast, and when she sees you standing there with your hat in hand like Bashful in *Snow White and the Seven Dwarfs*, she will surely laugh in your face. That's the feeling I had walking through the front door of Jam Action.

* * *

I STEPPED INTO A DARKENED ROOM—a cavern really. I stood for a moment near the door, letting my eyes adjust to the darkness that surrounded me. The club was enormous: three stories high with a long bar at one end and tables and chairs scattered on three levels around a raised stage. The room was definitely designed for performers. A bank of red, white, and blue lights washed the stage that was at the moment home to a bebop jazz quartet led by a gifted Montpellier-adopted trumpet player from Guadeloupe, Frank Nicolas. They were cookin'.

As my eyes adjusted to the room, I realized that the place was packed. I noticed a blond woman sitting in a chair to my right. Her legs were propped up on a second chair, which appeared to be the only available seat in the house. She must have noticed me caressing the chair with my eyes because she immediately set her feet on the ground and swung the chair around to accommodate me.

"May I?" I said in French.

"Oui."

I sat down and turned my attention to the band. In addition to the trumpeter, whose melodic lines were reminiscent of a brooding Miles Davis, the quartet included a guitar, contrabass, and drums. They were playing intricate jazz standards like "Nica's Dream" by Horace Silver and "Straight, No Chaser" by Thelonious Monk. The sixty-eight-year-old drummer, René Nann—a former percussionist for the famous Belgian singer, Jacques Brel—was explosive, changing rhythms every two measures. The guitarist and arranger, Thomas Fontvieille, held the band together with rich, full chords and melodic solos. Finally the bass player, Lonnie Plaxico—former accompanist for such legends as Dizzy Gillespie and Chet Baker—treated his instrument more like a guitar than a standup bass, fingers flying up and down the fret board.

The band was dynamite—melodically and rhythmically exploring tunes in a manner that was miles over my head. They took my breath away. And I was beginning to wonder what I was doing with my cornet at my feet. I nudged the horn deeper under my chair.

Between sets I decided to open a conversation with the woman who had offered me her temporary footstool. She was dressed entirely in black with her long blond hair held back in a ponytail. I placed her in her early twenties.

"Are you familiar with this band?" I asked in French.

"No, this is my first time here," she said in English.

If anything gets my goat, it's being smacked in the face with an English response to a perfectly good, grammatically correct French sentence. I knew this woman for ten seconds, and I was already steaming. "Tell me," I said in my surliest French, "why would you respond to me in English?"

"Because I don't speak French," the girl in black said. "I'm Canadian."

I felt my face flush in the dark. Oh, boy, how do I get out of this? "I'm so sorry. I thought you were French."

"No, I'm just here for a few weeks—language school."

"I see." Now I was trying to act like a human being again. "And then what?"

"I'd like to stay in France for as long as my money will hold out. As a matter of fact, I'm looking for a job right now."

"Uh-oh. That's going to be tough with a Canadian passport."

"I also have an British passport."

"That's a different story."

"Plus, I'm fluent in Spanish. I lived in Guatemala for a couple of years. I thought that might help."

I was beginning to like this young Canadian. The French phrase came to mind: *Elle est bien dans sa peau* (she is happy or comfortable with herself). There was a self-confidence about her that was endearing.

"I'll tell you what," I said. "I've been in correspondence with the director of personnel at L'Ecole des Roches, one of the most prestigious boarding schools in France. They're just one hundred kilometers west of Paris. At first I thought that I might land a job there myself as an English teacher, but with an American passport, it's nearly impossible. Maybe they could use someone who is fluent in both English and Spanish. Would something like that interest you?"

"You bet."

"Are you online?"

"Yes."

"Good. Why don't you give me your email address, and I'll see what I can do."

"That would be wonderful."

"What's your name?"

"Sara."

"Okay, Sara. My name is Allen. This may be a long shot, but we'll give it a try. How does that sound?"

"Sounds perfect."

I wondered if Sara was at all nervous about exchanging email addresses with an old guy from the States. From what I could see in the dim light, she seemed to be at ease and genuinely thankful for the help. The test would come when I sent her my first email message. Would it bounce?

The band was starting its second set. This time they paid tribute to some of the French standards: *"La Mer"* ("The Sea") and *"Un homme et une Femme"* ("A Man and a Woman"). There were times when they were so far out on the fringe that I had to strain to recognize any resemblance to the chord changes I knew.

Finally, the last note of the last song was played, and Frank Nicolas announced that *le boeuf* would begin after a five-minute break.

"I've been dreaming about this moment for a long time," I said to Sara, "but these guys are so hot. I just hope I don't make a complete fool out of myself."

"Oh, you'll do fine," Sara said. "Go for it."

"Right, easy enough for you to say—sitting there smugly with your arms folded."

"Just soaking up the atmosphere," Sara said with a smile.

I exhumed my cornet from under my chair, smiled weakly at Sara, and picked my way through the crowd to the foot of the stage. I found an open chair and sat down to unpack my instrument. The original quartet had kicked off the first number of the jam, the Miles Davis tune "All Blues." A pianist and a trombone player had joined the group, and they were both sensational. I was beginning to think there wasn't one average player in all of France. At the end of the song, Frank Nicolas looked at me and gave me a nod, the sign for me to join the group.

"How about 'The Nearness of You' in F?" I asked.

Frank smiled. "No, we do *jazz* standards."

I knew what Frank meant. The 1940 Hoagy Carmichael melody, "The Nearness of You," has certainly been covered by jazz singers, but a pure bebop jazz musician is looking for something a little more recent and, often, more complex—something from, say, Dizzy Gillespie, John Coltrane, or Thelonious Monk. The problem was I was more of a George Gershwin, Rogers and Hart kind of a singer.

"How about 'I've Got You Under My Skin'?"

"No."

"'There Will Never Be Another You'?"

"Can't do it."

I knew I was calling for titles that were not bebop jazz standards, but the 1940s big band tunes were all I knew.

"Would 'My Funny Valentine' work?" I asked meekly as a last resort.

Frank's eyes brightened. "We do that," he said. "What key?"

"E flat."

"Good."

I set the tempo as a slow ballad, and the band started vamping on a figure that sounded more like a Latin bebop version of "Yes, We've Got No Bananas" than the laid-back swoon tune I was accustomed to.

With my cornet under my arm, I stepped up to the microphone and started singing. Nothing was there. I could feel my voice resonating, but I couldn't hear a thing. I stopped singing. An American in the front row said, "We can hear you."

I listened to two more measures of vamp and opened my mouth to sing again. Still nothing. I was beginning to sweat. I checked the microphone; it was switched on. When I looked at Frank in desperation, he walked up to the microphone and tapped on the head. Then he looked at the sound booth at the back of the room and pointed at the monitor that was stationed at my feet. *"Un, deux, trois,"* he said into the mic. The monitor sprang to life.

There is one thing I have learned in all my years of singing. It does not matter if the audience can hear you perfectly. If you cannot hear yourself, you are lost. Your brain needs the feedback to register how you are doing—to make subtle adjustments as necessary. Singing without a monitor is like a pilot trying to fly in the clouds without the benefit of instruments. The plane would be in a spiraling nosedive in an instant.

The band was still vamping.

I know enough about entertaining to know that an audience will feel anxious if the performer is unsure of himself. I wanted to let them know that I was all right. I placed my lips against the microphone and spoke to the audience in French. "I have been dreaming about this moment for a long time—the chance to play with real French jazzmen. Thank you for being a part of my dream."

I heard a voice from the darkened audience say, *"C'est gentil."* That's sweet.

I took the microphone from the stand and started to sing. My voice leapt from the monitor; I could hear myself! The band was playing dense, rhythmic patterns behind me—driving me through the song with an electric energy that I had never felt before. The power of the band was churning under me—no, *through* me—like a runaway freight train. So this is what it's like to play with the big boys, I thought to myself.

I embraced the song. I was beginning to feel the familiar and welcomed heat in my chest.

After my vocal solo, the trombonist, guitarist, and pianist took a chorus. Their improvisations were as clean and inventive as any bebop solos I've ever heard. Frank sat out to give me, I thought, my day in the sun. Now, it was my turn to play a solo on my cornet. I started by playing close to the melody and then, little by little, began to reach higher and higher, culminating in a high C, which is rare for me—I prefer lingering on the staff in a register that is safer for me. With one screaming riff, I ripped the horn off my lips as I had seen Frank Nicolas do. I glanced at him standing in the shadow at the side of the stage and wondered if he caught the tribute. He laughed, nodded, and shook his finger at me as a mock scolding.

At the end of my cornet solo, I picked up the microphone to sing the "head." By this time my chest was on fire. A few times in my life, I have felt what many have called "being in the zone"—the feeling of being out of your body, just riding on the wave of divine inspiration. That is the way I felt on that final chorus. I felt like I could do anything, sing anything. And when I reached the end of the tune, I stopped before the last note, signaling the band that I wanted to improvise a scat arpeggio in *a cappella*. My voice rose and fell with ease, the preposterous syllables tumbling from my mouth like alphabet soup. And when I returned to the final word— "valentine"—the band was right there to stamp the ending with a soaring, fanciful bebop coda.

As the audience was applauding, Frank stepped onto the stage, took a cluster of keys from his pocket, and placed the keys on my chest like a medal for valor in the field of battle. I could not have been happier if he had presented me with the Légion d'Honneur. He put his other arm around my shoulder and spoke into my ear. "Bravo." I think it may have been the sweetest sound I have ever heard. I immediately stepped down from the stage, knowing that anything I did after that would be anticlimactic. It was the legendary circus promoter, P.T. Barnum, who said, "Always leave them wanting more." Good advice—especially since I had nothing more to give.

As I was winding my way back to my chair near the door, a handsome young man with dark brown eyes grabbed me by the wrist. "*Chapeau—* well done," he said.

"Thank you. You're very kind."

The young man still held me by the wrist. "My name is Emmanuel," he said. "Would you stay to hear me sing?"

"Of course."

"I would like to know what you think."

"I don't know what I can offer," I said, "but I would be happy to listen to you. It would be a treat."

With that Emmanuel smiled and headed for the stage. I turned and walked to where Sara was seated.

"You were perfect," she said. "I will never have your talent, but some-day I would like to have your courage."

"For my money, a young Canadian woman on her own in France is pretty courageous."

"Maybe," Sara said. "Anyway this courageous young lady has to head home. I have an early class tomorrow morning." She looked at her watch and saw that it was just past midnight. "Make that *this morning.*"

"Have a good night," I said. "It was a delight to meet you. I promise to check with my contact at Ecole des Roches. No idea if there is anything available, but it can't hurt to try."

"I really appreciate it."

"Like the French say, '*C'est normal.*'"

Sara kissed me lightly on both cheeks and said goodbye.

I sat down just as Emmanuel was sitting on a stool on the stage. He was speaking into the microphone. "Bonsoir mesdames, bonsoir messieurs. I have become interested in singing free form—improvising without any melody in mind. Let's see what happens."

The pianist began by playing an airy modal scale with no hint of a mel-ody. (Modal scales—any of seven patterns of notes over an octave using only the white keys—are as old as ancient Greece. They have a haunting, oriental quality.) The drummer picked up his brushes and rolled lightly on the big crash cymbal.

Emmanuel closed his eyes and began to sing. His tones were pure and accurate with no trace of misgivings. I could tell in an instant that he knew his instrument. There was no faltering to find a note, something that is so often heard among young singers. He sang with ease, one note leading to another in surprising combinations of rhythm and melody. He was a gifted singer.

At the end of his song, Emmanuel threaded his way to where I was sitting and sat down beside me.

"You are incredible," I said with full conviction.

The young man smiled, revealing a perfect set of teeth. "Really?"

"Really."

"What advice do you have for me?"

"Understand, any thoughts I have are just my ideas. They may not have any value for you."

"Yes, I understand."

"Ready?"

"Ready."

"First, I think I would lose the stool. Try to allow your body to be as free as your voice—a supplement to your voice. It can help you tell the story."

"Yes, I can see that."

"You might also think of your voice as an instrument. What would you sound like if you were a tenor sax or a trumpet or a guitar or a drum kit? If you don't have it already, get Al Jarreau's CD, *Look to the Rainbow*. He's the best."

"I know of Al Jarreau, but I don't have that CD. I will look for it."

"There is something else that might help."

"What's that?"

"From time to time you might try to make a musical reference to a piece that is known to the audience. Not only does it demonstrate your depth of musical knowledge, but it also lets the audience share a joke with you. The reference could be anything—a jazz standard, a children's song, a classical piece—anything. For example, sometimes I'll use the octave jumps in 'On the Trail' from Grofé's *Grand Canyon Suite* or a two-measure reference to 'Santa Claus Is Coming to Town.' Even a reference to the French national anthem could work."

"Cool." (The French actually use the word "cool," a legacy from dubbed versions of the American TV series "Happy Days.")

"But I really want to stress that these are just ideas. You are a wonderful singer. I think your own instincts will serve you beautifully. Just keep learning and having fun."

Emmanuel thanked me. Then we exchanged phone numbers and said goodbye.

When I left Jam Action that night, it was just past 1:00 a.m. I was feeling pretty high. For me, it had been the perfect night, the fulfillment of a personal dream. I had played with a brilliant French jazz band. And, along the way, I had touched, however slightly, the lives of two outstanding young people, Sara and Emmanuel. It doesn't get any better than that.

As soon as I got home, I went to my laptop and sent off a message to Jean-Paul, the personnel director at L'Ecole des Roches. Two days later Jean-Paul said that he might have a spot for Sara as an English teacher for students whose first language was Spanish. It actually sounded like it might work. A day later I received a call from the president of the prestigious boarding school. He wanted my assessment of Sara. I told him that although I had only met her once, I thought by virtue of her poise, intelligence, and experience, she surely warranted an interview. That meager recommendation must have been enough because that very day Sara told me that she was flying to Paris for an interview. At that point I knew she would land the job. Two weeks later, settled in at L'Ecole des Roches, Sara sent me this email message:

Bonjour Allen!

Wow, this school is beautiful! The campus is a great place to jog, and the staff is energetic and very friendly. I am living in La Prairie with sixty girls between fourteen and eighteen. So far, so good.

My experience up to now has been very privileged, to say the least. On Saturday, my first day, all the boarders and housemasters went to Rouen, the town where Jeanne d'Arc was burned at the stake (as I'm sure you know). Of course, the kids were not interested in seeing the eleventh-century cathedral, so we spent most of the time at the annual winter fair riding roller coasters.

On Tuesday, I was one of the lucky six profs who got to chaperone the kids to Euro Disney! I was the biggest kid there. I saw Mickey and Minnie, the Christmas parade, and rode every single ride (except the lame ones, of course).

Yesterday, Thursday, we had another school trip to Versailles. Although I wouldn't tell the French, I was not all that impressed with the opulent palace. I think I was expecting something more Renaissance, but the Château itself is much more bureaucratic looking and quite plain really. Excessive use of gold paint and busy English décor is not my favorite, but it was worth seeing.

Today, Friday, I had my first English class. The students were well behaved and excited to have a native English speaker. The young ones are going to be easier to teach than the older students. My role here is still confusing for me and perhaps for some of the students as well. I am not used to the kids calling me *Mademoiselle*.

I haven't worked on my French this week at all, which is a bit disappointing. So many kids and profs want to practice speaking English with me. For some reason I have begun feeling a bit shy about speaking French. I hope it doesn't last long.

I will write more soon. I just wanted to send you a note of first impressions and thank you once again for making this all possible.

Allen, you're the best.

Talk to you soon,

Sara

CHAPTER 12

In the Shadow of Renoir

IN 1971 I VISITED PARIS FOR THE
FIRST TIME. I climbed over 1,500
steps to the top of the Eiffel
Tower (today, the last section
is only accessible by elevator). I
stood under the Arc de Triom-
phe, strolled along the Left Bank
of the Seine River, and marveled
at the Gothic architecture of the
Cathédrale Notre-Dame. But of all
the glories of Paris—and there are
thousands—nothing was any more
enchanting for me than the thirty-
two- by twenty-five-inch painting,
Étude, Torse, Effet de Soleil (Study,

Torso, Effect of Sun) by Pierre-Auguste Renoir, now exhibited in the Musée
d'Orsay. Although Renoir entitled the painting a "study," it was exhibited at

the Second Impressionist Exposition in 1876, heralding the importance that Renoir attached to the work.

The image of that sensual portrait—the nude torso of a rounded woman with long auburn hair, her body dappled by the shadow of leaves in the morning sun—has settled in my consciousness and stayed there as rooted as the opening refrain of Beethoven's *Fifth Symphony*. The woman's head is tilted slightly to her right, her full lips are softly closed, and her downward gaze is quiet and wistful and completely at peace. Although lesser known, it is by far my favorite impressionist painting.

So it was with that image in my head, the *Nude in the Sun* (as it is often listed in the States), that I signed up for a painting class in Pérols. I did not have the temerity to think of myself as an American Renoir—he casts a shadow that curls around the planet. I thought of myself more as a house painter with a couple of four-inch-wide brushes and a flare for color.

The class was held in the arts and crafts room above the police station in Pérols. The room was well lit by virtue of generous windows on both ends of the room. Pressed against one wall were stacks of padded chairs and wooden easels. When I arrived, several students—mostly middle-aged women—were already encircling a still life of a teapot, a bowl, a bottle of J&B, and a half loaf of French bread. They were all setting up easels and twenty-four by thirty-inch canvases. I, on the other hand—thinking it would be less expensive than acrylics or oils (it was not)—had purchased watercolors and a seven- by ten-inch pad of watercolor paper. I found two lightweight sawhorses and a plywood plank and erected a makeshift table for myself.

To my right was a statuesque woman with short hair and a beautiful smile.

"This is your first time here," she said.

"Yes, my name is Allen."

"My name is Armelle."

When I was in France, I worked at memorizing names. I learned that if I did not register the name the first time, I was likely to fumble it for weeks to come. And the French (not unlike Americans) always seemed politely miffed when I asked for their names a second time. I wasn't sure that I had Armelle's name right, so I asked her to repeat it.

"Armelle," she said, smiling.

I leaned my ear into her. "Ar . . ."

"Armelle. It's difficult, isn't it?" she said. (It wasn't, really, but she was sweet to let me off the hook.) "Here." Armelle took a pencil from her paint box and jotted down her name on the corner of her canvas.

That was my introduction to Armelle. We became friends instantly and have remained friends to this day.

By this time about a dozen students were settled in and working. The instructor, Pierre, a lanky but graceful man, walked over to where I was sitting.

"So you are working with watercolors," Pierre said.

"I thought I would give it a try."

"Good, good."

I had already penciled in the teapot and bottle of J&B.

"Don't you think the format is a little small?" Pierre asked gently but with a raised eyebrow, signifying that the correct answer in this situation was an unqualified "yes."

"Maybe a little," I said timidly. "I have a second pad of paper that is a little bigger, but since I don't know what I'm doing, I thought I'd start small."

"Yes, but if you work small, you will not see your mistakes."

"In that case, perhaps I should work on the back of a postage stamp."

Pierre laughed. "*Ah non.* You see, if you work with a small canvas and blow it up, you will see all the mistakes. If you work with a large canvas and reduce it, you will see only a perfect painting. You do want a perfect painting?"

"Absolutely," I said. "That's what I'm going for. The perfect painting."

Pierre started making his rounds to other students while I continued working on my diminutive drawing. When I was satisfied with my sketch, I broke the cellophane seal on my box of watercolors. Inside were twelve tiny bricks of pigment, ranging from yellow to black. I had no idea what I was doing, but I dipped my brush in water, sloshed it across a brick of color, smeared the loaded brush on a piece of scratch paper, added a little of this and little of that, and then made my first stroke of color on the drawing.

A moment later, Pierre was looking over my shoulder. I really don't like the feeling of someone—even a teacher, *especially* a teacher—scrutinizing a piece of unfinished work. I'm sure that uneasiness has to do with ego—the anxiety of being seen as anything short of perfect. (Humility has never been one of my strong points.) But I sat back from my work so that Pierre could see what I had done and waited for his critique.

"*Pas mal*—not bad," Pierre said, which my brain registered as "not good." Pierre took a second look. "The shading on your teapot is not right. It should be more gradual."

"*Oui*, I see that."

"And your bowl is sad."

"That's no good," I said with a laugh, perhaps trying a little too hard to compensate for my insecurity as a painter. "We can't be having a sad bowl. No sad bowls in this league."

A number of students chuckled. Pierre fell into the spirit of things. "Well, I'm not talking about the morale of the bowl."

"Oh, you were just speaking metaphorically."

The class oohed and aahed, astonished that I would have the word "*métaphore*" in my French vocabulary.

"It's not any big thing," I said to Armelle. "The word *'métaphore'* is the same in English."

"Yes," Pierre said, "it is a metaphor. Your bowl should be a happy bowl."

With that Pierre moved to the next student, and I returned to my work. The shading on my teapot remained a little ragged and my breakfast bowl a little sad, but next time . . .

I think that Armelle could sense my discomfort in being on the pointed end of criticism. "I like your teapot," Armelle said with a smile that proclaimed "You can do it; I have faith in you."

"It's not a bad teapot," I said. Then, emulating French humility, added, "Although the handle on the lid is a little off-centered."

"Sometimes it's fun to be a little off-centered," Armelle said with just enough affection in her voice to make me think she knew me already.

At the end of the class, Pierre announced that we would have a nude model at the following session. Oh my. I immediately thought of Renoir and his *Nude in the Sun*—the magic of the sunlight laced across the soft, sinuous torso of a woman at ease, the pink and blue tint of her skin, the shimmer of the leaves, the sanguine bloom in her cheeks. A symphonic orchestra was beginning to swell in my head.

"We will be sketching," Pierre said, and suddenly someone pulled the plug on my orchestra. EEEeeaahhoow.

Sketching? You must be joking. How am I going to match Renoir with a sketch? I needed color and a billboard canvas, and, most of all, I needed the sun.

"Will we be working outside?" I asked.

The class laughed, as I knew they would.

"Where did you have in mind," Pierre asked with humor in his voice, "the church square?"

"It was just an idea," I said meekly. "I'm not married to it."

After class, Armelle and I walked side by side down the stairs and into the fresh air. The sun was low in the sky, which lengthened the shadows on the cobbled street.

"Have you ever sketched a nude before?" Armelle asked.

"Well, not exactly. I did sketch a naked vase once. Does that count?"

"I don't think that counts."

"How is it done?"

"How is what done?"

"I mean . . . well, that is . . . how does the model set up?"

"Set up?" Armelle said as a half question, half statement.

"Yeah, does she just drop her clothes right there in front of God and everyone?"

"Oh, Allen, you're really not that naïve are you?"

"No, of course not," I said straightening my backbone. "Are you kidding? Hey, I've been around. Maybe not *all* the way around, but still . . ." When I find myself in trouble, especially when I'm coming across as unsophisticated or, worse, incompetent, I resort to humor to save face. So I added, "You know, Armelle, I was born at night but not *last* night. What I'm trying to say is . . . that is what I was wondering was . . . you know . . ."

Armelle came to my rescue, bless her heart. "Allen, there is nothing to worry about. It's handled very discreetly. Usually the model will go into another room, remove her clothes, wrap a sheet around herself, and then step into the studio. She will sit on a stool and then allow the sheet to slip off her shoulders. It's all very *mesuré*."

"I see. Measured, huh?"

"*Oui, mesuré*. Not everyone is able to do it. The last model we had looked very pale sitting on the stool in the middle of the room. Suddenly she fainted."

"Oh my."

"It was just too stressful for her."

"I'm afraid that I may be the one who faints this time," I said, only half-jokingly.

"You'll do fine," Armelle said, patting me on the shoulder.

The next week when I walked into the studio, the room was full of student artists. I soon learned that a nude model was a big draw.

The windows were closed, and with all the extra bodies, the room was stuffy with the scent of a wet dog.

"May I open a window?" I asked of no one in particular.

"*Mais non,*" Pierre said. "We have a nude model today, and we must think of her."

"*Ah oui, bien sûr,*" I said. "Of course, I knew that. That makes sense."

It was then that I saw the model standing in a corner of the room, her back to a window that overlooked the main street of Pérols. She was wearing a pair of black cotton pants and a ribbed coffee-brown turtleneck sweater. I could see by her form against the window that she was not wearing a bra, a piece of information that suddenly, curiously carried less intrigue than usual.

She was a tall, full-bodied young woman with dark brown eyes and a tousled crop of auburn hair. She was not fat, but, as one student later described her, somewhat masculine. When I had asked about opening the window, her eyes met mine. I did not know if I should look into the eyes of a woman who in a moment would be posing naked. What is the rule on that anyway? I smiled weakly, apologetically, and she looked away.

I found a chair and, imagining where the model would sit, placed it at an angle that I thought would replicate the point of view in *Nude in the Sun*—in other words, full-body center.

I glanced at the model again, and she at me. I wondered if she thought I was positioning myself to take full advantage of her nakedness, to be a sanctioned voyeur. I'm sure I flushed; I felt the heat on my face.

When all the students had set up and it was time to begin, the model did not go into another room to change, nor did she have a sheet to cover her body. While other students were talking to me, asking me about my health and the week before, and while I tried to respond in a voice as routine as saying "how ya doin'," the young woman pulled the brown turtleneck over her head and tossed the sweater like dirty laundry into the corner of the room. She then slipped out of her shoes by holding down the heel with the toe of the opposing foot. She unzipped her pants and let them drop to her feet. She then stepped out of one leg and then the other and deftly kicked the trousers into the corner alongside the abandoned sweater. I could see all that peripherally, dimly as if veiled in the shadow of Renoir.

When she hooked a thumb under the waistband of her white panties (Is there another word more difficult for a man to say?), I looked away, deciding that my pencil desperately needed sharpening.

The model walked to the center of the room and leaned against a three-foot stool that was draped with a white sheet. Pierre instructed the model to place her foot here, her hand there, giving her a small oriental fan that she held unopened in her right hand. It suddenly occurred to me that, with the exception of my wife, this was the first time I was in the same room with a woman who was entirely naked.

"Respect the angles of the model," Pierre said to the class. "Use the full length of your pencil to gauge the proportional relationship of her head to her shoulders to her breasts to her hips."

My God, he was talking about her like she was an assortment of building blocks. I looked at the woman, at the blank page of my sketchbook, and at the woman again. I did not know how to start. I felt that putting my pencil to paper would somehow violate her.

The room was feeling warmer. I took in a breath and began to sketch her face—slowly, carefully. As I was drawing I could see how perfectly lovely she was—perhaps not in a classical sense, but still beautiful, as are all women with a story to tell and dreams to realize. I began to explore her face—to caress it really—with each tentative stroke of my pencil. Gradually, I worked down her body: her neck, her shoulders, her breasts, her waist.

Pierre moved to where I was sitting and examined my drawing. "Not bad," he said, "but your proportions are not accurate. Look where you have placed her navel. That is not right."

Now that he mentioned it, the navel on my sketchbook did look a little high. If the model were Route 66 from Chicago to LA, I had her bellybutton in Oklahoma City—and not Amarillo, Texas, where any schoolboy knows it belongs.

"Draw in her pubic hair," he said, sounding curiously nettled. "That will help orient you."

I had been avoiding the pubic hair; it just seemed so . . . *private*, so intimate. I made a few squiggles where her legs came together—feeling certain that the model was glowering at me (she was not). I sighed so deeply that Armelle, who was sitting next to me, asked if I was all right.

To hear a woman's voice disturb that sequestered moment felt like a stern sanction—as though my fourth grade teacher, Miss Chess, had just caught me in a hiding place during recess with a *Playboy* magazine opened to the centerfold. "Huh? Yeah, I'm all right."

Of course, I was not all right. I was not all right at all.

I began drawing the legs and feet of the model where I felt considerably safer. That brief respite allowed the blood to drain from my face. It was then that Pierre called for a break. The model straightened her back and rolled her head this way and that. She walked calmly to the corner of the room where she had heaped her clothing and quietly slipped into her pants and sweater.

Most of the students were gathered around a table, pouring doses of coffee and munching on chocolate-covered wafers. I sat immobile in my chair, staring blankly at my drawing, only to be awakened by the voice of the model, who was now standing beside me. She was carefully studying my sketch.

"I like it," she said. Her voice was soft and airy—just short of a whisper.

I did not know what to say. How do you talk to the model of a nude sketch, a stranger at that, who is standing there beside you with one hand on her hip and the other holding a cup of coffee as if she were waiting for her nails to dry? What do you say? I think I captured your thighs all right, but your left breast is a little off? No way. It made me wince just thinking about it.

"Uh, thank you," I finally muttered. And then, regaining a small semblance of sophistication, I asked, "What does it feel like to see your likeness on paper?" (I was using the formal "you" all the way here.)

"Sometimes I see myself in the drawings," the model said. "Sometimes I see someone I don't recognize at all."

Did I dare ask? "What do you see in my drawing?"

"I see myself," she said smiling.

"You are too kind," I said.

"Yes, I see myself although I think you made my face prettier than it really is."

I looked at her—her smooth caramel-colored skin and perfectly shaped nose—and then at my crude drawing. "Oh no," I said, "I don't think I have done you justice." For heaven's sake, was I flirting with the girl who only moments ago was standing ten feet from me cloaked in a blanket of . . . air? What's the rule on *that*?

Pierre called for work to begin again. The model returned to the corner of the room and, just as before, stripped her clothes and tossed them in a pile. She took her place on the stand. This was harder yet. However short the conversation, I had established a relationship with the model. She was a person. And now she was once again a drawing lesson. I decided to change my position and start a new sketch. I walked around the room, stopping at an angle that caught her back and the side of her face. I found a chair and settled in to draw.

I finished the second sketch and then a third. The minutes passed, and the class came to an end. The model stretched, got dressed, and in the next moment was gone. She had been paid thirty-three euros for her time. My contribution, like everyone else, was three euros. For just under four dollars, I had entered the private domain of another human being.

After the model had gone, most of the students lingered. Armelle, two other students, and I stood in a circle at one end of the room.

"What did you think about that experience?" Armelle asked.

"I did not feel adequate," I said, using the French word *"adéquat."*

"No," Armelle said, correcting my grammar, "we only use the word *adéquat* to describe things, not people. You want to say that you did not feel *à la hauteur*, equal to the task."

"Yes, that is what I mean," I said. "I did not feel *à la hauteur*."

"But was this your first time?" another student asked.

"Yes, it was my first time, but that's not the point."

"What is the point?"

"The point is that we were sketching a person."

"Of course."

"She was not a chair," I said. "She was a person. She is important. She has feelings and dreams and a whole life ahead of her. And I, with my awkward hand, could not do her justice."

"But you are just beginning," someone argued.

I was feeling frustrated that I could not explain my feelings. "I *know* I am just beginning. That's not it. You see, if I am drawing a still life, it is not a problem. The apple doesn't know that my drawing is crude. The bowl doesn't care if my proportions are not correct. But a person is different. She is real. She is beautiful and intelligent. And, more than anything else, I wanted to capture that beauty and intelligence. What right do I have to scrawl a few ugly lines? Don't you see? It's just not right."

"Oh, you shouldn't feel that way," one of the students said.

I heaved a sigh, as people do when, despite everything, they are not comprehended.

"Yes, he should feel that way," Armelle said. "He should feel exactly how he feels—whatever that might be."

I could have kissed Armelle.

"The feeling is not wrong," Armelle continued. "It is how he feels, and that is perfectly all right. You may not agree with him. That's your right, but it doesn't have anything to do with Allen's experience."

"Thank you, Armelle."

Armelle said nothing more. She just gave me one of her beautiful Armelle smiles.

The other students turned, shaking their heads, not out of disgust or even disagreement, but out of incomprehension.

The image of Renoir's *Nude in the Sun* came to me. I saw the woman's face in soft, undefined strokes of pink and blue, shadow and light, rendering an elusive, enigmatic illusion. And, yet, the model for Renoir's study was no illusion. She was real. Her name was Anna-Alma Henriette Leboeuf. She was born in the village of Chenoise, fifty miles southeast of Paris on February 11, 1856. In 1879, three years after posing for Renoir, she died in Paris at 47 rue Lafayette. She was twenty-three years old. A letter has survived, written in Renoir's hand to a Dr. Gachet—a friend to Renoir, Van Gogh, and other French impressionists—asking him to see the ailing model.

Other than those scant facts, no other details of Anna's life remain. But I can imagine:

Anna-Alma Henriette Leboeuf was a beautiful child. Although she left school when she was ten years old—she was too valuable doing chores on the small family farm—she was naturally bright and vivacious. But the winters in Chenoise were cold and wet, and she could feel her passion for life draining like the sand in an hourglass. She longed for something more, something new, something exciting. She longed for Paris. She left home in the middle of the night with nothing more than a round loaf of bread wrapped in the only thing she valued, a silk scarf that her papa had given her on her sixteenth birthday.

Life in Paris was not easy. She worked for one year in a textile sweat-shop, but the work was long and tedious and the money a pittance. At night she would go to a neighborhood café where young university students would flatter her and buy her drinks.

One night a particularly good-looking young man asked if she might like to see his apartment. She agreed. Before the sun had risen, she lay with him, naturally and without guilt. She felt overwhelmed, even giddy, with passion. The act of lovemaking with such abandonment was so sublime that she was sure that she had finally found her reason for living. But the next morning when she awoke, the man was gone. There was a note, a key, and a few francs on his pillow where his head had rested. She read the note slowly once and then again.

Chère Anna:
Merci. Please take these few francs with my gratitude.
Lock the door and slip the key under the door.
Perhaps we will meet again.
Jean-Claude

Anna sat motionless for a long time on the side of the bed, and then she cried. When she had stopped crying, she was a different woman. She took the francs—it was more money than she could make in a week at the textile factory. She got dressed, snatched the key from the pillow, and whisked out the door. She bent down to slip the key under the door but suddenly had another idea. She stood with the key still clutched in her hand. Then she turned, descended the stairs, and walked directly to the nearest bridge that crossed the Seine, le Pont de la Concorde. At the crest of the bridge, she tossed the key into the river.

After that there was another boy and another and another. And with all of them, she made love, and with all of them, she was paid. In time, Anna stopped working at the sweatshop.

One night she slept with a Paris art collector, a Monsieur Choquet, who knew of an artist who was looking for a model.

"Would you be interested?" Choquet asked.

"Perhaps," Anna said. "What is the artist's name?"

"Pierre Renoir."

The name sounded vaguely familiar to Anna and so on sheer impulse she said, *"Pourquoi pas?"*

When Anna met Renoir for the first time in his Paris studio, she was immediately enchanted. There was a gentleness in his eyes that she found disarming. She felt that she had known the thirty-five-year-old artist for a lifetime.

Renoir was himself not a stranger to adversity. Before becoming famous at the First Impressionist Exhibition in 1874, Renoir knew what it was like to go without eating for a day or two. In some ways he was not so different from Anna. They were both seeking a mode of self-expression. He was sure that Anna felt as he did: One's destiny was not invented, it was revealed.

Anna felt an uncanny kinship with Renoir. He was unlike the crude university students she knew so intimately—boys who were boisterous, arrogant, and relentlessly sardonic. In stark contrast, Renoir was soft-spoken, pensive, and what Anna found most charming, compassionate. From the start she felt at home in his presence.

As for Renoir, the artist was delighted with Anna. When he was nineteen years old, he was given permission to copy in the Louvre. The first painting he adored was *Bath of Diana* by the eighteenth-century mythological and pastoral artist François Boucher. The luminescence of Anna's face reminded him of that cherished painting.

Anna loved sitting for Renoir. For the first time in her life, she felt like she counted for something. She did not understand art—she had never even stepped into a museum—but somehow she knew that what Renoir was doing was important, and she was part of it.

Anna posed for Renoir for three days. It was then that Renoir was commissioned to do portraits for a wealthy family in Paris. Renoir said that he would contact Anna on his return. He did not. One commission led to a long sequence of projects. He lost contact with Anna. Nearly three years later Renoir heard from his good friend, Claude Monet, that Anna was deathly ill. He decided to visit her in her one-room apartment at 47 rue Lafayette.

Renoir knocked on the door, but there was no answer. He placed his ear close to the door. He was sure he heard a small voice. He turned the doorknob and stepped into the room, which was nearly bare. There were only empty wine bottles, a single straight-back chair, a small table, and finally a cot where Anna lay. At first Renoir thought he had the wrong apartment for he did not recognize the woman lying on the cot in a slip that was torn along the hem and stained with wine. She was gaunt, nearly skeletal—the body of a grotesque imposter—with a yellow pallor that smelled of death.

Renoir set the chair by the cot and sat down alongside Anna. He placed her hand in his. It felt like a collection of brittle twigs.

"Anna," Renoir said, "it's me, Pierre."

Anna looked at Renoir—at least looked in his direction—but the artist was not sure she recognized him.

"It's me, Pierre," he said again.

"Monsieur Renoir."

Renoir strained to recognize her voice, which was distant and airy, like a winter wind whistling through bones.

"My friend, Claude, told me you were ill, but . . ." Renoir felt the emotion building in his throat. "But I never imagined." He slowly stroked her hand.

"I have been very stupid," Anna said.

"Yes," Renoir said, "but that is over now. You will get better."

"You are very kind, Monsieur Renoir, but . . ."

"*Si, si.*"

Anna suddenly began to cough—a deep, barren cough. She covered her mouth with her hand, which was now spattered in blood.

Renoir scanned the room with his eyes, searching for a pitcher of water. There was none. "Anna, my dear Anna," he said.

The woman got control of her cough. She wiped her mouth with the back of her hand, and with the other she unconsciously stroked her hair, which lay flat and matted against her head.

"Oh, Monsieur Renoir," Anna said, "please don't trouble yourself for me. I know I'm dying."

Renoir shook his head. His eyes downcast and his face blanched, he realized that he was speaking to a dead woman. The guilt and terror of that thought made him sick to his stomach.

"Yes," Anna said, "I'm dying, but that's all right."

Renoir could see a thought play in Anna's eyes.

Anna smiled. "After all," she said, "I have done something good. I have posed for the great Pierre Renoir. How many farm girls can say that?"

"And you were the best," Renoir said. "You were the very best."

When Renoir left Anna's apartment, sick with grief, he went immediately to his studio and composed a letter to Dr. Gachet, pleading with him to see the girl who, just three years earlier, was the radiant and sensual figure in his masterpiece, *Étude, Torse, Effet de Soleil.*

A few weeks later, the woman from Chenoise was dead.

Like Anna, the nameless woman who sat for us in the studio above the police station in Pérols was a real person. She had a history and she had a future. She also had a soul, and, consequently, she was sacred. I will always be grateful for the gift of herself to me, a plodding artist in the long, long shadow of Pierre-Auguste Renoir.

CHAPTER 13

The Holidays in the South of France

A FEW DAYS BEFORE CHRISTMAS, the townspeople of Pérols met at the church square. The air was crisp and the sky perfectly cerulean. In the middle of the square was a sled—an elongated tricycle with a small flat-bed—and six huskies. It was Santa's sleigh.

The children, bundled in scarves and bonnets, introduced them-selves to Santa's dogs, who stood quietly, seemingly impervious to all the attention. Then Santa, decked in the traditional white beard and red suit and not so traditional Air Jordan basketball shoes, stepped onto the tailgate of his sleigh and shouted a command to the huskies. *"Allons-y."* Let's go.

The huskies sprang to life, their tails swishing, happy to be on the road. The townspeople fell in behind, chatting with their neighbors about the morning frost as they wove through the narrow streets of Pérols. The parade had begun—a two-mile stroll to the beach at Carnon. It was an annual tradition: a fundraiser for "Restaurants of the Heart," an associa-tion that distributes meals and groceries to the needy—an example of France's social conscience.

By the time we had reached the sea, our small band of Santa's helpers had swelled to a crowd of eight hundred. This was going to be a party. A tall, slender man with white hair and a New York Yankee's baseball cap was tending a six-foot-diameter sandpit grill. He leaned over the fire and expertly flipped the steaks, sausages, and slabs of pork, occasionally pausing to rub the biting smoke from his eyes.

A dozen booths were set up around the perimeter. Vendors were selling pizza, elephant-ear pastries, and spicy hot wine—all you wanted for just two euros.

Four white horses from the Camargue—the same horses that would guide the bulls through the streets of Pérols during the summer *abrivado*—were tied to the fence where the beach shrub turned to sand.

An announcer strolled through the crowd with a wireless microphone. "Look to the sky," he blared. "Here come the parachutists!"

And, true to his word, out of the sky eight, nine, no, ten skydivers with rainbow-colored chutes sliced left and right and landed perfectly on their target and into the arms of a jovial Saint Nick.

"Don't forget," the announcer boomed, "all those taking the 'polar-bear plunge' must sign up at the registration booth."

"That's me," I said to Nita.

"You're really going to do it?" Nita asked.

"Oh yeah. It's the French way."

After adding my name to a list of one hundred Christmas swimmers, I walked to the nearby bathhouse to change. The room was jammed with bathers—both men and women—and I, being somewhat modest, slipped out of my blue jeans and into my trunks in a flash while other men moved more leisurely, evidently unconcerned about dropping their drawers among a mixed crowd.

On the beach again the bathers circled up near the water's edge, whacking their arms to generate heat.

My friend, the ebullient and irrepressible Roger, was the swimmers' self-appointed cheerleader. He faced the bathers on stick legs, his arms undulating at his sides like a manic hula dancer. "Are we ready for a swim?" he shouted.

"Yes!" the bathers called back.

"Are you sure?"

"Yes!" the bathers roared.

"Then let's go!" Roger hollered, leading the pack.

And with those words, all swimmers—men and women, boys and girls—rushed for the sea.

There is something unsettling about stepping into water that dips just below fifty degrees Fahrenheit. It is rather like a sharp wet-towel snap to the behind—not life threatening but definitely galvanizing.

Most of the bathers sprang swiftly from one wave to the next, hooting their approval of the frigid brine. Meanwhile, I was more tentative (distinguished, I thought), wading in oh so slowly until the water slapped against my chest. I took in a deep breath, closed my eyes, and dropped to my knees for—how long was it?—oh, yeah, long enough to register agony. The water lapped over my head, which qualified me as a genuine member of the Polar Bear Club.

As I headed back to shore and the admiring crowd, I tucked in my gut ever so slightly and pulled back my shoulders, the conquering hero, returning triumphantly from the frigid baptism of honor. When I reached the shore, my friend, Henri, greeted me.

"Bravo, Allen," he said. "I want to introduce you to the mayor of Carnon."

I looked at the short, balding man standing next to Henri. He wore a dark blue suit and a solid red tie against a starched white shirt. He looked like the French flag and completely out of place among the crowd of holiday beachcombers.

"This is my American friend," Henri said to the mayor.

"*Bonjour*," I said, shaking the soft hand of the sartorial town official.

"How are you?" the mayor said in English.

"Very well."

"What part of the United States do you come from?" the mayor asked, still in English.

"From the state of Washington. Not Washington, DC, you understand, but the . . ."

The mayor's eyes drifted away from me, and I realized that the interview was over in mid-sentence. Ah yes, politicians; they are the same the world over.

After the dip, Nita and I paraded home, my teeth chattering like castanets. When we arrived, Nita led me to my favorite chair, propped up my feet, wrapped me in a blanket, and gave me a cup of hot chocolate. I was asleep before the chocolate was half drained and dreamt about swimming in the Mediterranean with Santa Claus and six huskies.

On Christmas Eve we had dinner with the Ducros—another fabulous five-course spread—watched a movie at a local theater and then drove into the village center for the Christmas Eve midnight mass.

We filed into the nineteenth-century church and found an open pew (a simple, straight-back bench) toward the front of the church. There was a yellow glow on the old stone walls. Within the alcove to the left, the pianist played a hymn, accompanied by two teenage girls who coaxed a timid melody from flute and clarinet.

There was an anthem from the choir and a brief and rather thin message from the priest about a mouse who lived in the church. But the highlight for me was the children's choir. Twenty boys and girls, ranging in age from five to twelve, stationed themselves on the altar steps. I was immediately drawn to a seven-year-old boy who held a tinfoil star over his head. There was something in his eyes that said, "I'm trouble."

As the children sang praises to the baby Jesus, the star became a heavy burden for the youngster. Slowly the silver star slipped from the sky and then, for reasons that only children can understand, the boy thought the star made a wondrous sword and started slicing the weapon into the arm of his neighbor, who, as you can imagine, was not at all keen on the idea. There were whispered words spoken by someone in the front row, which must have been sufficiently stern, for the boy snapped to attention and lofted the bent star overhead again.

Later in the service (after the message about the church mouse), the same children's choir entered singing from the back of the sanctuary, marching slowly to a simple hymn of exaltation. Leading the procession was a small boy clutching a manger the size of a large shoebox. I was so moved by the pageant—the combination of procession and children's voices—that, for an instant, I dared not breathe. And then, miracle of miracles, I realized that the boy who so proudly bore the manger was the same star-flailing rapscallion of yore. I knew it was he because I recognized the mischievous glint in his eye.

At the end of the service, the parishioners filed out of the church, each greeted by the priest with "*Bonsoir, bonsoir, bonsoir.*" I stepped into the night air and smiled at the sight of the clear, glowing Christmas lights strung from the oak tree that adorned the church square. And there, among the twinkling bulbs, was the seven-year-old boy, perched in the grand oak like a mountain cat with a taste for fresh meat.

Merry Christmas to all, and to all a good night.

Christmas day was proof to me that the French are the masters of family, friends, food, and folly. Our Christmas was a gastronomical marathon: a rampage of champagne, foie gras, smoked salmon, lobster, shrimp, roebuck, rabbit, asparagus, potatoes, beets, carrots, zucchini, red peppers, assorted cheeses, and two traditional log-shaped cakes called *bûche de Noël.* It took me three weeks to lose the extra tonnage that I had packed on in less than twenty-four hours. I realize that so much food sounds inconceivable, but we were invited to three homes on Christmas day—a great honor—and no host was willing to hear the words, "No, thank you, I couldn't possibly eat another bite."

The day would not have been so ruinous (speaking from a dietary sense only), except for a small miscalculation on our part. Our third engagement of the day—after breakfast at Armelle's and lunch at the Ducros'—was planned for 8:30 p.m. Because the evening affair started so late, Nita and I were certain that our hosts—Georges and Monique—would be serving hors d'oeuvres and nothing more. So, to tide us over, we had a sizeable Christmas dinner in our little apartment before setting out for the *soirée.* We were mistaken; it was a full-fledged dinner party for twelve guests.

Indeed, the Christmas party did start with hors d'oeuvres (champagne and caviar), but from there we sat down to an elegant table and a five-course dinner. I exchanged a glance with Nita. She surreptitiously shook her head, her warning to say nothing of the dinner we had just eaten.

I was seated between two women I had never met. To my left was a pale-skinned, plumpish woman with shocking red curly hair and an orange and blue dress with puffy sleeves that dropped below her shoulders. Her name was Dominique and she talked incessantly. To my right was Yvette, a pretty woman with high cheekbones and a black, spaghetti-strap evening gown. She looked stunning. I found myself leaning more and more toward Yvette or, to be honest, increasingly *away* from Dominique. By the end of the evening, I was practically sitting in Yvette's lap.

After the first course—salmon and shrimp—our host, Georges, who was looking dapper in his white dinner jacket and red bowtie, introduced the first game of the evening.

"This game is a test of your literary skills. You must select three slips of paper from this bowl," Georges said, brandishing a cut glass crystalline basin. "You will find a French expression on each snippet. Your task is to weave the three expressions into a true story—something that has happened to you in the last year."

"Oh, I just hate these kinds of games," Dominique squealed. "I am just such a twit."

I leaned a little closer toward Yvette.

The game was a hit. The guests strung the phrases into funny anecdotes about misadventures, intrigue, and, of course, sex. Everyone laughed out loud, only a shade overly exhuberant.

Then it was Dominique's turn. "Oh, I just don't know. You are all so clever. *Oh là là!* What can I say?"

I looked over at Nita, who pursed her lips and shook her head ever so slightly.

"What can I say?" Dominique repeated.

"Well, say something," Georges said, with only the sound of good humor in his voice.

"Yes, I must say something," Dominique said. "All right, here we go."

Dominique took in a deep breath and offered a convoluted story that had something to do with turtle soup, a beach ball, and a girdle. I couldn't make any sense out of it whatsoever, but the French seemed to enjoy the story well enough.

After the "phrase game," the second course was presented. Fish and more shrimp. Then Georges, who was a doctor before his retirement, said,

"Let's all move to the operating room," meaning the living room where he set up the next game.

"This is a test of agility and speed," Georges said, sounding more like a boardwalk barker than an operating-room physician. "Allen and Pierre will stand on these chairs," he said, positioning two straight-back dining room chairs in the middle of the room. He then selected two plump oranges from a fruit bowl and handed them to Yvette and Dominique. He paired Pierre with Yvette and Dominique with me—not my first choice, but I was trying to remain in the jaunty spirit of things.

"Your job," Georges said to the women, "is to pass the orange up the left pant leg of your partner and down the right pant leg. The fastest contestant wins."

"Oh, I couldn't do that!" Dominique squealed. "I just couldn't."

"Then perhaps we can find another contestant," Georges said, reaching for Dominique's orange.

"Not so fast," Dominique snapped, ripping the orange away from Georges's clutches. She stepped up to me like a bowler approaching the line, the orange positioned just under her chin, scrutinizing my "pins" as if they were a seven-ten split.

"Please be gentle," I said to my partner.

"One, two, three, *go!*" Georges whooped, and the race was on.

The first "leg" of the race was easy going. Dominique inched the cool orange up the inside of my pant leg with relative ease, but when the orange reached midpoint in the course, there was a bit of a traffic jam.

The dozen revelers howled with laughter and started clapping rhythmically. "DO-MI-NI-QUE, DO-MI-NI-QUE." Meanwhile, Yvette had adeptly run the course, leaving Dominique, the orange, and me center stage. Dominique was doubled over with laughter, her right hand on her side, her left hand holding the reluctant orange in place at twelve o'clock high.

"Go for it," I said to Dominique, squirming now to make room for the barricaded citrus.

Dominique was doing nothing—still doubled over, holding the orange in place with a straight arm. She looked at Georges. "Anything in the rules about unzipping?"

"Ah no," I said, gyrating more vigorously now.

Finally, Dominique stood upright and gave the orange a punch with her fist. It was one of the more frightening moments of my life. Luckily, she hit her target, and the orange popped through and down the right pant leg in an unattended free-fall. I stepped down from the chair and readjusted my belt. I looked at Nita, who shrugged her shoulders and said with her eyes, "That's life in the big city."

We all returned to the dining room where we were served roast beef, string beans, and mushrooms. By this time I was thinking I would not have to eat for a week. The conversation bounced along from one topic to the next. At one point Dominique leaned over toward me and said in a half whisper, "I hope I didn't hit anything vital."

I smiled demurely. "Oh, that's okay," I said in my best Mickey Mouse voice. "We didn't want children anyway."

After the main dish, Georges was up on his feet again. "It's time to dance," he pronounced.

We all filed back into the living room. Georges put on a Latin CD, and we all gave our best renditions of the salsa.

"Change partners," Georges shouted.

We all dutifully obeyed.

"Change partners again," Georges called out fifteen seconds later.

Again, we obliged.

At this point Georges was linked with Nita and I with Dominique.

"*Don't* change partners!" Georges boomed.

We danced like that—alternating between rock and roll and Latin melodies—for the next twenty minutes. Then it was a conga line, as Georges led the string of Christmas dancers from the living room into the hall and back again.

I'm generally not a stick-in-the-mud, but frankly, I much prefer a quiet evening of discussion to a frenetic Mardi Gras, but that's just me.

At three o'clock in the morning—after the salad and cheese, after the *bûche de Noël*, after the fruit and coffee, after two grueling tangos with Dominique—I whispered to Georges that I thought it was time for us to be going home.

"So early!" Georges protested.

"Well, yes," I said, "unless you have an extra pair of pajamas."

"I can accommodate that," Georges said, sounding deadly serious.

"Just the same . . ." At that moment, I was wishing I could say I had a dog that needed tending. Not that we were ungrateful for an incredible, once-in-a-lifetime cultural experience. We were just bushed.

By 3:30 a.m., after having kissed everyone good night, we finally worked our way to the door where we said good night all over again and wished everyone a *Joyeux Noël*.

On the drive home Nita said, "The French sure know how to throw a party."

"You can say that again."

"How do you feel?" Nita asked.

"I feel overwhelmed and grateful, truly grateful."

"I feel the same way."

"But I'm also thinking that finding a friend—whether French or American—with whom you have a real kinship is rare and very precious. I think those friendships need to be protected."

"And do you have such a friend?" Nita asked.

"You mean besides you?"

Nita smiled. "Yes, besides me."

There was a pause, and then we both said in unison, "Terry Barber."

Terry is a former neighbor and retired elementary school principal. In 2002 he was studying to become a Catholic deacon. He is a man with a noble soul who always ends his letters to me with "Love, Peace, and Joy," which pretty much describes his character.

When Nita and I arrived at our little apartment, we listened to our phone messages. There was only one: a Christmas wish from Terry calling from his home in Olympia, Washington. Terry's last words were, "I love you guys." And I thought what a perfect ending to a perfect day.

* * *

During our year in France, friends often asked if we missed anything in particular from the States. When I answered "not really," I was not being entirely truthful. There was one thing I did miss: an old-fashioned American hug. I am not talking about a no-contact teepee hug. That's not a hug. It's more like, I don't know, a litigation. I'm talking about a full-body bear hug. Although there are a fair number of Americans who have a problem with a full-contact embrace (those who confuse intimacy with sexuality, for example), in comparison with the French, we Americans are champion huggers.

During conversation, Americans will often touch each other with, say, a tap on the hand or a squeeze to the forearm. The French are less likely to accent their conversations with physical touch. It is a cultural preference. To high-touch Americans the practice is thought of as friendly and positive, but to low-touch French men and women physical contact is more likely to be viewed as intrusive and even improper.

On a few occasions—even though I knew it was taboo—I tried giving a French friend an American hug (sometimes I just can't help myself). Their reactions were almost comical: head bolted back, arms to the side, and eyes at full flame. And when I had the temerity to hug a French-woman, eyebrows were raised all over Languedoc. *"Oh là là,"* they would howl in dismay. That's just not right!

During my entire year in France, I met only one person who felt at home with a hug. Her name was Nicole.

It was New Year's Day. The hiking club had planned an excursion in the Alpilles mountain range, including a visit to the medieval village of Les Baux-de-Provence. It was going to be a long day, so all the hikers met at the town's community center at 7:00 a.m. As people were pulling gear out of their cars, I noticed Nicole driving up in her compact VW. I smiled. She had been away on a two-week vacation in Morocco, so I was delighted to see her pull in.

She was parked about twenty yards from where I was standing. At first she didn't spot me. But when she pulled her backpack out of her trunk, our eyes met. She actually squealed. She dropped her pack and sprinted the twenty yards with her arms open like she was running to her lover home from the war. When she reached me, she jumped into my arms and wrapped her legs around me, which nearly toppled me to the ground.

As I swung her around full circle, I caught a glimpse of the faces of the other hikers with their mouths agape and eyebrows at full mast. The last time I saw faces like that was in sixth grade at an elementary school basketball game. "Johnson, get in there," the coach barked. I was so excited that when I pulled down my sweatpants, I didn't notice that my shorts went along for the ride. For three long seconds I stood there in my bare butt and jockstrap. Imagine the look in the eyes of the fans. The French had the same look.

Later I asked Nicole where she learned how to hug.

"It's part of my job," she said. "I'm a physical therapist. I touch people. It's what I do."

"It is so rare," I said. "You are the only French person I know who knows how to give a decent hug."

"That's true," Nicole said. "It's just not done." She paused for a moment and smiled. I could see she was running a movie in her head. "I want to tell you a story," she said.

Nicole explained that one of her favorite male clients was blind. Whenever she worked with him, it was her custom to take the man's arm and guide him from the waiting room to the therapy room.

One day, unbeknown to Nicole, the blind man canceled his appointment, and the timeslot was filled with a new client, a man who, coincidently, resembled the blind man. Mistaking the new patient for her regular blind client, Nicole took the man by the arm and folded it over her own, tapping his hand affectionately. The unsuspecting man jumped back in horror. He must have thought, "Just what kind of massage do you have in mind!"

"The French are like that," Nicole said.

"I've noticed," I said. "The French don't touch. Sometimes, when I like someone, I'll greet them with a two-handed handshake. I've learned even that is too intimate."

"Certainly," Nicole agreed. "That kind of gesture is reserved for lovers."

"I've noticed, too, that the French have difficulty in *verbally* expressing intimacy," I said. "For example, I get the feeling it is difficult for the French to say 'I love you.' Am I right?"

"Yes. Again, that is for sweethearts. I think you Americans are much more liberated in that sense."

Nicole reminded me of an American CEO who ended his letters to his employees with the words, "I love you." That's pretty unusual, even by American standards, but for the French it would be inconceivable and probably laughable.

That was how the New Year's Day hike began. Just as memorable was how the hike ended.

We were now in the hilltop village of Les Baux-de-Provence with its narrow streets and terra-cotta roofs. We were all tired and more than a little thirsty, so we stopped at a terraced café along the main street to have a drink. It was one of those crisp, sunny days in Provence. A couple of us leaned backward on the hind legs of our chairs under the broad-leaf shade of an enormous sycamore tree.

We were all laughing about the events of the day, including Tani's mischief. When we had pulled off our packs and sat down to take a breather, Tani had slipped a five-pound rock into my backpack when I wasn't looking. I labored under the extra weight for ten kilometers until Tani's compunction got the best of him, and he confessed his crime. I knew the joke on me was part of my initiation to the family of hikers, so although I made a melodramatic show of outrage, I was actually flattered that I had been tapped as the hapless victim.

Our bodies were weary, but our spirits were high. We felt at home with each other.

I ordered my drink, a *limonade*, the French equivalent of a 7UP, and my hiking chums immediately started ribbing me about my relative disinterest in wine. That led to a general criticism of American behavior, especially what the French liked to call the "cowboy" tactics of President George W. Bush. The tone was lighthearted but not without a prickly undercurrent. I took their criticism in stride—I had heard it all before—and even contributed a jab or two of my own (knowing that, at times, the best defense is to slip the criticism by agreeing with the "enemy").

Although the assault was still in good fun, the French were starting to pile it on.

Maurice was a man in his late forties with a quick wit and a flair for storytelling. "Here's a joke that sums up American attitudes," he said with a mischievous smile.

A recent world survey included the following question: "If you please, what is your opinion on the shortage of food in the rest of the world?"

The survey was a complete failure because:

- In Africa no one knew the meaning of "food."
- In Western Europe no one knew the meaning of "a shortage."
- In Eastern Europe no one knew the meaning of "an opinion."
- In South America no one knew the meaning of "if you please."
- And in the United States no one knew the meaning of "the rest of the world."

Now I knew that the French loved a round of retorts, so I was not going to go down without a fight.

"Have you heard this one?" I asked. "What is the difference between an American corporation and a French corporation?"

They shook their heads.

"If an American corporation is given two cows, they sell one, buy a bull, and build a herd."

"That's right," Maurice said with a chuckle.

I held up my hand. "But, if a French corporation is given two cows, they go on strike and riot in the streets because they wanted three cows."

The circle of French hikers erupted with laughter. Maurice slapped the table with one hand and pointed at me with the other. "Touché, you got me."

In the middle of the friendly repartee, I noticed that François, a sturdy seventy-year-old hiker, was sitting quietly, even solemnly, at the end of the table. I wondered what he was thinking.

After bantering for nearly an hour, we paid our bill and started to stroll along the narrow streets of the village. I was looking in the window of one of the tourist shops that displayed an array of tawdry replicas of twelfth-century swords, daggers, battle-axes, and maces. Suddenly, I felt a firm hand on my shoulder. It was François. He was a big man with a ruddy complexion, round rimless glasses, and a baseball-style fishing cap. He reminded me of Teddy Roosevelt.

"Allen, come over here," he said in a voice that was just above a whisper. He led me to a bend in the road that was clear of tourists. He held my arm snuggly as if worried that I might suddenly bolt and threw a glance over his shoulder to make certain that no one was within earshot.

"I want you to know something," François said, looking at me intently. "We may joke about Americans, but I don't find it particularly amusing. You were the ones who came to our rescue in 1917 and again in 1944. Too many of us have forgotten that. I have not forgotten. I was there when American troops liberated Paris. That was August 25, 1944. I was just a boy, but I still remember that day."

The eyes of François were beginning to well up with tears. "We are quick to protest American policies," he said, "but you are the first ones we run to when we are in trouble."

I was quiet for a moment. From time to time throughout the year, I would hear other French men and women reflect the same idea but never with such emotion. I threw my arms around François and gave him an American-style hug, forgetting for a moment that he was, after all, still French. I felt François stiffen in my embrace. I released him quickly, mercifully.

I was looking deep into his eyes now, my own eyes suddenly tearing. "Thank you, François, thank you."

"I just thought you should know," he said, as he turned away, a little embarrassed by his own display of emotion.

I don't think I really knew François before he proclaimed his gratitude for the United States. Nor did I fully understand the complexities of the French personality. François was my guide to a deeper understanding. I think he may have adopted me as his special project.

A month after our hike to Les Baux-de-Provence, François invited me to go fishing on his eighteen-foot motorboat in the Mediterranean. It was a still and sunny day. We were sitting comfortably in lawn chairs at the boat's stern, poles in hand, with bread, cheese, and wine on a small table between us. I didn't catch a thing, but I was hooked on the conversation.

François began talking about the virtues of the French culture. "Sure, we have all the tangible treasures—the incredible monuments, unforgettable museums, and diverse landscape—but that's not '*la France profonde.*'"

"*La France profonde*" was a familiar expression. The phrase is meant to capture the deep village and agrarian culture of France. I interpreted the depiction as "France plain and simple," without the ostentation and feverish pace of Paris or Lyon.

I asked François to elaborate.

"*La France profonde* is joyful and proud. We love our history and traditions. We care about the next generation and the next and the next. We have a fondness for simple luxuries: a walk on the beach, a conversation with a next-door neighbor, a dinner with family. That is *la France profonde.*"

We sat in silence for a moment, watching our lines rise and fall with the gentle swells. I think that François was allowing the ideas to penetrate my American psychic. I tore off another chunk of French bread and slathered it with a generous layer of goat cheese.

"There is something else," he said.

"*Oui?*"

"We are a small country."

"About the size of Texas," I offered.

"Yes," François said with a smile, "but not quite so *va-t-en guerre*—so ready to go to war. Which leads me to my point. We know the bitter taste of war. Our beaches and hillsides are soaked with our blood and, as we both know, American blood. Enough is enough, don't you think? Don't you think it's time to stop the killing?"

"I get the sense that you are leading up to something François. What is it?"

François smiled the way a man does when he has been found out. "Yes, I do have something in mind."

François explained that there was going to be a public demonstration in Montpellier to protest President Bush's push for a war in Iraq. Would I like to go?

I thought for a moment. I knew that the war drums were banging in the States. After 9/11 American flags seemed to be fluttering on every pickup antenna in the country. Yellow-ribbon bumper stickers called for all Americans to "Support Our Troops." The country was in a fever pitch. Only a small minority wanted anything to do with talk about peace and understanding, but I was a member of that minority.

"Yes," I said. "Count me in."

Twenty thousand French citizens turned out for the march in Montpellier. The streets were jammed with protesters, all walking slowly as though in a death march from the Jardins du Peyrou to La Place de la Comédie. Appropriately, the procession began at the feet of two nineteenth-century sculptures by Jean-Antoine Injalbert: a pair of roaring lions tamed by two smiling cherubs. The theme of these sculptures was "love vanquishes force."

François and I were in the middle of the throng, shuffling down the street, taking it all in. Most of the banners were very simple, slogans calling for peace and reason. Other signs were less anti-American and more anti-Bush, one sign reading Ni Coca-Cola, Ni MacDo, Ni Bush. Another read Largons Bush, Pas des Bombes (Drop Bush, Not Bombs). A third was even less flattering. Something about "Saddam-izing Bush."

At one point I turned around to see the crowd behind me and caught sight of an American delegation toting a twelve-foot long banner that read in French, Americans for Peace and Justice. One of the American protesters wore a placard that read, Bush Stinks.

"I want to talk to that woman," I said to François.

"Go ahead," he said. "I won't be far."

I threaded my way through the crowd and touched the elbow of the woman who sported the sign.

"Those are harsh words," I said to the woman in English, hoping that she might elaborate.

She did not say a word. Nor did she dare look at me. Suddenly, I realized that she had no way of knowing my intentions in questioning her. For all she knew, I was a demented jingoist bent on leveling my wrath on anti-American protesters. She could not know that my interest did not go beyond journalistic curiosity. I looked at the woman again. With every step, she seemed to be turning increasingly pale. Out of compassion I quickly moved away from her.

It was then that something very curious happened. As the American delegation passed from one square to the next, the people who lined the streets and leaned out of their apartment windows applauded enthusiastically.

I caught up with François just as we rounded a corner toward La Place de la Comédie.

"What do you think of all this?" François asked.

"I think it is terrific," I said truthfully.

"Really. You are not just trying to flatter a French friend."

"No, not at all. I have to admit, it feels pretty strange being surrounded by all this anti-American sentiment."

"But it's not anti-American sentiment," François said. "It is antiwar sentiment."

"Yes, I think I understand that now."

"Your American press has been very hard on us, but I don't think they understand."

It was true that the American press had crucified the French. They reported with little objectivity that the French were cowards, that they did not remember D-Day, that America should dig up every GI casket at Normandy and ship them back to the United States for a proper burial. And, if that were not bad enough, they seemed to revel in reporting pure blatherskite. For example, there were scowling commentators who idiotically claimed that we should change the names of "french toast" and "french fries" to "freedom toast" and "freedom fries."

"What does the American press not understand?" I asked.

"I don't think they understand our motivation. Some American reporters suggest that we are against the war because we have economic interests in Iraq."

"Yes, I have read that."

"And they may be right. We may have economic interests in Iraq—I don't know. But tell me, do you think all of these people are protesting for economic reasons?" François waved both hands over the crowd that jammed the boulevard as if offering a benediction.

I smiled. "No, I don't think so. I think they are protesting because they love peace."

"Absolutely. They love peace. And is that so bad?"

I looked again at the teeming crowd, moving slowly, solemnly like a sacred religious processional. Then I looked into the eyes of my friend again. "No, François, there is nothing bad about that. Nothing at all."

CHAPTER 14

A Citizen of the World

OUR FIRST YEAR IN FRANCE WAS COMING TO AN END. It was time to go home, which was a strange thing to say because we felt that we were already home. In one year, we had expanded our homeland to include the landscape and people of Pérols, France.

A week before our departure, our friends, Armelle and her husband, Gil, invited Nita and me to dinner. They took us to one of only two restaurants in Pérols, Restaurant L'Estelle. When we entered the dining room, forty of our new French friends sprang to their feet, applauded, and sang the opening strains to the "Star Spangled Banner." Although the lyrics dribbled off after "Oh, say, can you see," it was the sweetest chorus I had ever heard. And when the song had faded, they stood there with open, childlike smiles and raised their glasses to us.

"Please give me a glass of wine," I said. "If ever there was a time for a toast, it is now."

Armelle poured and handed me a flute of champagne. I surveyed the room. They were all looking back at me with the most genuine, joyful faces. There was Odette and Tani and Marie-France and François and

Nicole and, of course, Armelle, who had organized the entire farewell dinner. They were all there, filled with such goodwill I wanted to cry.

"You are incredible," I said. "I know it is not something that you say naturally, but there are no better words to express what I am feeling tonight. I love you. I love you all."

In attendance was Roland, a former IBM engineer who had lived in the States for several years. "We love you too," Roland said in perfect English.

"We love you too," the crowd echoed.

"How I am going to miss you all," I said. "I wish I could squeeze you all into one big beautiful woman and take you back home with me. But that would never work. My wife would take one look at her and say, 'You put that thing right back where you found it.'"

The crowd laughed politely, which made me think that my little joke translated awkwardly into French. "So, I will just say, thank you for making our dreams come true. Most importantly, you must understand that our adventure is not yet over. It will only be over after all of you have come to visit us in the United States. But not *all at once.*"

I was beginning to feel my eyes well up with tears. "Oh, there is one other thing that you should know," I said. "We are coming back in a year. So, don't forget us. We will not forget you." With that I raised my glass, and we all sipped the sweet fruit from Champagne. I felt so giddy with joy that had there been an open fireplace, I swear I would have flung the drained wine glass into the fireback.

I did not want that night to end. We ate a five-course meal, opened gifts (a Provençal serving platter for Nita, a tome on modern art for me), and danced until two in the morning. It was a night I will never forget.

The sweet sorrow of saying goodbye was softened by the knowledge that four of our dearest friends—Jean, Juanito, Roland, and Marie—would be meeting us in Seattle in a month's time. We would hike the Washington Cascades and Canadian Rockies. I called us the French-American Hiking Team.

The morning we left France, Jean-Marie and Monique drove us to the Montpellier Airport at seven in the morning. Twenty of our friends were there to see us off. When we went through customs, the security guard asked me to open my bag.

"What is this?" he asked.

"It's a cornet," I said.

"You are a musician then," he said.

"Of sorts."

I looked through the gate. Our friends were still standing there, not willing to move until we had rounded the corner and were completely out of sight. I had an idea.

"Would you like me to play it?" I said to the guard.

"No, that won't be necessary," he said.

I leaned forward and half whispered. "Do you see those people over there?" I said, nodding to the band of brothers and sisters on the other side of the gate. "They are our friends. Let me play a phrase for them."

The guard smiled, and I knew it was okay.

I placed the horn to my lips while the guard motioned to a French soldier with a side arm that it was all right. I played the opening line of the French national anthem, "La Marseillaise." Our friends looked puzzled for a moment, looking over their shoulders for the music's source. Then they realized the music was coming from my breath, through my horn, to their ears, and they actually leapt off the ground. I did not have a better exit than that. I quickly wrapped up my cornet, thanked the guard, waved one last time to our new family and disappeared.

* * *

SHORTLY AFTER ARRIVING IN THE STATES, I decided to send a newsletter to our friends in France (a list of about fifty names). I wanted to keep in touch. I also wanted them to understand what I was feeling on reentry. The following is the first newsletter, which serves as an appropriate epilog to our first year in France. Most of our French friends can read English. Still, I included a few translations of American idioms.

Mes Amis:

There are many things in the States that are refreshing to me after our yearlong sojourn in France—things that I truly relish. At a four-way stop (*un croisement*) most American drivers wait politely for the other to pass, standing by for his or her rightful turn to cross the road. That would never happen in France where the rule of the road is "every man for himself."

People say "hello" on the street in the States. The first day I went for a bicycle ride, a young woman greeted me with a big smile and said, "Good morning. How are you? Have a nice day." And she was a total stranger. We all know that's not done in France. So there is much that I adore about America, much that I am proud of, but there is also much that is troubling.

I saw familiar images with fresh eyes. I noticed the little things that changed after 9/11:

The American flag behind the Delta Airlines counter.

A new name for CNN morning news: American Morning.

American flags sewed to the jerseys of university and professional athletes.

American flag emblems pinned to the lapels of American journalists (Lou Dobbs), entertainers (Jay Leno), and politicians (most notably George W. Bush).

A car salesman, who said, "Even if we don't find arms of mass destruction, we know they are there anyway."

A waitress, who said, "We stand behind our president, right or wrong."

Bumper stickers (*autocollants*) that read, "Together we stand," "I pledge allegiance," and "One nation under God."

These were all things that I had seen and heard before, but now they had new meaning. Suddenly, they seemed less about pride and justice and, sadly, more about fear and power.

Little by little, I found myself feeling uncomfortable (*mal à l'aise*). I had the feeling that I did not fit in. A week after our return to the States, I spoke to my good American friend, George, about the problem.

"I don't know what it is," I said. "I feel unsettled (*mal dans ma peau*). I am an American, but I don't feel like an American. I know I am not French, so who am I?"

"Why, don't you know?" George said. "You are a 'citizen of the world.'"

My quest for a personal identity was briefly set aside when the French-American Hiking Team flew into Seattle. We spent two weeks hiking in the Mount Rainier National Park in Washington and the Jasper National Park in Alberta, Canada. It was a joyous experience for everyone, generating enough material for another book.

On their last day in the United States, I drove the French delegation to the airport. We arrived early, so we had some time to circle up one more time and embrace each other. As I stood there looking at my good friends, I was overwhelmed with emotion. I could not control my voice. I could not stop the tears. At one point I practically collapsed in the arms of Jean (*être sur le point de m'effondrer*), sobbing with the grief of saying goodbye to my friends.

Much of my sorrow emerged from the realization that I was not going to see our new family for a good long time—at least a year. But there was something more. I realized I was grieving over the loss of an old idea that was so important and reassuring (*rassurant*) to me for so many years: the unconditional, almost blind, trust in my American heritage. After all, we Americans were raised to believe that we are always, without question, the standard of virtue, that all our actions are motivated by the highest ideals. I had been disabused of that dream. The Bush doctrine of "Preemptive War" was not noble. It was based on power, fear, and intimidation. It was not the policy of a citizen of the world.

As the five of us stood in a circle in the Seattle airport, I began to express to my dear friends how I felt. I repeated what I had said to George:

"I don't feel like an American," I said, "and I know I'm not French. Who am I?"

And amazingly, the French-American Hiking Team said, almost in a single voice, "Why, Allen, don't you know? You are a citizen of the world." They did not say words that were close to what George had said; they said the exact words: *Tu es un citoyen du monde.* That confirmed it for me.

Since that conversation, I have allowed the voices of George and the French-American Hiking Team to sink in (*faire son chemin*). Gradually, I was able to describe what it meant for me to be "a citizen of the world." That new awareness became my personal mission statement:

I am no longer committed to policies or regulations or doctrines. I am not driven by governmental mandates or religious exhortations.

I am driven by higher, immutable ideals—principles that surpass any institutional mandates. In the end, I have nothing to prove because it has all been proven before. Principles endure.

As a citizen of the world, I am committed to peace, tolerance, and understanding. I am stirred, not by aggression, but by genuine kindness.

As a citizen of the world, I have no nationality, no religion, no political affiliations. I am in tune with the climate of the world. I feel the joys and sorrows of all people, regardless of national borders (*frontières*).

Is that radical, even dangerous? Throughout history principle-centered men have been condemned and even crucified by those who were guided by ignoble doctrines. Nelson Mandela, Mahatma Gandhi, and Jesus Christ come to mind—all "citizens of the world" in the greatest sense of the phrase.

I do not mean to place myself among such giants of virtue—I am just an incipient traveler (*un voyageur naissant*) struggling to understand—but I must say that today I feel more at peace. I feel more in control of my own life. I feel more relaxed (*détendu*), more able to walk calmly on the streets where, all too often, the person with the biggest stick rules.

I am not anti-American. A citizen of the world is not against something—that is for Pharisees, for bigots, for extremists. A citizen of the world is for something. I am still an American. I will always be an American, but I believe that I am an American who is trying to live by the American ideal. I am attempting to live by the words—if not the spirit—of Thomas Jefferson and our founding fathers who wrote in our most sacred document, the Declaration of Independence, these immortal words:

"We hold these truths to be self-evident, that all men are created equal, that they are endowed by their Creator with certain unalienable Rights, that among these are Life, Liberty and the pursuit of Happiness."

That is what I am for: protecting the rights of life, liberty, and happiness for all human beings because we are all created equal. The fact that Jefferson's creed was a sanctuary for white, wealthy men—and not for women or poor citizens or black slaves or American Indians—does not invalidate the correctness of the principle.

There is one other Revolutionary War American who has stirred me with his words. It was the political activist Thomas Paine who wrote this beautiful mission statement.

"The world is my country, all mankind are my brethren, and to do good is my religion."

That is a mantra that I can live by.

These ideas are burned into my heart. To express my thoughts publicly, I decided to send a few lines to the editor of our local newspaper. My words were published a week later. I called it "An American Anthem for 2004":

Let us try again.
Let us open our hearts,
Shoulder the burden,
Offer a hand to those in need:
The ghetto boy,
The Indian brave,
The Latino field hand,
The teenage father,
The single mother,
The disillusioned,
The dispassionate,
The betrayed,
The forgotten.
Let our voices ring—
Not for "preemptive war,"

But for international law.
Not for oil, rubber, copper, and slave labor,
But for bread and shelter,
For education and immunization,
For honest work and an honorable wage,
For comfort, safety, and children's laughter.
Let us not allow something good
To get in the way of something better:
Let us be,
Not one nation under God,
But one world under God.
Let us blunt our swords
In the name of humanity.
Let us suspend judgment,
Seek understanding,
And give tolerance a chance.
Let us be citizens of the world
And unrelenting warriors
For Love, Peace, and Joy.
Let this be our American Anthem.

That is the news from Richland, Washington, USA. I miss you all. I am already looking forward to our reunion in one year.

Love, peace, and joy,
Allen

CHAPTER 15

The Americans Return

WE RETURNED TO PÉROLS IN ONE YEAR. When we arrived at the Montpellier airport, I felt like a kid on Christmas morning. It felt so good to be
back that I could hardly contain myself as we weaved our way through
airport security. When Nita and I finally walked through the glass doors
into the terminal, we were greeted with hoots and whistles. My eyes followed the clamor, and there they were—the beautiful lot of them, led by
the French-American hiking team. I picked up Marie, who is as light as a
feather, and lifted her above my head.

"You'll hurt your back," she squealed.

"Oh no, never," I shot back.

It was not French, but I gave American hugs to everyone. We were
hugging so tightly, laughing so loudly that I suddenly realized that we had
created quite a stir in the airport.

"*Oh là là,*" a woman in her forties said in half astonishment, half
delight.

"*Oh là là* is right," I said with a toothy grin. "Would you like me to
give you a hug too?"

She was speechless, so I kissed her on both cheeks, knowing that an outright hug had the potential of creating an ugly international incident.

"Welcome to France," she said flushed and popeyed.

Admittedly, I was now performing for my friends. "My name is Allen," I said to the nameless woman. "Would you like to be my friend too?"

"I think I would," the woman said, "but I have to catch a flight now."

"That's all right," I said. "If you want to find me, just go to Pérols and ask for the American, Allen."

She left smiling, but I think she was shaking her head when she said once again, *"Oh là là."*

I think the French are both puzzled and intrigued by my social style. (And I'm sure there are a few who are put off.) But I cannot do otherwise. It is something that I inherited from my mother, who, as they say, never met a stranger. I don't mean to be rude. I'm just genuinely curious about the lives of others. And if you don't mind me saying so, I think it is that very quality that makes the ideal world traveler: someone with an unquenchable sense of curiosity and a willingness to appear childlike.

There is a second quality that is even more indispensable to becoming a world-class traveler. To always say "yes." When you are in another country, and you are invited to a dinner, even a dinner with strange food, say "yes." When you are invited to dance, say "yes." When you are asked to attend an antiwar march, say "yes" (if only to observe if you cannot, in good conscience, participate). When you are invited to attend a wedding or visit an unfamiliar village or simply go for a long walk along the beach, you must always say "yes." Saying "no" is tantamount to saying, "I don't care about you, your country, or your customs." It is the height of boorishness.

The subtitle of this book is entitled *How a Grumpy American Fell in Love with France.* It's true that I can be cantankerous (you've read about some of my more snippy moments in these pages). But that's not where the story ends. That crankiness was ultimately and inexorably overpowered by love.

Here's what I believe. Every "yes" releases a pinpoint of light until that beam burgeons into a blaze of clarity. That blaze is called awareness, understanding, and intimacy—a blaze that transformed this grumpy American into a lover. That is the power of saying "yes."

* * *

SAYING "YES" PAID RICH DIVIDENDS early into our second year.

I was standing in line, waiting to check out my shopping cart of weekly groceries. It was Saturday, so it was a slow-moving procession.

Standing behind me was a tall, distinguished gentleman with a friendly face. I mentally practiced and then articulated one of the acceptable French phrases for interrupting someone's solitude.

"*Excusez-moi de vous déranger monsieur.*" Excuse me for bothering you sir.

The man smiled a warm, inviting smile. "Oh, you are not bothering me," he said. "How can I help you?"

There was an intelligent iridescence in the eyes of this dignified gentleman, which made me think that he might be willing to be playful with me. So I used one of my pat opening lines for starting a conversation. "I am an American," I said.

His eyebrows arched.

"I can't imagine that you thought I was Parisian," I added.

"Well, I was vacillating between the two. Is he Parisian and or is he American. Which is it? It's so hard to say."

Oh, I definitely liked this guy.

"Yeah, right." I almost punched him in the arm, but that would have been too risky, even for me. "Are you from here?"

"Montpellier," he said.

"I love the backstreets of Montpellier. They have so much character."

"I live on one of those backstreets. Not far from the Cathédrale Saint-Pierre."

"Ah, do you? You're very lucky. I love that part of the city."

"Would you like to come visit my family and me?"

This man cannot be French, I thought. "I beg your pardon?"

"I asked if you would like to come visit us. Are you married?"

"Ah . . . well, yes, I am married. And yes, absolutely, we would love to visit you. I'm just astonished that you would invite me without even knowing my name."

"Do you think your name might make me change my mind? What is your name?"

"Allen. My name is Allen."

He threw both hands over his shoulders. "Oh, I'm sorry, forget everything I said. That's a terrible name. We can't possibly have you at the house."

I looked down at my shoes, impersonating both sorrow and embarrassment. "Yeah, that's what I figured. I'm so sorry to have troubled you."

The man laughed at my charade, and when I lifted my head, I saw that his hand was extended.

"My name is Benoît," he said.

I shook his hand. "My name is Allen. But you know that already."

"It's a pleasure to meet you Allen."

We exchanged contact information, and Benoît explained how I could easily take the *tramway* to his apartment. We set a dinner date for Saturday night.

My wife has always been more conservative than I. So when I told her that we were invited to dinner at the home of a friend in Montpellier, she was at a loss.

"Who do we know in Montpellier?"

"Benoît."

"Who's Benoît?"

"He's a man I just met."

"We're having dinner with someone you just met?"

"Right."

"How did you meet him?"

"Standing in the checkout line at Carrefour."

"Standing in line?"

"Yeah, it was crazy. We just started talking, and the next thing I knew we had an invitation for dinner."

"That's not like the French."

"That's what I thought."

"Well, do you think we should go?"

"Why would we *not* go?"

"Because you don't know who he is."

"I know enough. He's a good man."

"How can you tell?"

"Trust me, I can tell."

So when Saturday arrived, Nita was feeling a little apprehensive. That malaise came to a peak when, after two *tramway* connections and a half-mile walk, we stood in front of the gated apartment house. The courtyard looked like a scene from the pen of Edgar Allan Poe. Unkempt vines were a tangle along the crest of the eight-foot wrought-iron gate. As we peered apprehensively through the railing, we spied a tenebrous courtyard strewn with dead leaves from a half-dozen autumns. A bicycle with rusted chain and spokes leaned against the ashen three-story apartment wall like a dead horse.

If that were not enough, a scowling crow perched on a leafless tree branch cawed at us with incessant acrimony. Was the bird's call a presage of unimagined horror that awaited us on the other side of the gate? We could not help but wonder as we surveyed the courtyard that looked increasingly like a worn sepia photograph stained with time.

"Do we ring?" Nita asked.

Even I was feeling a little shaky. "Sure," I said with false bravado. "We've come this far. What do we have to lose?"

"How about our lives?" Nita said in a tone too serious for my liking.

"Nah," I said, pressing the bell once and then again.

We waited thirty seconds. "Well, I guess nobody's home," Nita said, as she turned and started to walk double-quick down the street toward the *tramway* station.

Just then the front door swung open, and Benoît greeted me with a wave.

"He's coming," I said in a stage whisper to Nita.

Her head and shoulders went slack as she slowly looped back and rolled her eyes at me.

"*Bonsoir,*" I said, waving back to Benoît.

As the friendly Frenchman crossed the courtyard, Nita said, "I don't know about this," which I ignored.

Benoît unlatched the gate, and I did the introductions.

"So happy to meet you," Benoît said to Nita, kissing her cheeks one, two, three times.

"Happy to meet you," Nita said with an almost genuine tone.

We walked across the courtyard, up a three-step stoop, and through the front door. We were greeted by a stairwell that was no more inviting than the courtyard. The wallpaper was water stained and peeling. Halfway up the staircase an old placard announcing a concert scheduled for the last decade hung askew by a single tack.

Benoît mumbled an off-handed apology for the condition of the foyer.

"Oh, this is quaint. It has character," Nita said.

I glanced at Nita, who looked like she actually meant it.

"It's not fancy," Benoît said, "but it's home."

Stepping into Benoît's apartment was like walking into a fine antique shop. There was a long hallway with bedrooms on the left and a sitting room and dining room on the right. A very small kitchen was at the far end of the hall. The hardwood floors were dark oak, and the walls were adorned with beautiful watercolor paintings. The entryways into each room were decorated with hand-painted flowering vines.

"Who is the artist?" I asked.

"That would be me," a silky voice said behind me.

I turned and faced a beautiful, slender, dark-haired woman in her early forties. Benoît, who was twenty years her senior, introduced the woman as his wife, Elisabeth.

The four of us sat down in their sitting room. As is the French custom, Elisabeth had set out one bowl of pistachios and another of green olives. Benoît poured the drinks.

We moved easily into animated conversation. We learned that Benoît had been a professor of biology at the University of Montpellier. He had written several books on vegetation and ecology. As for Elisabeth, she was indeed the artist—particularly gifted at working with watercolors. But, like her husband, she was also a charming conversationalist.

It was then that we were introduced to their two teenage sons, Joseph and Antonin. The elder of the two was Joseph, a tall and slender teenager, who was an ardent hip-hop dancer. I quickly realized that dancing was a good choice for him. His high-octane energy was ideal for a youngster who wished to make a name for himself by spinning on his head. Let me give you a sense for Joseph. As the adults were happily chattering, he must have become bored. Without fanfare, he lifted and wrapped both feet behind his head, all the while pretending to be engrossed in a scientific journal. It was my first introduction to a human pretzel.

"That's gotta hurt," I said.

"Nope," Joseph said. "It's what I do."

Antonin was a little more sedate but not by much. He, like his brother, seemed to be interested in comic books and video games.

When it was time for dinner, we were led through the dining room and onto a magical balcony that overlooked a five-hundred-year-old park.

"This is why we choose this apartment," Benoît said. "The apartment is small, but this—this is heaven."

And he was right, it was heaven. The night air was warm, and the tiny tree frogs were croaking. After a delicious salad, we were served an equally delectable main course of veal, sliced bell peppers, and *une tarti-flette* (potatoes, Reblochon cheese, and chopped bacon and onion). Then we all sat back in our chairs and sipped the red wine.

"This is one of those moments," I said to Nita with a slow sigh of satisfaction.

"What kind of moment is that?" Elisabeth asked.

"It is a *perfect* moment," I explained. "It does not happen often, but sometimes, if everything is right and the gods are smiling, you know that nothing could be more perfect. This is one of those moments. You are both such gracious hosts. And Elisabeth, you are a master chef. The conversation is bright and funny, and the evening air feels like a warm bath. It is all being played out right here, this moment, overlooking this incredible French garden." I shrugged my shoulders. "What can I say? This is one of those moments."

That was the beginning of a lifelong friendship. Over the years, we have hiked together, picnicked together, and gone to concerts together.

Today, one of Elisabeth's paintings hangs in our home; one of Benoît's books is in my library. We have found summer homes for both Joseph and Antonin in the States to give them a boost to their English fluency. In turn, we have had American students stay with Benoît and Elisabeth.

When we are with Elisabeth and Benoît, we are at home. When we are separated, we miss them. They are truly our dear friends! Even if their courtyard does have a rather shadowy, gothic ambiance.

* * *

THE SECOND HAPPY ENCOUNTER OF OUR SECOND YEAR was a Spanish treasure. Juanito was thirteen-years old when he immigrated to France from Barcelona just after World War II. When he arrived, he was intent on becoming absolutely fluent in French. With the help of his French teacher, he drilled and drilled until he was a master of the language. When I arrived in Pérols, I asked who was considered to be the most elegant and well-spoken Frenchman in our village. I was told to look up Juanito. And so I did. I soon learned that his French was, indeed, impeccable. With time I discovered that his character was equally flawless.

I first met Juanito on a hike. He was leading a group of twenty on an easy fifteen-kilometer trek. At one point we crossed a vineyard on our way to a dirt road on the other side. Before we got to the road, the owner sprinted from his home with his shotgun in hand.

Juanito immediately spotted the angry man and met him half way. I followed at a distance just to hear the conversation.

"Who the hell do you think you are?" the owner shouted.

"Evidently, we are fools who do not belong here," Juanito said.

"You've got that right," the owner said, his venom already diminishing.

"I am so sorry," Juanito said.

"You should be sorry."

"We are a hiking club from Pérols, and I was under the false impression that our route had been approved. Obviously that is not the case. We were trying to get to that dirt road." Juanito pointed to our destination. "But we will backtrack if you prefer."

At this point the owner opened the barrel of his shotgun as a sign of appeasement. "No, you don't have to do that," he said. "But next time talk to me first."

"That is only right," Juanito said. "And thank you for your kindness."

"Not a problem. You know, if you are ready for a lunch break, there's a stand of trees on the edge of my property that's ideal."

"That would be wonderful. Are you sure it is not an inconvenience?"

"Not at all," the man said, shaking hands with Juanito.

That's when I decided to make Juanito my friend. Any man who could so deftly defuse an angry Frenchman with a shotgun was a man I wanted as a buddy.

Juanito and I did indeed become friends. Over the years, we have traveled throughout the United States and Canada, from New York City to New Orleans, from the Glacier National Park to the Grand Canyon, from Seattle to Prince Albert Island. In France we traveled throughout le Midi. But our most memorable European excursions took us to his beloved homeland, Spain.

Fluent in Spanish, Juanito was the perfect guide for me in Spain. He adopted my traveling style, which is characterized by frequent stops in hidden places to talk with the townspeople.

Juanito often said that by traveling with me, he came to truly know the United States. "The French who have vacationed in the United States think they know the country," he would say. "They don't. I know the States, thanks to my American friend."

I echo Juanito's gratitude. I came to know Spain through his eyes. In fact, the time we spent together wandering through Spain, engaging in conversation about his childhood and the Spanish Civil War, was the inspiration for my novel, *The Awakening*. The book is dedicated to my dear friend Juanito.

One weekend Juanito took me to his summer home in the Cévennes, eighty-five miles north of Montpellier. Isolated and bucolic, it was a tiny village called La Moline. Juanito was reenergized with each visit. He especially loved restoring the village well and the domed wood-fired bread oven.

I once asked him why he took so much pleasure in restoration.

"It is our history," he said. "This is the France that should never be forgotten. The highways will come. The malls will be built. But this is *la France profonde*, and it must always be embraced as sacred."

Our first evening there Juanito prepared paella, a wonderful Spanish casserole mixture of Valencian rice, green vegetables, beans, and in this case, rabbit. (Other variations substitute chicken, duck, sausage, snails, or seafood.) I could see that Juanito took pride in his cuisine and rightly so. It was exquisite, and I ate enough for at least two.

At the end of the meal, Juanito asked if I would like a little more wine.

"Yes, I think I would. It's quite good."

"That's all you have to say about my wine? It's quite good?"

I looked askance at Juanito. I thought I detected a hint of playfulness in his eyes, so I went along for the ride. "I know that you think that wine is a food group, but I'm not ready to join that club. Besides, what would you like me to say? That your wine is the quintessence of virtue, as seductive as a beautiful woman, as sumptuous as a warm summer night on the French Rivera? Come on, it's a glass of wine. I don't want to make love to it; I just want to slug it down."

Juanito was absolutely silent for five long beats, his eyes burning into mine. Then, perfectly expressionless, he said, "I forgive you."

It made me laugh out loud, but Juanito was not laughing.

My God, had I really offended him? "You're not laughing," I said.

"You noticed that," he said, as chilling as a northeasterly mistral wind.

"Juanito, I'm . . . I'm so sorry."

Only then did Juanito allow a slow smile to brighten his face.

"You dirty dog," I said in English. "You had me worried, you know."

"Well, you were talking about French wine. There are some things you just don't trivialize."

"*D'accord.* I will try to be more reverent in the future."

"See that you are."

To help digest our meal (not to mention settle my stomach after that lowdown trick), Juanito suggested a game of *pétanque*, which I had never played. He led me to a flat piece of terrain near his home, picked up a stick, and drew an eighteen-inch-diameter circle in the dirt.

"Stand inside the circle," he said, "and keep both feet on the ground at all times."

"Okay, I can do that."

Then he threw a small bright-green ball about twenty feet from where we were standing.

"That's your target," Juanito said. "That green ball is called *le cochonnet*."

"Ah, the piglet," I translated.

"Yes, the piglet. That's your target. Try to get as close as you can to *le cochonnet*."

"Sounds easy enough," I said with American swagger, to which Juanito gave me a wily smile. I did not like that smile. He handed me a hollow metal ball *(une boule)* that was a shade smaller than an American softball. It weighed about a pound and a half.

I felt the heft of the *boule* in my hand, sighted the *cochonnet*, bent my knees, and launched the metal sphere into the air. The ball rolled to about two feet of the *cochonnet*.

"Hmm, I think I like this game," I said puffing up my chest. I didn't step out of the circle; I *hopped* out, landed on one foot, and froze like a sprinter crossing the finish line. "Beat that monsieur, if you think you are man enough."

"Well, I'll give it a try," Juanito said softly.

He took his position and squinted his eyes at the target. "Well played Allen. But I'm not ready to give up quite yet."

"Don't stiffen up," I mocked. "You're not as young as you used to be," which was silly because although Juanito was a dozen years my senior, he was as agile as a teenager.

"Oh, I think I'll manage all right," he said in that truly annoying deferential tone of his when he knows that he has everything perfectly under control.

He slowly crouched and with his hand placed on top of the ball, flipped the orb with a perfect reverse spin. His *boule* cracked into mine, which sent it flying, while his ball rolled serenely to within two or three inches from the *cochonnet*.

Now, I should tell you that I keep my competitive impulse on a short leash on most occasions. I am calm, dignified, and sportingly magnanimous. This was not one of those times. "So it's going to be that way, is it?" I snarled. "Well, let's just see about that."

I stepped into the circle and, imitating Juanito's stylish reverse spin, lofted the ball into the air. My *boule* landed with a thud some four or five feet off the mark. "The sun was in my eyes," I whimpered, which was ridiculous because the sun had already slipped behind the mountain crest.

"Yeah, that sun can be merciless this time of day," Juanito said with a wink.

The match continued like that—me unloading disparaging wisecracks as my balls landed in the brush, and Juanito coolly planting his steel balls with pinpoint precision. Boy, he was irritating.

After a while, Juanito stopped keeping score, either out of boredom or compassion.

As we walked back to the house, I put my arm around Juanito and said, "If I have to lose so horribly, I'm glad it was to someone with your character. You almost make losing a pleasure. *Almost.*"

When I put my arm around Juanito, he put his arm around me. Over time, I discovered it was something he would invariably do. Some men, maybe most, have difficulty expressing affection, especially a physical gesture of affection. Outside of the obligatory greeting kisses, the French are even more reserved than Americans. Juanito was not like that. Although he was Hemingway-esque in his manliness, he was never shy about being tender. (Just in case you were wondering, no, we were not lovers. We are both too much in love with women in general and with our wives in particular. It is just that Juanito is one of those rare men who feels completely at peace in his own skin—a quality that I find irresistible.)

La Moline is three-thousand feet above sea level, so it can get cool when the sun calls it a day. Juanito stoked up a fire in the little house, and in a few minutes we were seated comfortably in front of the fire, our feet propped up on the hearth, a glass of wine in hand.

We started talking. We covered a wide range of topics: family, work, politics, women, even death and dying. That was one thing about the two of us. We could talk freely about anything.

When we got to the topic of religion, I recounted a favorite joke of mine.

One day in the Garden of Eden, Adam told God that he was feeling lonely.

God pondered for a moment and said, "Hmm, I'll make you a woman."

"That sounds like a good idea," Adam said. "What will she do?"

"She will take care of all of your needs," God said. "She will wash your clothes (when you have clothes that is), cook your meals, support your decisions, and satisfy all your sexual desires."

"Wow! What will that cost?" Adam asked.

"Well," God said, not one for pulling punches, "it won't be cheap. Frankly, it will cost you an arm and a leg."

Adam grimaced. "Yikes, what can I get for a rib?"

After telling the story, Juanito stared back at me with a flummoxed expression—a look that said, "*Et alors*—so what happened then?"

Granted, the joke probably didn't warrant a horselaugh, and, yes, some might be offended by its sexist overtones, but I was still surprised by the deadpan reaction. The joke always seemed to work in the States.

Suddenly, I had a hunch that Juanito didn't get the joke because he didn't know his Bible.

"Are you religious?" I asked.

"I'm Catholic," he said.

"Then you believe that God sent his only begotten son to die on the cross for your salvation?"

Juanito shook his head. "No."

"Then you are not a Catholic."

"Yes I am."

"No you're not."

That went on for a few rounds until Juanito explained that being Catholic in France was not necessarily about being *croyant*, a believer. It was about being a part of a long tradition. I could not convince Juanito that he was not Catholic because he *was* Catholic in a much broader sense than sheer doctrine. He was Catholic by two-thousand years of history: the grand cathedrals, the religious holidays, the Christian pilgrimages, like the long trek to Santiago de Compostela in northwest Spain, which Juanito had hiked more than once.

(By the way, over the next few weeks I conducted a short experiment. I told the Adam-and-God joke to a dozen French friends. None of them got it because none of them knew the Bible story. Of the twelve interviewees, only one described herself as a "true believer." So I tested her knowledge of the Bible by asking her to name the four gospels of the New Testament. She didn't have a clue.

My intent is not to ridicule the French but merely describe what I discovered. The French are overwhelmingly Catholic by tradition, but they are not religious. Only a small percentage—less than ten percent—attend weekly mass.)

After discussing religion, our conversation turned to politics and, after another glass of wine, to sex. Juanito had a joke of his own, which he told with an English accent. You haven't heard anything if you have not heard Juanito tell a joke in French with an imperious English dialect.

A duke and his duchess are reposing in the library. The duke is smoking his favorite pipe and reading *The London Times*. At a side table is a glass of port, which he sips from time to time. After a moment, the duchess says, "Oh, dearie, I am afraid that you must speak to our son, Randolph."

"Oh?"

"Yes, I think it is time that you spoke to him about the birds and the bees."

"Really? The birds and the bees you say."

"Oh yes, indeed."

"Then I will do just that," the duke says, not looking up from his paper.

The next evening, the duke and Randolph have a private conversation in the library.

"Oh Randolph old chum, I wonder if we might have a little chat."

"Why, of course, Papa."

"Jolly good. Randolph, do you remember when you and I visited London last spring?"

"Oh yes, Papa."

"And do you remember the beautiful ladies we met when we were there?"

"Oh yes, Papa."

"And do you remember what we did with those beautiful ladies?"

"*Oh yes*, Papa."

"Well, your mother would like you to know that the birds and the bees do the exact same thing."

Juanito had me doubled over with laughter. Yes, the joke was funny, but the telling of the story was priceless.

When I had finally collected myself, I revisited a conversation that Juanito and I had with his friend, Dario, on the coast of Spain.

"It is important to have a mistress," Dario had said, without the slightest qualm. "In fact, it is thanks to my mistress that I can have a deeper, more loving relationship with my wife."

At the time I asked Dario if he was serious, and he assured me that indeed he was.

Dario's reasoning was absolutely convoluted to me. "I could never do that," I confessed to Juanito. "I just cannot be that duplicitous. I mean, how can you expect to have an intimate relationship with your wife while living a secret life with another woman? Sure, I've been tempted. Who hasn't? But in the end, it would be a despicable act of betrayal. I could never do that to Nita."

It was then that I told Juanito about Caroline and the acting camp: the seduction, the temptation, the drive home in the early morning hours, the suspicion, and, ultimately, the warm and tender embrace of two devoted lovers.

Juanito listened carefully to my story, laughed at the characterization of my clumsy modesty, and finally grew solemn when the story came to a close. He nodded his head, smiled, and said, "You're a good man, Allen." His eyes were shining.

We continued talking freely, contemplating the meaning of sex, romance, and love until the fire burned itself out, and we finally called it a night.

As I drifted off to sleep, I thought about Juanito's character. There was an openness about him that could only come from supreme self-confidence. It was not an arrogant self-confidence, but a simple, unruffled sense of peace.

I wanted more of that internal serenity for myself. Oh, most of the time I can rest easy, but when I'm tired, I can quickly become irritable.

Here's an example. Juanito and I were on one of our trips to Spain. It was the end of the day, and I was exhausted after a long drive. We pitched our tent and sat down at a picnic table for a makeshift dinner. I hunched over my bowl of soup like a prisoner of war guarding his meager rations.

Sensing my fatigue, Juanito asked me how I was doing.

That innocuous question was all it took. I snapped. "I'm doing fine. Just leave me alone for a few minutes. Is that too much to ask?"

Juanito did not say another word. He took a short walk, and when he returned, we hit the sack in silence.

The next morning, I apologized to Juanito.

"It's all right," he said. Then after a moment he asked, "Do you know where that comes from?"

I was still embarrassed by my own actions, so it was not a question I particularly wanted to entertain. Still, I knew that Juanito merited a thoughtful and genuine response. Plus, maybe talking about it would help me get to a better place.

I thought for a moment. "Well, it would be easy to blame it all on my father. He was always quick to anger. I basically stayed clear of him my entire life."

"I see."

"But that's unfair. I need to take charge of my own actions. Now that I think about it, I think it may have something to do with my quest for perfection."

"What do you mean?"

"Well, to pick on my dad again, I always thought that I had a shot at earning his love by being perfect. And when I was not perfect, like last night, I hated myself for it."

Juanito let that register for a moment. "You know, Allen, we all have our demons to fight. The trick is not to be beaten down. I like your facility for self-examination because that is what makes us all better men."

Juanito's choice of words did not elude me. When he said, "that is what makes *us all* better men," he was including himself in the injunction. Although he could have easily and rightly excluded himself, I did appreciate the generous inference.

Juanito and I became very close. We had a number of common interests: travel, hiking, tennis, music, conversation. Another shared passion was bicycling. On one of our biking day-trips, we rode along the canal from Pérols to Aigues-Mortes, a thirty-mile roundtrip excursion. Aigues-Mortes was always a favorite destination of mine. The walled medieval village was the starting point of the seventh and eighth crusades, led by Louis IX in the thirteenth-century. Whenever I'm there, I feel like I should be entering, not on a bicycle, but on a faithful, fully armored steed.

We rode through the gate and into the heart of the medieval city, the Saint-Louis Square, with its magnificent nineteenth-century sculpture of Louis IX at its center. We leaned our bikes against the wall of a café and sat down for coffee and a pastry. After a long ride, it was a luxury to sit back, extend our legs, and watch the tourists and townspeople stroll by.

"I have something on my mind," I said to Juanito.

"*Oui.*"

As I leaned across the small table, my voice became softer and more deliberate. "Juanito," I said, "I think of you as *mon âme sœur*," which literally means "my soul sister" but is translated into English as "my kindred spirit." Yes, using the word "sister" has always seemed a little strange to me, but that's the expression.

Juanito smiled. "Me too."

"In fact, I have come to think of you as my brother. Would you be willing to be my brother—if not in blood, in spirit?"

Juanito's smile grew even wider. "Of course I would. That would be a great honor."

And so he and I became brothers at that moment in the Saint-Louis Square of Aigues-Mortes. Then we talked about what it meant to be a brother—mostly how important it was to be there when the other was in need. We both agreed on that creed, a creed that Juanito upheld two weeks later.

It was another sunny morning in Pérols. I was late for a doubles tennis match that paired two friends against Juanito and me. I strapped on my tennis racket, straddled my bicycle, and started pedaling furiously. By the time I had gotten to the town center, I knew I was making good time, but there was still another half mile to the courts. I stood up on my bike to kick it up a notch.

When I'm bicycling, I never feel completely safe sharing the road with French drivers. So when I spotted a driveway cut into the sidewalk, I leaned into the ramp. I was almost parallel to the curb when my tire caught the lip of concrete, went into a slide, and smacked me to the cement faster than I could say, *"Aïe aïe aïe!"*

I lay there shaken for a moment, wondering if everything was in one piece. I wiggled my toes and was happy to learn they still worked. My right elbow was a bit sore but not badly enough to turn me around.

I looked up and down the street to see if anyone had seen the accident. I already had my jaunty quip in mind. "I meant to do that," I would say. But the street was deserted. With no one to console me, I had no alternative but to get back on my bike and ride on to the tennis courts. When I got to the clubhouse, Juanito and the others were already there.

"Ah, there you are," Juanito said. "We wondered if you were going to make it."

"I wondered too," I said, and then told the story of sliding into second base with my bicycle.

"Are you all right?" Juanito asked.

"I think so although my elbow is a little sore." It was then that I raised my elbow to take a look for the first time. "Holy crap!" I said in English.

"Mon Dieu!" Juanito said in French.

We both stared in disbelief at a hole the size of a quarter on the inside of my elbow. The sight of it made me dizzy.

"I don't think I'd better play tennis today guys."

"We've got to get you to the doctor!" Juanito said. "You're coming with me."

Five minutes later, we were standing in the office of our village physician. The receptionist took one look at me, now the color of paste, and said the doctor would see me immediately.

The physician was a sixty-something, gray-haired man with a pleasant smile. "What do we have here?" he asked. He gently turned my arm over, stared at my wound, and said, "Oh, that's not good."

"Exactly my sentiment."

Then the doctor did something I will never forget. He grabbed a tin box the size of an abridged dictionary and popped open the lid. There was a collection of naked scalpels, scissors, tweezers, and I'm sure a good deal of rust. He rummaged around in the box with his bare hands until he found a pair of tweezers that suited him. Then, without sterilizing the instrument, he came at me like a maniac with a hot poker.

"This may hurt a tiny bit."

I swear that's what he said. It must be part of the universal Hippocratic Oath.

He poked at the wound with the tweezers. He lied. It did not "hurt a tiny bit." It hurt like hell!

"I almost have it." He poked at the wound again. "Wait, wait, wait. Aah, got it. That's quite the stone monsieur," he said, holding up a bloody chunk of gravel the size of the tip of my thumb—okay, the tip of my little finger, but it was big.

Then he tossed the bloodstained tweezers back into the tin box and closed the lid. I looked at Juanito, who cocked his head and pumped his shoulders.

"Are you going to sew me up now?"

"I can't do that."

"Excuse me?"

"I'm not set up for that. This is a serious injury. You need to go into Montpellier."

"I do?"

"Oh, yes."

"And do you think I'm going to be all right?"

"Oh, sure, you'll be fine," he said in a tone that didn't sound entirely convincing.

"But I need to go to Montpellier."

"Yep. Montpellier is where you want to go."

"Okay. Then that's where we'll go." I turned to Juanito. "Are you up for that?"

"Of course," Juanito said. *"Tu peux compter sur moi."* You can count on me.

In the next few minutes, we were on the road again. Naturally, Juanito knew the way. When we arrived and got out of the car, I started to feel dizzy again.

"Can I help you?" Juanito asked.

I think I could have made it just fine into the emergency room, but it felt good to have Juanito there for me. "I'd like that. I feel a little shaky."

Juanito put his arm around me, and we walked side by side into the clinic.

A few minutes later, I was sitting upright on an operating table. The young doctor knew what he was doing. He gave me a local anesthetic and thoroughly cleaned the wound.

At one point, when the inner stitches were going in, I felt a twinge and grabbed Juanito's hand.

"I got you," Juanito said.

I know all of this sounds as if I'm an absolute milksop, but I don't see it that way. True, I'm not ready to put my hand into a nest of rattlesnakes or kick over a stand of Harley Hogs at a roadside tavern, but I have mustered enough courage to climb Mount Rainier and swim with the sharks in the Caribbean.

No, I don't think it was cowardice that made me lean on Juanito. I gave Juanito my hand because it was reassuring to know that I had a brother who would stand by me. That may sound mawkish to some, but so be it. It is the voice of that kind of loyalty and compassion—from so many friends and especially from Juanito—that calls me back to France.

CHAPTER 16

The Garden

ROGER IS AN EPICURE. I imagine that he thinks more about food and wine than anything else. However, the first thing you notice about him is that he stammers. I am not being mean in saying that. His rapid-fire stuttering is completely congruent with his personality. Roger is constantly on the move, a freight train of energy. If a word does not come quickly enough, he simply reloads until he gets it right. He doesn't seem to be bothered by his unique elocution. His friends (I am proud to include myself in that fortunate circle) pay it no mind.

My attention to his speech quickly dissolved the first time I was invited to his home for dinner.

"You must taste this," Roger said.

"What is it?" I asked, looking at something that looked like pig ears.

"Pig ears."

"Oh, that's what I thought."

"I-I-I think you'll like the flavor."

"Okay," I said, examining the *oreille*. It had been fried crispy. I gave it a sniff. Hmm, not surprisingly it smelled like fried pork. I took a hardy bite. The surface layer crunched between my teeth while the inner layer was, well, chewy. I let my tongue become acquainted with the morsel of cartilage. It had a rich, sweet porky flavor. It actually tasted pretty good.

"It tastes sweet," I said.

"I added just a touch of honey," Roger said. "Nah-nah-not bad, huh?"

"Not bad at all. I just hope I haven't insulted the pig."

"Oh, he got over it long ago."

Later that evening I asked Roger one of my favorite questions. "What are you passionate about these days, Roger?" His eyes immediately lit up. "The garden." He thought about his response a moment and then nodded his head in approval. "Yep, the garden."

"Tell me about it."

"Well, I talked to the mayor, an-an-and he agreed to let me work a plot of ground on the edge of town. Then I talked to my friends—Jean-Marie, Roland, Jean, Juanito—and we formed an association of gardeners. Would you like to see it?"

"Yes I would," I said honestly.

The next day Roger took me to the garden: a half acre of land bounded by a welded-wire fence.

"Right this way," Roger said, as he opened the gate to the enclosure with a ceremonious flourish of his hand. "So what do you think?"

I canvassed the garden. It was a bountiful supermarket. A few white chickens pecked at the ground between the rows of cabbages and melons. A rock-lined pond was teeming with glistening trout. As for vegetables, there was a cornucopia of lettuce, zucchini, spinach, tomatoes, onions, scallions, carrots, radishes, and beets. Toward the back of the plot, there were cherry and apricot trees and a metal six-foot-diameter water reservoir. *"C'est un beau jardin."* It was indeed a beautiful garden.

"Oui. I-I-I think so too."

"What about theft? Does that bother you?"

"It has happened. But so what? If people are that hungry, they should help themselves."

"Still, a thank-you note would be nice."

"It-it-it doesn't matter."

When Roger walked to the back of the enclosure, he pointed out a somewhat rusted barbecue grill, a twelve-by-sixteen-foot slab of concrete, and a half-dozen four-by-four sticks of lumber. "We are going to build a shelter," he said. "A place where we can have a fine meal and a glass of wine."

"That sounds like fun."

"It will be fun. And we want you, as our honorary American, to cut the ribbon on the day of our grand opening. Would you do that for us?"

Now I was the one who was stuttering. "I-I-I don't know what to say."

"Say 'yes.'"

"Of course, yes!" I said, taking Roger in my arms and giving him an American hug.

"Well, that's good. That's perfect," he said, recovering from my Yankee embrace. *"C'est décidé."* It's decided.

A month later was the grand opening of the neighborhood garden. What a celebration! Jean-Marie and Monique Ducros were there, as were Tani, Odette, Marie-France, Armelle, Roland, François, Marie, Jean, and, of course, Juanito.

Roger was in typical high spirits. When Nita and I arrived, he was already stoking the grill. "We are going to eat well today," he announced, all the while poking a metal spatula into the sky.

The shelter, which looked like a typical American carport, was well constructed. There was room enough for two picnic tables that were already loaded with bread, red wine, and a huge salad made fresh from the garden. Along one side of the shelter, a blue ribbon was wrapped around the joists and tied in a bow at the center.

Everyone was in a festive mood. We were circled up around the picnic tables with Roger just off to the side of the grill.

"Tell us the story again," Tani said to me.

"What story?" I knew what he was talking about, but I was playing dumb.

"You know, the story about the club bike ride last week."

"I'm not talking about that anymore," I protested. "There are some stories you just have to let go."

"Wha-wha-what story?" Roger asked, waving his spatula like an orchestra conductor.

"Oh, you see, Roger doesn't know the story." Tani spread his hands over both tables as if parting the Red Sea. "All of this is thanks to him. It's the least you can do."

Tani whipped the family of friends into a frenzy. They started to chant, "Al-len, Al-len, Al-len," clapping on each syllable.

"Okay, okay," I said, "but this is absolutely, positively the last time. An American has to retain some semblance of dignity."

"Americans have dignity?" Tani said. "I thought Americans only had money."

I looked at François, just as he flashed Tani a disapproving frown. "That's enough, Tani," I said. "I don't want to have to send you to your room."

Tani raised both hands to say he was done.

"All right," I said. "For absolutely, positively the last time—the biking story." I stood up, heaved a sigh of resignation, and faced my audience. "There were about twenty of us."

"Twenty-five," Roland corrected.

"Thank you, Roland," I said in English. "Just like an engineer to obsess about the numbers."

"You're welcome," Roland said, also in English.

"Get on with it," Jean-Marie said.

"I'm trying to get on with it," I groaned. "It was like this. It was near the end of a four-hour ride. We were all bouncing along on a bumpy dirt road. I was feeling weary. That was when I noticed what looked like a canal that followed the road. But the canal was not filled with water. It was filled with what looked to be baked mud, finely cracked by the sun. It was perfectly smooth.

"I thought this was silly. Why should we struggle to dodge the rocks and ruts on the dirt road when there was an amazingly flat surface just six feet away?"

"I love this part," Tani said.

I gave Tani a dirty look. "Sooo, I stood up on my bike and rode down a gentle embankment onto the flat, sun-cracked bed of mud."

"Except it wasn't mud," Roland said.

"No, it wasn't."

"What was it?" Marie-France asked, hearing the story for the first time.

"*C'était un flux de déchets industriels*. It was a stream of industrial waste. I had ridden my bicycle into a river of shit! I was up to my waist in the sludge, and my bicycle was buried."

A barrage of laughter bellowed from my listeners.

Roger actually fell to one knee with laughter. "Oh, th-th-those Americans are bizarre," he guffawed. "They bathe in the strangest places."

"What do you expect from such a new nation?" Tani added. "They're still learning how to groom themselves. You can see that Allen hasn't learned how to use a comb yet."

I slid my hand over my perfectly smooth cranium. "That's it. You crossed the line, Tani," I said with a wink. "No more hair jokes. Besides I don't need a comb; a little floor polish works perfectly fine for me."

"That's enough, Tani," Armelle said, always the one to come to my defense. "What happened? How did you get out of that, that . . . well, you know?"

"'*Merde*' is the word you're looking for," Tani said.

Armelle blushed. "*Oui.*"

"Well, I reached down into the muck, grabbed hold of the rear tire, and somehow managed to drag my bike to the bank."

"Did anyone help you?" Monique asked.

"We were not going anywhere near Allen," Tani said. "He stank to high heaven."

"Then what?" Armelle asked, coming to my rescue again.

"Then I wheeled my bike up the bank. I didn't say a word to anyone. I peddled as fast as I could to the nearest marsh. I rode right in, tipped my bike over, and sat in the pond like an American Buddha. After a long moment of reflection on divine retribution and my place in the universe, I scrubbed down my bicycle and myself as best I could. It took me days to get the foul scent out of my nostrils."

"You poor thing," Armelle said.

"Yes, you-you-you poor thing," Roger said, unable to stifle another burst of laughter.

With the story told, I caught Tani's eye and wagged my finger at him. He just screwed up his face like a guilty schoolboy playing innocent.

Roger clanked a cowbell with a metal serving spoon. *"Madame est servie,"* he called out, which means "Madame is served"—a fancy and, therefore, satirical way of saying, "Let's eat."

When we all gathered around the two picnic tables, Roger presented a two-foot-diameter meat platter, piled high with sausage, chicken, rabbit, and pork.

"Oh là là," the French said in unison.

The feast had begun. The stories began to spin out about hikes and fishing excursions and world travels. There was a typical foray into politics, but it was always laced with humor and a good dose of hyperbole.

After the main dish and before the dessert, I suggested it was time for a song. Nearly two years earlier, Juanito and I had worked up a duet of *"Les Feuilles Mortes"* ("Autumn Leaves") in both French and English. We often sang the ballad as a way of thanking our hosts. It was our theme song throughout every country we explored—France, Spain, and the United States. We stood up, each with one arm around the other, and crooned the tune to an enthusiastic reception.

"Quand même, those Americans do-do-do know how to entertain," Roger said.

"As do the French," I said, offering a deep bow to Juanito.

Our little performance was all that was needed to prime the pump. The French started belting out folk songs, most of which were unfamiliar to me but common fare for them. It was a joyous time.

After the singing, after the apple and peach tarts, after the wine, bread, and cheese, it was time for the official ribbon-cutting ceremony.

Roger hammered the cowbell again. "It is time for the speeches."

"Oui!" the French shouted.

Roger cleared his voice. "This is our garden. It is where we come to seed and har-har-harvest our crops. It is for our delight and the delight of our neighbors. It is our place of community."

"That's true," Juanito said.

"But our community is not just French," Roger continued. "It is also American. We are international! So, we decided that our favorite American should have the honor of cutting the ribbon that joins the uprights of our little home."

"Unfortunately, our favorite American couldn't make it," Tani quipped.

"Hey-hey-hey, cut that out," Roger said. "This is serious." He then turned to me. "My friend, would you please say a few words?"

I have never been shy about public speaking. But at that moment my brain was scrambling for the right words. I scanned the faces of the people I loved: Nita, who gave my hand a squeeze; our oldest and most loyal friends, Jean-Marie and Monique; my swimming pal, Odette; my dance partner, Marie-France; my painting buddy, Armelle; my hiking cohort, Tani; my loyal fishing pal, François; and, of course, my brother, Juanito.

"I am nearly at a loss for words."

"Good," Tani said.

"I said 'nearly.' I am never totally out of words. The problem is choosing the right words. It was Mark Twain who said, 'The difference between the right word and the almost right word is the difference between lightning and a lightning bug.' So give me a minute."

I took a breath. "First, I need to thank you all for making us part of your family. We are so honored. And thank you, Roger, for all that you have done. We will never forget this day. We will never forget your friendship."

Roger smiled and tipped his head.

"I think I will leave you with this. When I was a boy, my mother used to sing a lullaby to me. It is a song that came out of the depression. The tune was written by an incredible jazz cornetist, Red Nichols. The title is 'Five Pennies.' I would like to sing it for you, but I'm afraid I did not come prepared. Do any of you have pennies in your pockets?"

The French have an expression when they are importuned for cash. *"Tu me prends pour un Américain?"* You take me for an American? So when I asked Tani to dig deep that was what he said. Still, he smiled when he managed to find a worn *centime* and placed it in my hand.

I quickly collected the five cents. "Whenever my mother sang this song, she would give me one penny for each line of music. It was her way of saying that she loved me. I would like to do the same for you."

I displayed the first penny to my audience and sang.

"This little penny is to wish on and make your wishes come true."

As I sang that first line, I placed the penny in Armelle's hand, curling her fingers over the coin.

"This little penny is to dream on, dream of all you can do."

I folded the second penny into Roger's hand.

"This little penny is a dancing penny. See how it glitters and it glows. Bright as a whistle, light as a whistle. Quick, quick as a wink upon its twinkling toes."

Naturally, I placed the dancing penny into the hand of my dance partner, Marie-France. When I wrapped my hand around hers, I could see tears in her eyes.

"This little penny is to laugh on, to see that tears never fall."

I placed the fourth "laughing" penny in Tani's hand, along with a pulled punch to his nose.

"This little penny is the last little penny and most important of all. For this penny is to love on, and where love is, heaven is there."

Normally I would have placed the last penny in my wife's hand. But this day was in celebration of an international family. So I pressed the last penny into the hand of my brother, Juanito. He tightened his fingers around the *centime* and pumped his fist, a gesture that said, "Yes, you are my brother."

"So with these five pennies, if they're these five pennies, you'll be a millionaire."

The last note disappeared into a zephyrean brush stroke, leaving only silence. And then, as if one, they all stood, faces shining, and applauded. Naturally, I responded with my most elegant curtsey.

"And now, the cutting of the ribbon," Roger pronounced. He gestured to me and then to the ribbon. "Monsieur Johnson, if you will."

I stood up and straightened my back. *"Monsieur le Maire."* Mister Mayor. "It is my honor. The scissors, if you please."

"Well-well-well, I'm sorry, we don't have a pair of scissors, but we do have this."

Roger handed me a small white box tied with a red, white, and blue ribbon.

"What is this?"

"It is a gift for our American friend."

"But your friendship is sufficient."

"We cannot do the ceremony without it," Roger said.

I opened the box and found a five-inch pocketknife, the famous Laguiole blade. The traditional Occitan folding knife, with the distinctive forged bee symbol at the base of the blade, was first designed in 1829. Every Frenchman owns at least one, and this one was a beauty. It had a polished rosewood handle and a scalloped spine. I had to take a deep breath. "Thank you, Roger," I finally managed to say.

"Do not thank me," Roger said. "It comes from all of us."

"Thank you all. Shall we see how well it can cut?"

"Ouais!" the French shouted.

I had the ribbon in hand. *"Mesdames et Messieurs,"* I said, "in the name of all that is sacred—good wine, fine cheese, hearty bread, a perfect salad, and cherished friends—I christen thee, this magnificent garden, *Le Jardin de la Famille."* The razor-sharp Laguiole sliced through the ribbon in a single, swift stroke, and as the blue streamers fluttered to their repose, the life of a French-American family was born.

Acknowledgments

IN PREPARATION FOR OUR FIRST YEAR in France, my wife Nita and I joined a French club in our hometown of Richland, Washington. Michel and Liliane Billaux, a Belgian couple with enormous hearts and abundant patience, were our guides to the subtle nuances of the French language. Their counsel saved us from countless blunders.

In France, our dear friends, Jean-Marie and Monique Ducros, greeted us with open arms. We first met this wonderful French couple in a Berber mountain village in Algeria in 1972. The four of us were teachers at the local high school—Nita and I teaching English, and the Ducros teaching science. Housing was difficult to find, so we shared the same cottage for the first two months of our two-year term. We stayed in contact over the years—first by letters and then by email.

Both Jean-Marie and Monique were raised in small villages—Jean-Marie in the Pyrenees and Monique in the Rouergue. Perhaps it was the influence of that quiet rural upbringing that produced a couple of such extraordinary generosity. Whatever the reason, we could not have made the trip to France without them. For our first month in France, while we were struggling to find lodging of our own, *their* home, a welcoming two-story stucco villa in Pérols, was also *our* home. They were our lifeline during our first year in France (and ever since): always accessible, always helpful, and always family. One would be hard pressed to find more loyal friends.

Jean Pommé was my language tutor when I lived in France. A former high school French teacher, Jean knew all the nuances and intricacies of the language. He graciously met with me for at least two hours every week to coach me on French grammar and vocabulary. Whenever I was unsure of the subtle meaning of a word or phrase, Jean could always set me on the right course.

My wife, Nita, has always been a trooper—not just for this adventure, but for every exploit that has ever tickled my fancy. As I have leapt from one passion to the next—entertaining, flying, motorcycling, scuba diving, mountain climbing, photographing—Nita has always been there to applaud my awkward forays. And when I systematically fell flat on my face, she would lift me up, dust me off, and give my bruised derriere a loving pat as if to say, "You can do it Bunkie. I have faith in you." Although we were both excited about going back to France, I think at least one of Nita's motivations for taking flight to the other side of the world was to support my dream. She is a wonder.

As always, my literary agent, Peter Riva, is an alacritous source of encouragement and guidance. It feels good having him in my corner.

I'd like to thank Doris Lisk, Michel Billaux, Patricia Johnson, and Annie Tchemitcheff for their gracious proofing of the original manuscript. Finally, Joanne DeMichele is a wizard of a copyeditor.

APPENDIX A

Twelve Secrets to Understanding the French

THIS IS REALLY A SUMMARY of *Pardon My French*. To my mind, these are the qualities that most characterize the French. Do not think of them as absolutes for there are certainly exceptions. But I would argue that they are strong tendencies.

1. *It's not personal.* Many Americans think that the French are cold. Other descriptors are even less flattering. Snobbish, arrogant, haughty. Those critics miss the point. The French are not cold; they are private and reserved. The French will seldom ask if they may help a foreigner who is obviously lost in a strange city (for that you will have to go to Germany). But if you ask for help, they are more than pleased to set you on the right path.

2. *The French like to be wooed.* Connected to the first secret, the French enjoy being sought out—it's easier for them. They love to be invited out for the evening—for a movie, for dinner, for a

concert. They like to feel that they are special and worthy of the pursuit. In this quality, they are not unlike Americans.

3. *Fashion is fundamental.* The French are very stylish and often sensual. A Frenchwoman knows how to make herself attractive with minimal accessories. For example, they can do wondrous things with a scarf or the basic black dress, the latter of which is a staple in nearly every Frenchwoman's wardrobe. Sometimes their style feels a little peculiar—like wearing blue jeans under a dress—but if you observe carefully, you'll realize they have thought it out. Besides, they walk down the street with such authority, such confidence, they invariably pull it off.

4. *Driving is a competition.* The French don't drive; they lift off. For the French, particularly the French of le Midi (southern France), driving is an aggressive sport—a competition—and for many an expression of macho bravado. They are notorious for speeding—whizzing through traffic circles as though they were annoying obstacles in a Formula 1 speedway. To live in France, one simply has to accept the idea that someone—probably in the next ten seconds—is going to tailgate. Live with it; it's part of their Latin heritage.

5. *To live happy, live hidden.* That is a French expression, and the French believe it. Their homes are walled, gated, and locked. Their shutters are fastened as soon as (or before) the sun sets. What is their concern? They say two things: (a) They don't want others (particularly the taxman) to see what they have, and (b) they want to protect themselves from thieves. This sentiment goes back a millennium. In the middle ages, castles were built for defense. As such, all the windows were small—very small—just large enough to let an arrow fly at the approaching enemy. When windows became larger—to let in more sun, for the old fortresses were dreary places—iron bars were added to cover the opening. Those iron bars are still in use today. Some things just don't change.

6. *Anonymity is a personal right.* The French avoid introducing themselves to others. I have bought a car, rented an apartment, and purchased insurance, and never has a salesperson volunteered his

or her name. Part of this tendency has to do with the French distaste for being held responsible. If you have a problem with a product, you go to the organization, not the individual. Of course, the French salesperson relishes that anonymity.

7. *The glass is half empty.* The French tend to be a bit pessimistic by nature. I think the characteristic has been influenced by their education system. Children are scored on a scale of one to twenty, and only God (and maybe the professor) gets a twenty. When students receive a high score—say a seventeen or eighteen—they are congratulated with, at most, a dispassionate "not bad." Even the way the French say "you're welcome" is couched in negativism: "It's nothing." For whatever reason, the French tend to be stingy with praise, and when they do receive praise (for their work is often impressive), they feel uncomfortable about accepting the tribute. More likely than not, they dismiss the praise with "Oh, it was really nothing."

8. *The customer is on his own.* The French have a curious notion of customer service. Basically, it doesn't exist. That's a little exaggerated but not by much. For the French, a customer is seldom right and certainly never king. There are a few exceptions. The people at the national telephone company, France Télécom, have been well trained. But most other companies have no idea of what it means to make the customer happy. Why? They have rarely been the recipients of excellent customer service themselves. How can they model what they have never experienced?

9. *Line of command is everything.* For the French, respecting the management hierarchy within a company is key. When the boss is in the room, the boss talks and the employees listen. There is no royalty in France any longer, but there are senior managers. As an American, I have asked to see the *patron* (boss) on a number of issues. My requests resulted in one of two responses: (a) a flat refusal (one woman at a welcome desk actually laughed at me when I asked to speak to the boss. "Oh, no," she said. "Not for a question like that.") or (b) the salesperson will become more attentive to the customer (fear is alive and well in French enterprises).

10. *Politeness still counts.* The French are sticklers for politeness. Although this custom is beginning to disappear among French youth (who are taking on a more relaxed—some would say "rude"—American attitude), it is still very correct to say "*Bonjour* Madame, Monsieur," when entering a shop. Not just "*Bonjour*," mind you, but "*Bonjour* Madame, Monsieur." There is something about a naked "*Bonjour*" that grates on the ears of traditional French shopkeepers. At the end of a transaction, saying "*Au revoir, bonne journée*" (goodbye, have a nice day) is always appropriate and expected.

11. *Eating and drinking is not a task.* Eating and drinking for the French is an exquisite pleasure. On the average the French spend two hours, fifteen minutes at the table each day. For myself, I have never spent less than three hours at the table (it is usually more like four hours) when invited for dinner at the home of a French friend. Meals are savored for the food and the fine wine, yes, but also for the fellowship, with conversation about people, experiences, current events, all seasoned with generous doses of humor—often below the belt, as the French say. As for the wine, I have heard Frenchmen rhapsodize about the virtues of wine. As one French friend told me, "It is not a drink, it is a way of life."

12. *Vive ma liberté.* More than all other secrets, this is the most important in understanding the French. The French are vigilant and tenacious guardians of their personal liberty. The problem is, by their own admission, their passion for personal freedom often violates the freedom of others. To draw from a favorite French expression, "All is permitted—even that which is forbidden is permitted." That personal liberty includes highway speeding, drunk driving, tax deception, and, perhaps the ultimate indulgence, suicide (with rates that are sixty-three percent higher than those found in the United States). Where does this indulgence come from? The French say it is part of the Latin culture—as old as ancient Rome.

Indulgent egotism got a boost in 1968 when the country was almost torn apart by a demand from students and factory workers for greater freedom. Unfortunately, the legacy has all too often resulted in chaotic classrooms and self-serving, shortsighted factory strikes. Unions have been instrumental in establishing a thirty-five hour workweek and twenty-five days of vacation. Many argue that such a relaxed work ethic has handed France an unstable economy, accentuated by an overall unemployment rate of ten percent, with a disturbing twenty-two percent unemployment rate for those younger than twenty-five.

APPENDIX B

How to Live in France for a Year

GOING TO FRANCE for three months is a lark. All you need is a passport. To live in France for a year takes the heart of an Ironman triathlete. You must be doggedly resolute.

The first step as a Washington State resident was to go online to the French consulate in San Francisco. (To discover what French consulate serves your region, go to www.france-consulat.org.) The problem is that the site is outdated and incomplete. And when you try to reach the consulate by phone, you will be greeted by an ice-cold answering machine and a maze of menus.

One day when I was feeling particularly tenacious, I stayed on the phone, jumping from one lifeless office to another until, by divine mercy, I was connected to a breathing receptionist.

"Oh my God, I am so glad to hear your voice," I said, unable to suppress my excitement. I wanted to be her best friend for life. "You have no idea . . ."

"What do you want?" the receptionist asked in English. Her tone was so snappy even her French accent could not soften the edge.

I heard the urgency in her voice and started speaking feverishly. "I-I-I am trying to get a long-stay visa, but I have a slew of questions. I need to find someone—*anyone*—I can speak to. But no one answers the phone."

"That is correct."

"And they don't respond to email."

"That is correct." I loved the sound of her "r's," but I was in no mood to be charmed.

"And . . . and . . ."

"Have you tried to fax?"

"Yes, I have. I've done that."

"Then, you've tried everything, haven't you?"

"Huh? Well, yes, I guess so." And then, with all the American sex appeal I could muster, I said, "Could you please help me?"

"Ah, that I cannot do," she said flatly.

"Okay, but what if . . ." and suddenly the world hiccupped, and I was speaking to a dial tone. "RrrrrrAAHHH!" I spun out of my chair, hopped on one foot, and wailed like a banshee. I marched helter-skelter into the kitchen, flung open the refrigerator door, glowered at a cantaloupe, slammed the door shut, and stumbled back into my office.

Sometimes being a world traveler is not easy. What I learned about getting a long-stay visa, I learned in bits and pieces, fragments from whispered hints from other expatriates.

I can tell you this—and it will help enormously: All American documents must be translated by an approved translator and then officially notarized. The authorized translator, who I discovered out of sheer luck, was Dominique of The French Class. And, best of all, she was located a few minutes walking distance from the French consulate in San Francisco (visit www.frenchclass.com). She was an invaluable resource.

It took nearly six months to complete our paperwork and finally receive our long-stay visa. What I did not know then is that I would repeat the process in France. Hint: Take all your official documents with you (birth certificates, marriage certificate, proof of financial independence, verification of health insurance, and a half dozen extra passport photos—everything the French consulate requires in the States).

Then, finally, after the research; after the paperwork; after packing 250 pounds of clothing, hiking and camping gear, bicycle paraphernalia, a trumpet, a flute, a laptop, shoes, cosmetics, guide books, and gifts for our French friends; after the goodbye dinners and retirement parties; after selling both cars and relinquishing our keys to the house sitter; after all that, we were ready to begin the adventure.

APPENDIX C

Suggested Further Reading

THERE IS NO SHORTAGE OF INFORMATION ON FRANCE. In fact, if you let it, the deluge of literature could boggle the mind. I sifted through a lot of books and surfed a gigabyte of Internet sites. These are my favorites:

Reading French Literature

The language. Who can resist the French when they look into your eyes and say, *"Comme je suis content de te voir"*—how happy I am to see you. Who is not swept away by the sound of the syllables flowing like a quiet stream, one word after another? Who is not charmed by the romantic rhythm of unaccented words whispering tenderly, lovingly, "Pick up your dirty underwear from the bathroom floor"? I swear, everything is poetry when spoken in French. So, the sooner you start reading in French, especially aloud, the sooner you will revel in the music of the language.

I'm not particularly gifted in learning a new language. It took me a long time to be able to read French, and when I started, I did not start with a classic by Voltaire or Camus. I began by reading the Jean-Jacques Sempé-illustrated series, *Le Petit Nicolas*, by René Goscinny. These little books recount the antics of the incorrigible, pint-size Nicolas and his gang of cohorts. They are funny and easy to read—an ideal selection for the beginning French student.

After reading *Le Petit Nicolas*, I felt more confident. It was then that a French friend in the States recommended reading the plays and screenplays of Marcel Pagnol—the complete works. This, too, was a good choice. First, Pagnol wrote about the people of Provence, particularly Marseille. The characters are colorful and immediately engaging. I can still hear their conversations in the bar by the port. Second, plays and screenplays are, of course, all dialogue. That was exactly what I wanted: to understand, not so much how the French *wrote*, but how they *spoke*. It took me a full year to read the two volumes, but I can still smell the saltwater of Marseille. I recommend starting with the classic Marseille trilogy: *Marius* (1931), *Fanny* (1932), and *César* (1936).

If you are going to do any reading in French—or any speaking, for that matter—you will need to build your vocabulary. My favorite book was *Mastering French Vocabulary: A Thematic Approach* (Barron's Foreign Language Guides). Written by Wolfgang Fischer and Anne-Marie Le Plouhinec, this vocabulary treasure comes with ten hours of MP3 audio, which, of course, is essential to getting the pronunciation right. I went through the book multiple times, highlighting the words I couldn't remember. Then I went back and drilled on the highlighted words. It was a workout, but it was a big boost to my fluency.

Reading about French Culture

I read a number of books about French culture, but my favorite was Harriet Welty-Rochefort's memoir entitled *French Toast: An American in Paris Celebrates the Maddening Mysteries of the French*. Harriet (I feel like I can call her by her first name) is an American writer who speaks with refreshing candor, clarity, and wit. She is the kind of unpretentious writer one would like to have over for dinner. Most importantly, she knows the French. She married a Frenchman and has lived in France for forty years. I have found her observations to be consistently accurate. Her book is only 224 pages long, but every page rings absolutely true. As a plus, it is currently available in hardcover, paperback, e-book, and audio CD.

If you enjoy *French Toast*, I also recommend Harriet's book, *Joie de Vivre: Secrets of Wining, Dining, and Romancing Like the French*. It's great fun.

Just for the pure joy of it, Peter Mayle's bestseller, *A Year in Provence*, is a must-read. And, by the way, the French were also big fans of the book. The 1993 mini-series starring John Thaw and Lindsay Duncan is priceless.

French Reference Books and Applications

On a more technical level, I discovered a number of books and applications that were indispensable. The first was *The Ultimate French Review and Practice* by David Stillman and Ronni L. Gordon. It is the best book on French grammar that I have seen. Any intermediate or advanced learner who has the discipline to work through it—cover to cover—will be amply rewarded. The paperback comes with a CD or, if you prefer, it is also available on e-book. (Be warned, this is not a textbook for beginners.)

Two of my must-have reference books were found in my favorite bookstore in Montpellier, the Librarie Sauramps. The first was the *Dictionnaire du Français* as edited by Josette Rey-Debove and published by Le Robert & Cle International. I will tell you that it is hard to find, but if you ever come across it, grab it while you can. This is not a French/English dictionary. It is a purely French dictionary, but one that is designed for the foreigner. It offers not only the meaning of the word, but—to name only three of a dozen features—the pronunciation, construction within a sentence, and examples of its use. I think it is terrific.

My second find in the Librarie Sauramps was the two-volume set of *Le Robert & Collins Super Senior Grand Dictionnaire Français-Anglais/Anglais-Français*. It was a happy day when I made that purchase. Sure, I have pocket-size French/English dictionaries, but I rarely use them anymore. The *Super Senior* has everything I need: all the meanings, all the expressions, and precise counsel on what is considered familiar or crude. It even includes a French and English thesaurus. There are not a lot of bargains in France, but at Sauramps I paid half the price posted in the States.

If you *are* looking for a French/English dictionary that you can slip into a purse or hip pocket, I recommend the six-by-four-inch *Langenscheidt's Pocket Dictionary*. One big plus about this dictionary is the inclusion of the international phonetic pronunciation of all French words. This is a must. What good is a word if you don't know how to pronounce it? Naturally, the user will have to learn the phonetic alphabet—indispensable if you are going to learn a language—but that can be done in a couple of sittings.

If you would like a bilingual dictionary for your handheld device, I recommend the *French English Dictionary* + by VidaLingua. Just tap on the word to hear it clearly and accurately pronounced. It includes both verb conjugations as well as essential French phrases, all of which are clearly and perfectly pronounced.

Another terrific resource can be found at www.sonicomobile.com. They have two wonderful programs: iTranslate and iTranslate Voice 2. Both programs allow you to translate complete sentences from English to French or French to English. Just record your voice and, voilà, your sentence is instantly translated. This is a lifesaver for those who are just learning the language. The spoken audio is superb.

Internet Sites

As you can imagine, there are innumerable Internet sites dedicated to understanding almost every dimension of France, including means of travel, conversion tables, and facts and figures. These are the ones I found to be the most useful.

General information

www.info-france-usa.org: This French Embassy site literally includes information from A to Z, including a French news magazine, information on visiting France, and a delightful section just for kids.

SUGGESTED FURTHER READING

https://www.cia.gov/library/publications/the-world-factbook/: This CIA publication offers a wealth of facts and figures regarding, among other things, French government, economy, military, and transnational issues.

Transportation

www.renaultusa.com: For those planning to stay in France for over eighteen days, consider a short-term car lease. The price can be attractive.

www.autoeurope.com/buyback_home.cfm: This site offers Peugeot's version of the short-term lease plan. As with Renault, the car is fully insured and may be picked up at a wide range of locations throughout France.

www.sncf.com: This site details how to get around France by train.

About the Author

ALLEN JOHNSON'S HISTORY HAS BEEN DIVERSE. With a doctorate in psychology, he was a popular keynote speaker and leadership development consultant. He is also an avid cyclist, actor, musician, painter, photographer, videographer, and screenwriter. When not in France, Allen and his wife Nita live in Richland, Washington.

His other book titles include:

The Awakening: A Novel of Intrigue, Seduction, and Redemption
The Power Within: The Five Disciplines of Personal Effectiveness
This Side of Crazy: 54 Lessons on Living from Someone Who
Should Know Better But Keeps Messing Up Anyway

allenjohnsonphd@charter.net
booksbyallen.blogspot.com
twitter.com/allenjohnsonphd
facebook.com/booksbyallen
amazon.com/author/allenjohnson